Dedication

On behalf of the Board of Directors, officers and employees of Terre Haute First National Bank, we are pleased to present *Terre Haute: A Pictorial History.* We extend our sincere thanks to the authors and to the many people whose photographs, memories and knowledge of local history helped to make this book possible.

Terre Haute First National Bank is proud to have played a prominent role in the city's development for 160 years. It is with special pride that we bring you this handsome volume. We hope it will be a valuable addition to your family library and a collector's item in the years to come.

We dedicate this book to the people of Terre Haute, past and present, whose faith, courage and determination established the foundation for our city's growth and progress.

Donald E. Smith
President and Chief Executive Officer
Terre Haute First National Bank

On June 6, 1988, First Financial Corporation opened First Financial Plaza on the southeast corner of Sixth Street and Wabash Avenue in Terre Haute. More than a building, it serves as a symbol of faith and confidence in the city's future.

1913 – 607 Ohio Street
Earl W. Kickler collection

1889 – Sixth Street and Wabash Avenue

Terre Haute:
A Pictorial History

by Dorothy Weinz Jerse
and
Judith Stedman Calvert

G. Bradley Publishing, Inc.
St. Louis, Missouri

Terre Haute: A Pictorial History

*by Dorothy Weinz Jerse
and Judith Stedman Calvert*

A limited edition of 4,000
of which this is...

_2266_

PUBLICATION STAFF
Authors: Dorothy Weinz Jerse
         Judith Stedman Calvert
Vigo County Historical Society Editorial Board:
   Elizabeth Bevington
   David Buchanan
   Brenda Christianson
   Susan Dehler
   Kenneth W. Martin
   Dr. William B. Pickett
   Dr. John Robson
   Joy Sacopulos
   Dr. Edward K. Spann
   Helene Clare Steppe
Consulting Historian:
   Dr. William B. Pickett
Cover Artist: D. Omer Seamon
Book Design: Diane Kramer
Publisher: G. Bradley Publishing, Inc.
Sponsors: Terre Haute First National Bank
         Vigo County Historical Society

Cover Artist

D. Omer "Salty" Seamon, Hoosier water color artist, was born in Gibson County in 1911 and has been a resident of Vigo County since 1931. The recipient of a Doctorate of Humanities presented by Rose-Hulman Institute of Technology, he was also recognized by the Indiana State Legislature for his contribution in art depicting the historical subject matter and rural scenes of Indiana. He was designated a Sagamore of the Wabash by Indiana Governor Otis Bowen in 1980.

Cover Illustration

The oldest remaining business building in Vigo County was built in 1834-1836 as the home of the Branch Bank of the State Bank of Indiana. Later known as Memorial Hall, the stately building was a meeting place for veterans organizations for many years. Recently restored and renovated, the former bank building now houses the law offices of Kesler & Kesler.

Copyright 1993 by G. Bradley Publishing, Inc. all rights reserved. Printed in the United States of America. No part of this publication may be reproduced, stored in a retrieval system, or transmitted, in any form or by any means, electronic, mechanical, photocopying, recording, or otherwise, without the prior permission of the publisher.
ISBN 0-943963-33-8
Printed in the United States of America

Table of Contents

Foreword		7
Chapter 1	In the Beginning	9
Chapter 2	Always Going Somewhere	15
Chapter 3	City Government	35
Chapter 4	The City, The Nation, The World	47
Chapter 5	Terre Haute in the Headlines	63
Chapter 6	At Work in the City	77
Chapter 7	The People and Their Neighborhoods	109
Chapter 8	Caring for Each Other	127
Chapter 9	The Downtown Churches	145
Chapter 10	Private and Public Education	149
Chapter 11	The Arts and Entertainment	167
Chapter 12	Leisure and Sports	177
Acknowledgements and Contributors		196
Bibliography		197
Index		198

The Indiana State University Homecoming Parade has been an exciting annual event since 1923. The 1953 Chi Omega Sorority float is shown here near the intersection of Seventh Street and Wabash Avenue. *Barbara Carney collection*

The Vigo County Historical Society

The Vigo County Historical Society, organized in 1922, was chartered as a not-for-profit organization in 1924. For years it met in the basement of the Emeline Fairbanks Library. John Biel, Juliet Peddle, Grace Davis and Walter Shriner were among the organizing members. The collections were stored in a variety of locations, including the library and the Sheldon Swope Art Gallery. The group disbanded during World War II and then reorganized with new vigor after the war.

The Historical Museum was purchased through a gift from the Hulman Foundation and opened in 1958. Dorothy Clark served as secretary of the society and later as curator. Rooms on the second floor were rented to help augment the society's funds; the last of those rooms was converted to exhibit display in the early 1980s. The society opened the Paul Dresser birthplace to the public in 1966. Strong community support helped raise the necessary funds to move the building and to restore it to an 1850s appearance.

In the late 1970s the efforts of Wayne Miller and Bill Pickett brought new vigor to the society through both business and individual membership drives. The society, again using funds from the Hulman Foundation, then purchased the Markle House. Plans called for opening the 1848 Greek Revival home as a third museum. Cost factors proved too much to support those efforts so the house was re-sold with covenants to insure its protection.

The Friends of the Historical Museum, organized in 1975, support the day-to-day activities of the Historical Museum and host a monthly program (open to the public) featuring a wide variety of speakers.

The society receives funding from a number of sources, including membership, grants and fundraising activities. The latter includes the Summer Celebration held each July. The first celebration at the Markle House in 1980 drew over 300 people. In 1992 more than 1200 people attended the musical variety show which differs from year to year, but is always based on some aspect of Vigo County history.

The Historical Society published its first book in 1983. *On the Banks of the Wabash: A Photograph Album of Greater Terre Haute, 1900-1950,* written by Dorothy Jerse, Judith Calvert and Kenneth Martin, celebrated the achievements of Martin's Photo Shop, 1906-1976. A second publication, *Juliet Peddle of Terre Haute: The Architect, The Historian, and Her City, 1899-1979,* was written in 1988 by Harriet M. Caplow, Joyce Lakey Shanks, Edward K. Spann, and Helene C. Steppe.

—David Buchanan, Executive Director

Vigo County Historical Society
Board of Directors, 1992-93

Janice J. Buffington; Martha Cowen; Robert Cundiff; Reta Decker; William E. Dever; R. Michael Dinkel; Kristine E. Felling; David Felstein; Harry Frey; George W. Gardner; Troy Helman; Cathy Hendricks; Samuel F. Hulbert; Kathryn Jarrett; Donald L. Layton; Nelson Markle; C. Don Nattkemper; James Nichols; Bette Rose; Peter Sacopulos; David W. Sullivan; Joseph A. Weist; John P. Woelfle

Paul Dresser Memorial Birthplace
Fairbanks Park

Historical Museum of the Wabash Valley
1411 South Sixth Street

Foreword

The story of Terre Haute, Indiana, is a fascinating part of the American drama. Located on the high east bank of the Wabash River, "Terre Haute" (French for high land) originated as a Native American village (the Wea tribe called it Orchard Town) and army outpost (Fort Harrison). The Terre Haute Land Company bought the site in 1816 from the U. S. government. A real estate venture and seat of Vigo County, it grew gradually into a grain- and lumber-milling crossroads.

The city's heyday came with the railroad construction that began in 1847. Located as it was at the heart of the Indiana-Illinois agricultural area and bituminous coal fields, local entrepreneur and landowner, Chauncey Rose, knew Terre Haute could benefit. He formed a company and proceeded to build the Terre Haute and Richmond (later the Vandalia) Railroad, which soon became the region's dominant enterprise. In the years that followed, Terre Haute became known for its manufacturing, food processing, and colleges—Saint Mary-of-the-Woods, Indiana State Normal and Rose Polytechnic Institute. Modest two- and three-room wooden cottages and bungalows where working class families clustered in ethnic neighborhoods surrounded the city's steel foundries, railroad and mine car shops, breweries and distilleries. Wealthy merchants, mine-owners, manufacturers, professors and railroad executives lived in two districts of sedate and stylish Italianate, Queen Anne, Four Square and Romanesque houses. In the early twentieth century, two of the nation's most important highways — U.S. 40, the Old National Road between Washington, D. C. and San Francisco, and U.S. 41, connecting Chicago and Miami — intersected in the central business area. Near the river was a drinking, gambling and brothel district. A city of various peoples and cultures, it was perhaps not surprising that Terre Haute was home of Daniel W. Voorhees, the state's longest serving United States Senator; Eugene V. Debs, the nation's most famous socialist presidential candidate; and Theodore Dreiser, America's best-known writer of realistic fiction, including *Sister Carrie* and *An American Tragedy*.

The decline in demand for coal that accompanied the advent of the internal combustion engine, along with federal prohibition of alcoholic beverages, brought Terre Haute's expansion to an end by 1920. The region's soft coal production declined. Automobiles and trucks began to supplant railroads. The population, having reached 70,000, stopped growing while the nation's population expanded elsewhere in geometrical fashion.

As years passed, Terre Haute was able to diversify its economy. By the 1960s pharmaceutical, chemical and musical record companies were on the scene. Construction of Interstate 70 three miles south of the city in 1969 formed a new crossroads with U.S. 41. Honey Creek Square became the retailing center. The bawdy entertainment district disappeared. Higher education replaced manufacturing as the service sector became the city's largest employer. Indiana State Normal became Indiana State University; Rose Polytechnic became Rose-Hulman Institute of Technology.

By combining photographs, quotations and narrative obtained through many years of living and working in their city and months of research and writing, the authors have revealed a Terre Haute heretofore little known even to many of its inhabitants, a city of unrelenting optimism and faith in American values.

William B. Pickett,
Professor of History
Rose-Hulman Institute of Technology

"The Wabash Valley Under Four Flags"

As we look backward, we see four national flags which have in turn floated over the Wabash Valley. There would have been five except that the Indians, the first inhabitants of this land, had nothing which took the place of a flag as we think of it today.

First then, there was the Spanish flag brought by the Spanish adventurer, DeSoto, when he landed on the shores of Florida about 1540. He did not get as far north as the Wabash Valley, but took possession of the whole country which was watered by the Mississippi River and its tributaries in the name of the King of Spain.

Then came the French "Voyaguers" — traders and explorers. They made way for LaSalle, Marquette, Joliette, Frenchmen who came and took possession of the country in the name of the King of France and raised the French flag, the Fleur-de-lis (1682). With the capture of Quebec in 1759, all French possessions in this part of North America passed to the hands and under the flag of England (1763).

Came then the period known as the American Revolution (1775-1783) and into the western country came General George Rogers Clark. To his successful campaign we owe the establishment of the western boundary of what was then the United States, making us a part of the great Northwest Territory (1784), and entitling us to the protection of the Stars and Stripes.

by Laura Briggs in *The Wabash Valley Remembers*, 1787-1938.

The mound builders had disappeared from the valley of the Wabash before explorers and fur traders arrived but left mounds containing their bones, ornaments and tools.

Later, the Miami, Wea, Piankeshaw, Kickapoo, Shawnee, Potawatomi and Delaware Native Americans lived in domed-roof wigwams as shown here. Pressures from movements of other tribes and from the French and English brought these tribes to the Wabash valley.
Watercolor by D. Omer Seamon

CHAPTER 1

In the Beginning

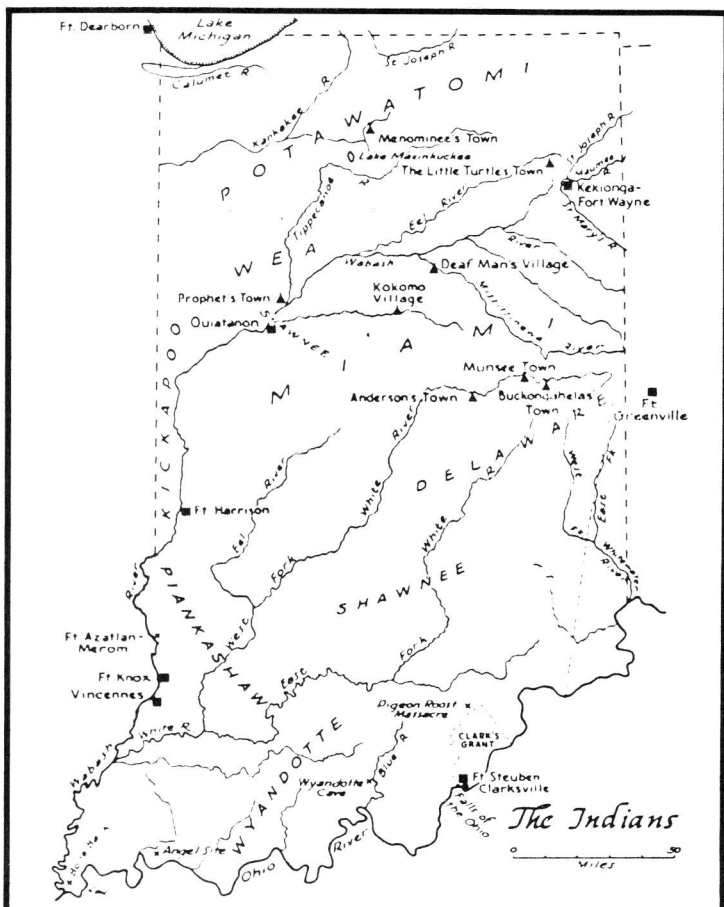

Map "Indians of Indiana" by Ray Clark for *A Pictorial History of Indiana* by Dwight Hoover; Indiana University Press, 1980.

> *"Terre Haute was a landmark 150 years before it became a city . . resting 50 feet above the water's edge on the east bank of the Ouabache (Wabash) this "highland" — "terre haute" in French — was like a beacon to early explorers and fur traders. The elevation could be sighted from several miles upstream and down."*

from *French Imprint on the Heart of America* by Mary Elizabeth Wood

---

The early history of the city of Terre Haute flows with the waters of the Wabash River. However, the earlier history of the area goes back millions of years to when the state of Indiana was covered by an inland sea. With slow upward movements of the floor, the sea withdrew leaving its evidence preserved in layers of sandstone and limestone.

The land was changed once again when vast glaciers from the north passed over the state. Temperatures warmed after this Age of Ice and enormous floods of water from the melting ice created the Wabash Valley.

The earliest human inhabitants were members of prehistoric tribes who left implements and bones as evidence of their cultures. Many years later, the Native Americans, whom the European explorers found and named Indians, came into the area from the north and then from the east.

The fur trade, a very profitable one to the European newcomers, gave the natives an incentive to hunt beyond providing furs and skins for their own use; these items could now be exchanged for tools, trinkets and liquor. Hunting in excess in exchange for the trader's products was destructive to the wild animal population and the liquor added to the destruction of tribal lifestyle.

Conflict was inevitable. The Native Americans believed the land belonged to all people; the Europeans had the concept of individual ownership. The wars between the French and the English and later the English and the American colonists caused each group to try to persuade the Native Americans to fight on "their side."

After years of bloody attacks and battles, treaties and purchases of lands from the Native Americans, the land became safe for settlers about 1814. They came in great numbers from the older states of the Union.

Patrick J. Furlong wrote, *Although the legendary American pioneer was typically a farmer who came west with his wife and a milk cow . . . there were also pioneers with no desire to face the backbreaking drudgery of agriculture. They came with a variety of ambitions, some hoping for easy wealth as land speculators and town promoters, others to ply their trades as millers, blacksmiths, or storekeepers . . .For everyone the frontier represented a hope for the future, and for some it was also an escape from demanding parents, unhappy marriages, eager creditors, or the sheriff.*

Whatever their individual reasons, both strength and courage characterized those who came to the valley of the Wabash to settle in the new real estate development called Terre Haute. In a speech given in 1873, the Rev. Blackford Condit praised these early residents, saying: *. . .for while the early settlements on the frontier at that time were characterized by ignorance and rowdyism, comparatively the early settlement of Terre Haute was characterized by its intelligence, good order, and by a certain gentility that has always marked the place.*

These people, the land, the river, the climate, and federal and state governments all contributed to the development of the city of Terre Haute.

FORT HARRISON – 1811

- - -September 26, 1811- - -

General William Henry Harrison, governor of the Indiana Territory, left Vincennes with a small army to confront a confederation of tribes under Tecumseh and his brother, The Prophet, at what has come to be known as the Battle of Tippecanoe.

- - -October 3, 1811- - -

Stopping on his way north, Harrison selected a site on a heavily wooded bluff overlooking the Wabash River for a fort to be built to protect his supply route. Construction was completed by the end of the month.

- - -September 4, 1812- - -

With Captain Zachary Taylor in command and at a time when many at the fort were suffering from "summer sickness," the fort was attacked and set afire by a war party of 600 Kickapoos, Potawatomis, Shawnees, Weas, and Winnebagos. Taylor and the men and women at the fort were able to repulse the attack, but they lost their stock and supplies. Major Willoughby Morgan took command in 1815 and was succeeded by Major John T. Chunn. The fort was de-activated in 1822.

William Henry Harrison, 1773-1841
9th President of the United States, 1841

Zachary Taylor, 1784-1850
12th President of the United States, 1849-1850

... the trees were felled, the timber hewn out, and the walls of the fort erected. These consisted of a rough palisade or stockade of heavy timber, about one hundred and fifty feet square. The northwest and south-west corners terminated in blockhouses ... two stories high, and pierced on both faces with embrasures, above and below, through which to fire on the enemy. This description was written by Attorney Charles Cruft for the first Terre Haute city directory in 1858. *woodcut print by Juliet Peddle*

Lodge No. 86 of the Benevolent and Protective Order of the Elks, founded in 1892, purchased the Fort Harrison Country Club in 1937. Their clubhouse, erected in 1970, is located on the site of the original fort. *Artie Harbaugh Photo*

WESTERN REGISTER & TERRE-HAUTE ADVERTISER.

VOL. 1. TERRE-HAUTE, VIGO COUNTY, INDIANA, MONDAY JULY 21, 1823 No. 1

EARLY PIONEERS

The *Western Register & Terre-Haute Advertiser* was the first newspaper to be printed in Terre Haute. J. W. Osborn, the printer and publisher who had moved to the new town from Vincennes, was described as "a man who, in my estimation, carried in his head all the knowledge of the world" by early resident Captain William Earle.

Osborn published the first issue on July 21, 1823. His editorial, "To the Public," reads in part:

The superior advantages of the northwestern country, present a most promising field for honest enterprise, and if we may judge from the acquisition of population, talents, enterprise & wealth it has received within the last seven years, together with its having been turned from a "howling wilderness," the haunts of prowling beasts of prey and the residence of ferocious Savage, into a comparative garden and the home of thousands of civilized, industrious and enlightened citizens, we may rationally look forward with the most pleasing anticipations to that happy era, when the combined energies of the citizens of the Northwest, will, by their irresistible exertions, carry into effect that grand system of internal improvement, which alone can render them independent—which will so materially add to their convenience and prosperity and raise our country to that splendid rank which the God of Nature has designed it.

Osborn's editorial reflects the feelings and prevalent attitudes of pioneers. Most believed that it was their responsibility to acquire the land and put it into production for their own gain even if this feat had to be accomplished through conflict with and removal of the original inhabitants to land west of the Mississippi River.

Arriving at Fort Harrison in 1815, Curtis Gilbert opened a trading store and served as postmaster there until the post office was moved south to Terre Haute in 1818. Gilbert was the town's first postmaster and clerk of Vigo County. He served as clerk and recorder for 21 years and was a member of the first two city councils. The house he built on the northeast corner of Water and Ohio streets, remembered as the first frame structure in the town, housed the first post office and county clerk's office, and one year later the first meeting of the Masonic lodge. The county jail was constructed on this site in 1882.

Sketch by Juliet Peddle

This log home photographed on Pioneer Days at Fowler Park in 1982 was constructed prior to 1830 in Riley Township on land obtained as a land grant in 1821 by John Jackson. A gift of the children of Dan and Iva Wood, it was moved to the park and reconstructed by the American Federation of Teachers, Local 734. A resource of the Vigo County Park and Recreation Department, this village and its volunteers recreate pioneer life to help visitors understand and appreciate Wabash Valley pioneer life. *Vigo County Park & Recreation Dept. Photo*

SALE OF LOTS
IN THE TOWN OF
TERRE HAUTE

WILL commence on the last Monday of October now ensuing, on the spot and under the superintendence of the proprietors, and continue for two days, if necessary, upon a credit of one and two years.

This Town has just been laid out upon one of the most liberal plans, as it respects healthiness and terms. It is not presumed nor intended that art can or shall counteract nature, but assist and promote her views; for any and all situations on the River Wabash either above or below Vincennes, Terre Haute is supereminently entitled to the precedency; not only from its elevated situation, being upon a high Bank of the river (from which circumstance it derives its name) immediately below Fort Harrison—the richness and depth of the soil, not only at the town but for miles of the adjacent and fertile plain, called Fort Harrison Prairie; and a country abounding with timber "fit for the builder's use," and extensive Coal Banks—Besides, it is a known and acknowledged truth, that there is no other eligible situation for a town for a number of miles above or below this site, other than the Lands owned by the proprietors of Terre Haute, and of their extensive claim they have selected the best; competition is therefore silenced. It is deemed necessary merely to observe, that the Wabash is navigable for Keels and Batteaux, at all seasons of the year, from its Rapids here, and for one hundred miles above.

Independent of those natural advantages, there are artificial ones such as few towns possess, for the Streets are from sixty-six to one hundred feet in width. Every Lot has the advantage of an Alley of sixteen feet. And ground has been appropriated for a Court and Market-Houses, and other public buildings, Churches, Schools, &c. It is rationally and confidently expected that ere long a new county will be formed in this part of the country and that Terre Haute will in all probability be the Seat of Justice. And those who are acquainted with the Geography of the country, do not hesitate to express their belief that a public Road will shortly be opened from the State of Ohio direct to this place, and hence to St. Louis.

CUTHBERT & T. BULLITT,
JONATHAN LINDLEY,
ABRAHAM MARKLE,
HYACINTH LASSELLE,
Proprietors, by their Agent,
Joseph Kitchel
Vincennes, Ind. Sept. 19, 1816

"A new village has been laid out at Terre Haute, three miles below Fort Harrison. This situation, for beauty of prospect, is exceded by none in the state."

Samuel R. Brown, 1817, in *The Western Gazetteer; or Emigrants' Directory*.

The plat of the original town of Terre Haute containing 268 lots bounded by Eagle St. (N), Fifth St. (E), Swan St. (S), and Water St. (W) was filed and recorded at Vincennes, Knox County, on October 25, 1816.

The above advertisement announcing the new real estate development of Terre Haute and offering lots for sale appeared in the October 7, 1816, issue of *Liberty Hall and Cincinnatti Gazette*. That same year the State of Indiana was admitted to the Union by joint resolution of Congress.

The town property was divided into 12 shares among the proprietors: Cuthbert and Thomas Bullitt of Louisville, Kentucky - 2; Jonathan Lindley of Orange County - 4; Hyacinth Lasselle of Vincennes - 3; and Abraham Markle of Fort Harrison - 3.

VIGO COUNTY FOUNDED - 1818

Vigo County (pronounced Vee´go) broke off from Sullivan County on January 21, 1818, by an act of the state legislature. Two months later Terre Haute became the county seat.

The county was named in honor of Francis Vigo, a successful trader, who had given financial and military intelligence support to General George Rogers Clark in his campaign to capture the Northwest Territory from the British for the United States, 1778-1779.

Warmed by the welcome he received on his visit to Terre Haute on July 4, 1834, Vigo bequeathed the county $500 in his will to purchase a bell for the courthouse. In 1875, many years after his death, the money he had given to equip the army of General Clark was paid to the executors of his will. The bell, purchased in part with $500 of the settlement of the claim, still hangs in the courthouse tower.

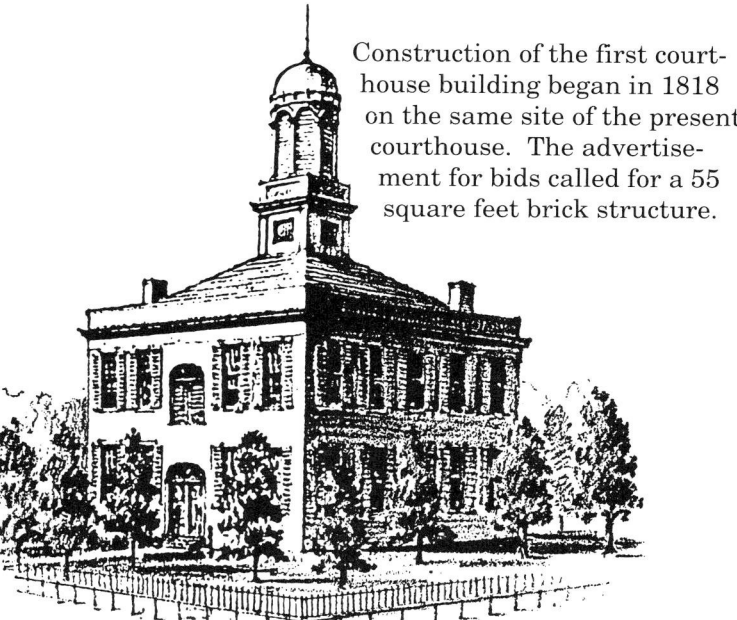

Construction of the first courthouse building began in 1818 on the same site of the present courthouse. The advertisement for bids called for a 55 square feet brick structure.

Sketch by Juliet Peddle

Charles Lesueur, the French naturalist who traveled through North America from 1815 to 1837, made this sketch of Francis Vigo.

Bruno Roselli wrote of Vigo: *The Italian-Americans have in Francesco Vigo, born at Mondovi, Italy on December 3rd, 1747, and laid to rest in his beloved Indiana (Vincennes) on March 22nd, 1836, a natural hero . . . no less unselfish as the great Lafayette.*

Artie Harbaugh photo

In 1966, Vigo County Commissioner Harry Brentlinger and three students checked out the two-ton Vigo Bell which hangs in the present courthouse. It has been called both the "liberty bell of Indiana" and the "liberty bell of the Northwest Territory."

Construction of the building, designed by Samuel Hannaford & Sons, Cincinnati, was completed in 1888, four years after the cornerstone was laid. The dome has become a symbol of both tradition and of the future to the citizens of the Terre Haute area.

A TOWN DEVELOPS 1817 – 1832

The appearance of Terre Haute changed from a pioneer village to a growing town once the county seat was established here in 1818. By 1823, J. W. Osborn's October 15th editorial in the *Western Register & Terre Haute Advertiser* reads:

The local situation of Terre Haute appears as favorable to health as that of any other we have seen in the Western Country, it is surrounded by a body of land, inferior to none in the Union. - A great part of this land is owned by industrious, wealthy, enterprising and enlightened citizens—and we believe that no part of our state can boast of such rapid improvements as have been made in this and adjoining counties within the last six years. The town of Terre Haute, however, has been impeded in its growth by many obstacles. — The immense prices at which lots were valued at the first sales — The severe change in the times which immediately ensued, and the then scarcity of lumber and high prices of other articles for building placed it beyond the power of those who did not possess large capital, to furnish themselves with lots, dwellings, shops &c. These obstacles, together with the afflicting disease, which this place, in common with almost every other in the West, was visited in 1820, have checked growth, which from its natural advantageous situation it would otherwise have had.

But, for two or three years past, while other parts have been visited, (as in the case this season) with the most fatal diseases, Terre Haute has been peculiarly favoured with health,—and notwithstanding the hardness of times the town has been increasing in wealth, improvements and population. It now contains about 50 buildings besides a most splendid Court House a Jail—&c.

There are established in this village five Stores, one Grocery, three Taverns, two Boot & Shoe Shops, two Blacksmiths and one Gunsmiths three Taylors besides several Carpenters and Joiners, Cabinet-makers &c., and from the liberal prices of labour, the demand of various other mechanics, and the great inducements which are held out to capitalists, we can but look forward with the most pleasing anticipations,—the local situation of our town, the fertility of the adjoining country, the intelligence, enterprize and worth of the citizens who surround us, combine in warranting the assertion, that Terre Haute will not long be inferior, to the most populous town in our state.

The 1830 U. S. Census reported a total of 5,766 individuals living in Vigo County. Two per cent of the county residents were free African-American males and females and 37 per cent were children ten years of age and younger; less than 100 persons were 60 years or older.

The Dewees-Preston-Smith house, once located at South Thirteenth and one-half and Poplar streets, was built between 1823 and 1827 by Major George W. Dewees who had come to Terre Haute from New Orleans. Known as the oldest dwelling in the city for many years, it was badly damaged by fire in 1979 and razed in 1988 despite the efforts of historic preservation groups to save and restore it.

David Linton built one of the earliest brick homes in 1830 in the middle of the block bounded by Ohio, Walnut, Fifth and Sixth streets. It was moved forward to 521 Ohio Street in 1879 and converted to commercial use. The TV Drive-in facilities of the Terre Haute Savings Bank now occupy the site.

CHAPTER 2

Always Going Somewhere

This member of The Motorcycle Club promoted Terre Haute with pride about 1914.

"In its early days the only way of getting to Terre Haute or away from it was by the river. Other towns were far distant. Man set to work to bring them together."

from *Art Souvenir of Terre Haute*, 1894.

The site of Terre Haute was chosen in part because of its proximity to the Wabash River. As historian William F. Cronin pointed out, it was selected not because of the beauty but for the utilitarian reasons of the river providing a water supply and an avenue of transportation.

Terre Hauteans, aware of their geographical location, later named it the "Crossroads of America." Promotional materials written throughout the years point out the advantages.

This account appeared in the 1890 volume, *The Industrial Advantages of Terre Haute: The great fertility and advantageous location of Terre Haute made it an important trading and distributing point when it was but a village. Flotillas of "broad horns," or flat-boats, and quite a fleet of little steamboats were loaded with pork and produce for the Mississippi River and New Orleans. When the line of trade shifted from north and south to east and west this point was still in the highway, and the great National Road, from Maryland to the Mississippi River, passed through it; the Wabash and Erie Canal, for a time such an important connection of the lakes and the Ohio, also passed through it, to be succeeded . . . by a railroad as an avenue for eastern trade.*

The National Road, with its stage coaches, was paralleled by the Terre Haute & Richmond Railroad, destined to be an important link in the greatest railroad system of the world—the pioneers of the nine railroads converged to this city . . . To the 5,000 people here just before the T. H. & I. was built may be added 5,000 for each new road—but the new census will probably show more than 45,000.

With nine lines radiating from the city, railroads did have a large part in employment and the prosperity of the city at the turn of the century. The steam locomotive had brought the death of river and canal transportation for both passengers and freight.

The first automobile appeared in Terre Haute in 1900 and electric street cars and interurbans also entered the transportation scene. More shoppers could get to the downtown stores. Workers no longer had to live close to their workplaces, and new real estate developments appeared on the edges of the city.

At first the automobile belonged only to the rich; it would take a few decades of electric interurban trains and intercity buses before improved roads, personally-owned vehicles, and the trucking industry would change the way of life from train depots and bus terminals to filling stations, auto repair shops, roadside restaurants and motels, and drive-in banking service.

Speed continues to be the big factor. Just as once Terre Haute residents and businesses thought horse-drawn vehicles had become too slow, they now choose to use Hulman Regional Airport and Interstate 70. No matter how the means and rate of speed change, transportation remains a matter of moving people and products from one place to another.

WABASH RIVER

The city of Terre Haute owes its location to the Wabash River which continues to flow through its history. The name "Wabash" has its roots in the languages of the Native American tribes; the Miami said "Wa bah shik ki" meaning "white" for the limestone on the river bottom which gave the water a bright, clear appearance. The French spelling was "Ouabache," pronounced "Wabash."

The dugout canoes of the Native Americans, explorers and traders were gradually replaced by the flat boats. Although they could only float downstream, they were the best means at the time to ship

The date of this photograph of an excursion on the steamer *Romeo,* owned by Uriah Shewmaker, is in question. However, on June 26, 1867, the *Terre Haute Daily Express* reported, "The *Romeo* with the Centenary Sabbath School got off in good season yesterday morning . . . The Prairie City band accompanied the excursion."

The limestone through which the water of the Wabash River flows makes the river a prime area for fresh water mussels. Shown here are men forking mussels from the river and a mussel buyer on the west bank at Tecumseh in the early 1900s. The shells were used in the manufacture of buttons until plastic buttons took over the market. Beginning in the 1950s, the Terre Haute firm of M. D. Cohen & Son, Inc. began exporting the shells to the cultured pearl industry in Japan. There a tiny piece of the shell is inserted into oysters to cause an irritation which forces an oyster to develop a pearl.
Logan Edwards collection

the products of the valley to New Orleans and other markets on the way. Keel boats, moved forward by men with poles, came up the river with goods during the summer when the water was low.

The arrival of the first steam boat was reported in the May 10, 1823 issue of the Vincennes *Western Sun and General Advertiser*. It was a joyous occasion. Local historian H. W. Beckwith described the event: *She landed at the old boat-yard south of the foot of Oak Street. Of course the whole town went to see her, besides the country round about. The steamboats were always welcomed by firing the "old cannon."*

In June 1831, the *Western Register & Terre Haute Advertiser* reported on the river traffic: *Eight years ago the first steamboat ascended the river. Since December 1st we have had 36 arrivals from below and 27 from above, in all 63 in six months. We believe 1,700 flatboats have descended the Wabash this spring.*

The steamboat era continued until the 1880s. Like the simpler boats before them, they provided transportation for people and commerce, but they were also used for pleasure excursions.

Shortly after the turn of the century and at other times since, efforts have been made to make the Wabash River navigable once again. It has not happened yet; however, the river continues to be used for recreation. Boating enthusiasts welcomed the construction of the 200 foot Ralph Tucker Memorial Boat Dock in Fairbanks Park. It was dedicated on October 10, 1992.

This crowd enjoying a river cruise on the *Eloise* in 1906 is said to be a group of Terre Haute saloonkeepers and their families. No doubt a good time was had by all.

Known as "the most stupendous, colossal showboat ever," the "Floating Palace" arrived in Terre Haute for 2 and 7 p.m. performances on Saturday, April 23, 1853, and once again on the return trip from Lafayette on April 30. The interior contained a circus ring, large theater and museum, and seating for an estimated 1,500 persons.

Wabash Courier, April 9, 1853

Spectators in Fairbanks Park watched this hovercraft in action on the Wabash River in April, 1990. Reporting that Neoteric-USA-Inc. and Eglen Hovercraft were manufacturing these air-cushion vehicles in the city, the October, 1976 issue of *Indiana Magazine* labeled Terre Haute the "Small Hovercraft Capitol of the World." *Tribune-Star Publishing Company* photo

The Wabash & Erie Canal, 1832-1874 - 468 miles

"On March 2, 1827, Congress provided a land grant to encourage Indiana to build the Wabash & Erie Canal. Work began five years later on February 22, 1832 in Fort Wayne. Construction proceeded west as the canal reached Lafayette in 1841. A second federal land grant enabled the canal to reach Terre Haute by 1849. The connection with the Evansville segment was completed in 1853 forming the longest canal in the United States."

—Canal Society of America

Construction was accomplished with simple tools including picks, shovels and wheelbarrows by crews of diggers, mostly Irish immigrants, who had to endure fever, dysentery and cholera. It has been said that "one laborer died for every six miles of canal built."

The boats, known as packets, brought new settlers to the area and gave residents a way to travel. The canal also opened more and larger markets to farmers and merchants all along the line.

In 1898 author Maurice Thompson described a canal boat as a "long, low, narrow structure, appearing like an elongated floating house, with ill-ventilated and dimly lighted cabin and sleeping berths."

He wrote: *It was drawn by one or two horses hitched to a long rope attached to the bow of the boat. The horses walked on a path called a towpath, at the side of the canal, and were driven by a man or boy, who sometimes rode, sometimes walked. The boat had a rudder with which a pilot kept it in its proper place while it crept along like a great lazy turtle on the still water.*

A "Bulletin of the Indiana Historical Bureau" (1971) reads: *People on the line regarded their canal with irritation, irony and affection. They grumbled about breaks stopping navigation, low water that left boats stranded in the mud, the negligence of lazy superintendents, exorbitant tolls . . . But they admired the big ditch and . . . relished the robust vitality of canaling.*

Competition from railroads brought an end to the canal era. The section south of Terre Haute was closed in 1860 and the canal trustees officially closed the canal in 1874. The whole line was offered for sale at an auction in Terre Haute in February, 1876. Canal historian Paul Fatout wrote this epitaph, "The Wabash & Erie Canal was no more . . . having died in debt for more than $18 million."

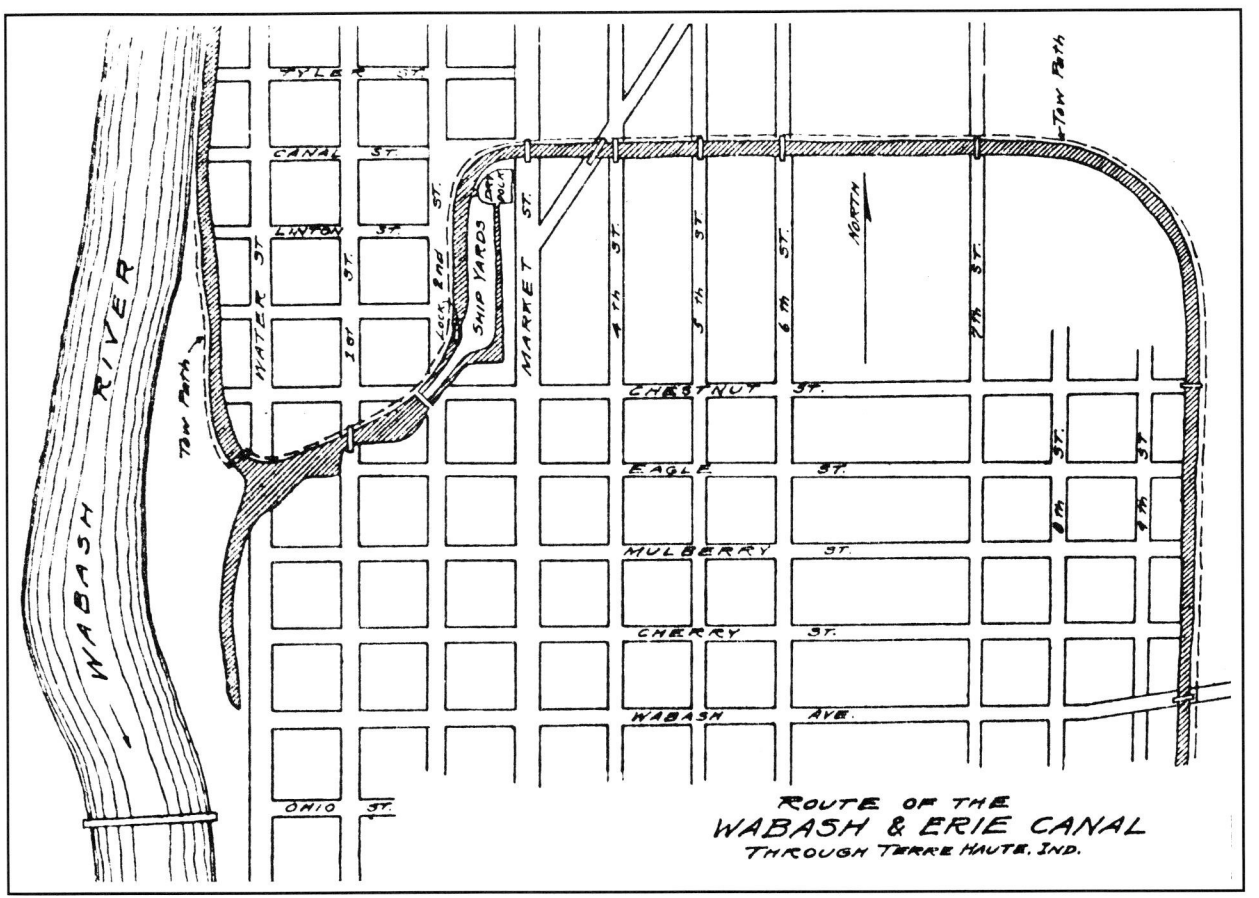

Traveling four to six miles an hour, the boats would enter Terre Haute from the north, pass through locks near the corner of Second and Chestnut streets and under wooden bridges on their way through the city to Lockport (now Riley). This map appeared with an article about the canal by F. H. Cash, Jr. in a 1907 issue of the *Rose Technic*.

This wooden bridge, the second to span the Wabash River at Terre Haute, was built by the Terre Haute Drawbridge Company in 1865. When raised, the draw of the bridge allowed steamboats to pass through.

Bridges Over The Wabash River

As the city and its business prospered, the demand for a bridge grew. The first wooden bridge was opened Christmas Day, 1846, at the foot of Ohio Street supplanting the Farrington ferry. The second and third bridges were located at the foot of Wabash Avenue, and the current twin structures are off Cherry and Ohio streets. The purpose remains the same; only the designs and materials used in construction have changed.

These men seem pleased to pose for a photograph on the draw near the west end of the bridge where the channel was at that time. First operated as a toll bridge, it was purchased by the county for $80,000 and made a free bridge in 1874.

This photograph, taken from the courthouse tower, shows the steel bridge in the center, which was completed in 1905, awaiting demolition. The new twin Theodore Dreiser (east bound) and Paul Dresser (west bound) Memorial Bridges were dedicated on October 15, 1992.
Artie Harbaugh photo

The National Road

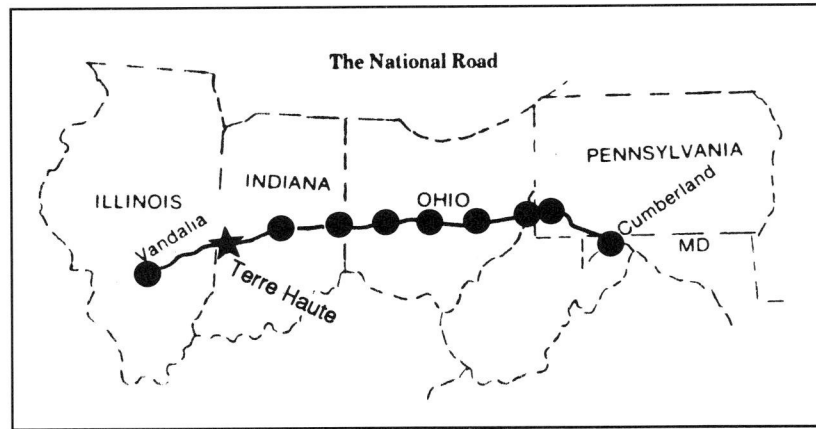

The first great east-west road across Indiana was the National Road, also known as "The Great Western Road," "The Old Pike," "The Government Road," "The Cumberland Road," and "The Main Street of America." Construction began in the east in 1811.

After the first federal appropriation for the Indiana segment was made in 1829, the superintendents advertised for bids. The road was to be 80 feet wide and graded. Lee Burns, road historian, wrote that the first specifications read, "remove the stumps in the central 30 feet," but that later ones provided that "no stumps were to be over 15 inches high and that those in the center of the road were to be rounded and trimmed so as to present no serious obstructions to carriages."

Construction was completed though Terre Haute and to the Indiana-Illinois line by 1834. Many years later it became State Road 3. The designation U.S. Highway 40 followed in 1926.

STAGES (1858)
WEST to ST. LOUIS—
Leaves Buntin's Hotel, Mondays, Wednesdays and Fridays, 3:30 P.M.
NORTH to ATTICA—
Leaves Buntin's Hotel daily at 6:30 A.M.
To CRAWFORDSVILLE leaves Post Office, Mondays and Thursdays at 7 A.M.

Located on the southeast corner of South Third (then Market Street) and Ohio streets and first known as the City Hotel, Buntin's Hotel was popular during the stage coach era. The proprietor at the time this advertisement and schedule appeared in the 1858 city directory was Touissant Cameron Buntin.

January 21, 1892
The first consignment of paving brick for Main Street (now Wabash Avenue) has been received by the contractors and are being stored along the north side of Main between Ninth and Tenth Streets. Two million bricks will be on hand before the work is commenced. The brick is furnished by the Canton (Ohio) Paving Company.
Terre Haute Gazette

The Crossroads of America

Terre Haute has been called the "crossroads" of America, of the nation and of the world because two major roads meet at right angles in the city. The east-west route, the National Road, has been variously named Wabash Street, Main Street, National Road Street, Wabash Avenue, State Road 3, and U.S. 40. Now the major east-west route is Interstate 70, south of the original city, but U.S. 40 still follows Wabash Avenue until it splits into Cherry and Ohio streets to bypass the courthouse on its way to and from the Wabash River bridges.

The north-south route has been known as Seventh Street, State Road 10, the Dixie Bee Highway, and U.S. 41. Now the route is on Third Street which has become U.S. 41.

The "crossroads" title also stemmed from the fact that the city was a railway center for steam and electric lines and for many years was located near the nation's center of population.

This highway billboard welcomed visitors to the city in 1945 with the hope they would drive on to the Terre Haute House at the "crossroads" of Seventh Street and Wabash Avenue. *Martin Photo*

Located six miles west of U.S. 41 on Interstate 70, the Clear Creek Welcome Center was opened in 1992 by the Indiana Department of Transportation. Eastbound travelers are welcomed at the center by the Terre Haute Convention & Visitors Bureau, which began operation in 1981. Its office is located just one-half block west of the original "crossroads" in downtown Terre Haute.
Terre Haute Convention & Visitor's Bureau collection

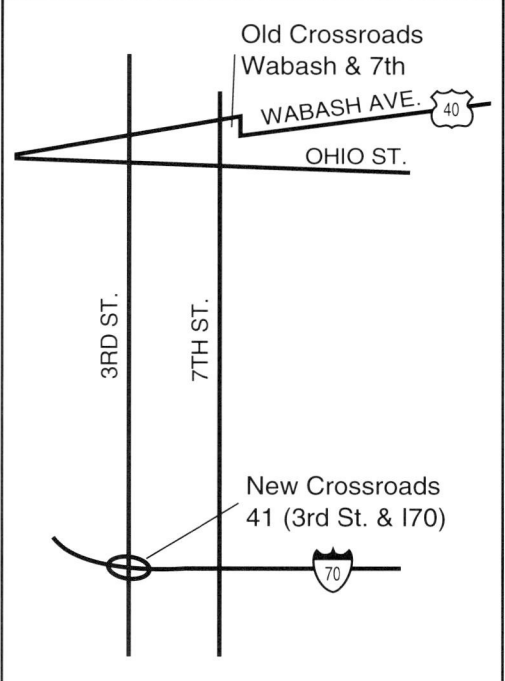

With the completion of Interstate 70 through Terre Haute in 1969, the crossroads moved south to the point where I-70 crosses U.S. 41. Now travelers are greeted at the Clear Creek Welcome Center and are persuaded by billboards along the way to stop for meals at restaurants and overnight stays in motels located near the junction of I-70 and U.S. 41.

Horses To...

Horse transportation was "the way to go," although the destination of these young people is unknown. Many businesses in the city were horse-related. In 1890 six transfer companies offered carriages, omnibuses and baggage wagons to and from all trains.

Milkman Earl Boyer and his twin sons, Jim and Jack, posed by his delivery wagon in the 1930s. For more than a third of this century, horse-drawn vehicles competed with trucks for the delivery of products. *James Boyer Collection*

Veterinarian S. V. Ramsey was one of nine veterinarians practicing in Terre Haute in 1900. An 1889 graduate of Chicago Veterinary College, he is shown here with a horse skeleton at his hospital at 222 South Third Street. A McDonald's Restaurant is now at this location.

Horseless Carriages

The delivery truck in this 1955 advertisement for the Model Milk & Ice Cream Company, 540 North Seventh Street, has replaced the horse-drawn vehicle. The milkman was one of the "efficient, courteous route men, who cover Terre Haute and vicinity." *Vigo County Public Library collection*

This photograph of Dr. George L. Dickerson with his automobile appeared in Volume I, Number One of the *Haute Magazine* April, 1904. Described as an "auto enthusiast," he was also a physician with office hours listed as "every day in the year from 8 to 12, 1 to 5 and 7 to 8 o'clock" at 22 1/2 South Sixth Street.

There were 12 automobile dealers offering new models in Terre Haute in 1947, one of which was this Packard dealership at 1800 Wabash Avenue. These new models were advertised as "out of this world . . . into your heart: Three Great New Packard Eights for '48."

Later this site became the location of Key Auto Sales, Bill Fowler Dodge, and then Vigo Dodge. Kasameyer Glass, Inc. has occupied the building since 1969. *Martin Photo*

Pennsylvania Railroad Shops - March 14, 1929
Little did these Pennsylvania Railroad workers know what was coming down the track . . . the stock market crash and the beginning of the Great Depression were just months away. Many workers would experience worry and hard times during the 1930s. *Richard Unger collection*

Car Shop Employees
...ute, Ind - March 14, 1929

RAILROADS

Vandalia Line Railroad Shops, Terre Haute, Ind.

This streamlined diesel-electric power locomotive was photographed at a stop in Terre Haute in December, 1945. Units like this one provided the power for the fastest passenger trains on the New York Central System.
Martin Photo

Opposite page: This solid and important system, grown up around the Terre Haute & Indianapolis, has its heart in this city where its shops and main offices have been located since its beginning . . . The distribution of its monthly pay roll and purchase of supplies making a very large business—not very often disturbed as this road is as uniformly busy as any in the United States. The Industrial Advantages of Terre Haute, *1890*

Railroad history in Terre Haute began with the charter of the Terre Haute and Richmond Railroad Company in 1847, with Chauncey Rose president and with its completion in 1852. The number of railroad lines serving the city first grew and then declined with the smaller lines becoming parts of larger systems during the next 140 years.

    1860:   Evansville & Crawfordsville — Terre Haute & Richmond — Alton & St. Louis

    1890:   Terre Haute & Indianapolis — Terre Haute & Alton — Indianapolis & St. Louis — St. Louis, Vandalia & Terre Haute — Terre Haute & Logansport — Evansville & Terre Haute — Chicago & Eastern Illinois — Evansville & Indianapolis — Terre Haute & Peoria

    1920:   Chicago & Eastern Illinois — Chicago, Terre Haute & Southeastern — Evansville & Indianapolis — New York Central (Big Four) — Pittsburgh, Cincinnati, Chicago & St. Louis (Pennsylvania)

    1940:   Chicago & Eastern Illinois — Chicago, Milwaukee, St. Paul & Pacific — New York Central System — Pennsylvania.

    1968:   The Pennsylvania Railroad and New York Central became Penn Central. The Chicago & Eastern Illinois Railroad ceased passenger service to Terre Haute.

    1979:   Amtrak's "National Limited," the last passenger train through the city, was discontinued.

    1990:   Conrail — Louisville & Nashville — Soo railroad freight lines.

The many railroad lines traveling through the city were an important factor in the city's economic growth, but also a source of frustration. When trains blocked crossings, street traffic stopped. After years of delays, three overpasses were constructed: Fruitridge Avenue, 1972; Fort Harrison Road, 1978; and North Third Street, 1986.

The photo above was taken by John D. Galloway, an 1889 graduate of Rose-Polytechnic Institute, for his senior thesis entitled, "A Review of the East Span of the Vandalia Bridge." *Rose-Hulman Institute of Technology collection*

Crossing guard houses were in use before the advent of automated signals. This one at left, photographed by John Galloway in 1889, was located across the street from Jacob Stump's grocery and saloon at 603 North Fourth Street. *Rose-Hulman Institute of Technology collection*

DEPOTS

Built by A. R. Monninger and C. J. Dressler and known as The Northern until 1907, the hotel contained 20 sleeping rooms, a cafe and a bar at the time of its grand opening on August 14, 1899. The building was torn down in 1969.

The Big Four Depot and the Great Northern Hotel were located across the street from each other at North Seventh and Tippecanoe streets. Both were built in 1899 where the Cleveland, Cincinnati, Chicago & St. Louis (later the New York Central Lines) stopped in the city. The depot was razed in 1986; the last passenger train had stopped there in 1979. *Judith Calvert collection*

August 15, 1893 - *The Vandalia's new union station was put into service today . . . The first train to stop was the 11 o'clock train of the Peoria division of the Vandalia . . . The depot is three stories high, with a two hundred foot tower and large rotunda center . . . Red stone is used for the first thirty feet and after that the material is pressed brick with red stone trimming.* Terre Haute Gazette

Designed by Hannaford & Sons and located on North Ninth Street between Sycamore and Spruce Streets, this remarkable Romanesque structure was razed in 1960.

The only building of the complex still standing is the site of the Afro-American Culture Center of Indiana State University. *Rose-Hulman Institute of Technology collection*

STREET CARS

1866 — Terre Haute Street Railway was granted a charter by the city

1867 — The first line (Union Depot to First Street) was put into operation with mules supplying the power.

1890-91 — The system was changed to electrical lines.

1904 — The Terre Haute Electric Company, which was organized in 1899, was consolidated with the Terre Haute Electric Traction Company. It owned the Terre Haute electric light system, the street car lines in Brazil, Clinton, Terre Haute and West Terre Haute and several interurban lines out of Terre Haute.

1907 — The operation was taken over by the Terre Haute Indianapolis & Eastern Traction Company.

1939 — The street car lines were abandoned and service was taken over by the buses of the Terre Haute City Lines.

The 1908 roster of equipment of the Terre Haute Traction & Light Company from the collection of W. C. Twigg lists car #93 as: "32', 1" long, 7' 6" wide and 11', 5" high over the roof and a 66/18 gear ratio." It was built in 1907.

The small, lightweight Birney Safety Cars, equipped with devices to permit one-man operation, dominate this Wabash Avenue scene. The Wabash Avenue line from the courthouse to Highland Lawn Cemetery, along with the South Seventh Street and North Nineteenth Street lines, were the last three to remain in operation before buses took over the service. *Judith Calvert collection*

BIRNEY SAFETY CARS
*in operation on Wabash Ave.,
Terre Haute, Ind., U.S.A.
··· April, 1920 ···*

Interurbans

Charles L. Henry of Anderson, Indiana, coined the word "interurban" for electric railways between towns in 1893. The trains were often called "windsplitters."

EAST — The first line in the Wabash Valley was completed from Terre Haute to Brazil in 1900. It reached Greencastle in 1907. The following year service from Terre Haute to Indianapolis via Greencastle was available.

NORTH — The Terre Haute to Clinton line was constructed to Ellsworth (North Terre Haute) and on to Clinton in 1903.

WEST — Reaching West Terre Haute and St. Mary's in 1905, the line to Paris was completed in 1907.

SOUTH — The line was built to Farmersburg, to Shelburn, and on to Sullivan in 1906.

Interurban service was discontinued on January 11, 1940.

Noted for the carved stone facades on the north and south sides, the Terminal Arcade, designed by architect Daniel Burnham, was constructed by the Terre Haute Traction & Light Company in 1911. Interurban passengers could walk through the building from the street to the north side to board the trains. Businesses occupied the ground floor and the basement. Vacant at various times, the building later served as a bus terminal and as a restaurant.

These two men, identified as Hess and C. B. Smith, are standing by car #29 on the interurban line from Terre Haute to Paris in 1920. Soon buses and cars would become more attractive to travelers and falling revenues would bring an end to the interurban era.

Buses

The story of Terre Haute bus service is divided between the commercial intercity lines, which competed with steam and interurban trains, and the city lines which replaced street car service.

INTERCITY — October 25, 1925 - *The motorized bus lines are a convenience and a necessity to thousands of people throughout the Wabash Valley. It is a fact that the buses serve many cities and towns whose other means of transportation is such that they can not arrive in Terre Haute during shopping hours. Also that the buses pass through many cities and towns where steam trains are only available once a day . . . A grand total of over 200 regularly scheduled bus trains are now operating in and out of the various bus stations in Terre Haute EACH AND EVERY DAY.*
        advertisement in the *Terre Haute Tribune*

CITY LINES — June 4, 1939 - *Evolution of Terre Haute's transit system from street cars to buses . . . will be complete Sunday morning when Terre Haute City Lines, Inc. takes over the entire system replacing all cars and buses now in service with new and modern motor coaches.*
        Terre Haute Tribune-Star

Located at 520 Cherry Street, this station was in use from about 1930 until 1949 when the bus lines moved to the Terminal Arcade at 820 Wabash Avenue. By the early 1970s the Greyhound and Trailways lines were using a newly-constructed bus station at 222 Cherry Street.

Pictured are the new diesel buses which arrived in 1948. The garage, constructed in 1939, was located at 101 Ohio Street. The city assumed operation of the buses on September 22, 1964. *Both photos Vigo County Public Library collection*

Early Air Travel

August 8, 1911 - *"Gee, it's great." This was the remark of Louis Johnson, who with his brothers, Harry and Julius, had been working for months to perfect a monoplane. The remark was occasioned by two highly successful flights at the "aviation field" on the Elroy Smith farm near Ellsworth (North Terre Haute) this morning. Terre Haute Tribune*

Louis, Harry, Julius and Clarence Johnson later became well-known for their success in the manufacture of the famous Johnson marine motors in Waukegan, Illinois. This model of their airplane, which was the first successful monoplane built and designed in the United States, was placed in the Smithsonian Institute, Washington, D. C. in 1960.

A second original plane built in Terre Haute was a tractor biplane designed and constructed by E. A. "Gus" Riggs in 1913. *Vigo County Public Library collection*

Early local pilots used unimproved fields at 25th Street and Wabash Avenue and at South Seventh Street and Davis Avenue, the latter of which would become Dresser Field. The site was approved in 1929, and it was made the Municipal Airport in 1930.

The name was changed to Paul Cox Field in 1933 in honor of Cox, who had died in a plane crash with William R. Root in 1932. The field was officially closed to air traffic in 1959. Terre Haute South Vigo High School now stands on part of the site.

Herman Brown, who had learned to fly at Paul Cox Field, opened his Sky King Airport north of the city. It was dedicated in 1962 with Kirby Grant, star of the "Sky King" television show in attendance.

Harry E. Fitch, vice-president, Dr. Albert M. Mitchell, president, and Raymond F. Thomas, secretary, of the Terre Haute Board of Aviation Commissioners posed with the attendants assigned to this Chicago & Southern airplane in 1941.

Hulman Regional Airport

Robert Kadel photographed Edward Whalen, president of the Chamber of Commerce; Mrs. Anton Hulman, Sr.; and Anton Hulman, Jr. at the dedication ceremony of the Terminal Building on November 29, 1953. The plaque reads: "This tablet is placed here in appreciation of the splendid effort and generosity of Mrs. Anton Hulman (and) Anton Hulman, Jr. for making possible this airport and terminal."

A 640 acre tract in Lost Creek Township was approved for an airport by the federal government on February 9, 1943. Just days later Anton Hulman, Jr., gave $100,000 to the city with which to purchase the land. Work began that summer.

The *Terre Haute Tribune,* reporting the dedication ceremony, declared, *Terre Haute's place in the imminent post-war aviation boom is assured, and numerous authorities credited Hulman Field with being the most advanced type of installation ever approved by the Civil Aviation Authority.*

Expansion and improvement continued. By 1977 more than 400 persons were employed on a full-time basis at the airport, 230 of whom were full-time Indiana Air National Guard employees. Indiana's only FAA Automated Flight Service Station opened at the field in 1985.

Flight 20 of TWA landed to pick up the eastbound mail when Hulman Field was dedicated on October 3, 1944. The ceremony attracted thousands of spectators, including students and employees of the city schools and retail stores which had been closed for the afternoon ceremony. Hazel Dodge Turman was the first Terre Hautean to make a round trip when TWA air service was inaugurated on July 1, 1945.

The commercial airlines and the airport administration moved their offices from temporary quonset huts into the new terminal at Hulman Airport in November, 1953. Pictured here in 1954, the terminal had been a half-million dollar construction project. The general contractors were Roehm Bros., Inc. *Martin Photo*

What's In A Name?

The city lies on the western margin of "Fort Harrison Prairie" and from this peculiarity of location, many years since received the sobriquet of Prairie City, by which it is now known far and wide.
  Terre Haute City Directory, 1860-61

July 3, 1939

Editor the Star:

"Terre Haute's nickname was Prairie City, and an apt one, too. It carried it for many years and until . . . older newspaper men had passed on and newer ones took their places who had no particularly sympathetic interest in Terre Haute, and treated it as if it were like a mule, without the pride of ancestry or the hope of posterity.

. . . The nickname Prairie City is just as applicable now as it was when 'the fairest city of the plain' was christened that, during or before the Civil War. . . . When we had two rolling mills, a nail factory and a glass factory we tried to give Terre Haute a new nickname, the Pittsburgh of the West, for some reason or other it did not 'take.' . . . Perhaps we can revive the good old name, Prairie City . . ."
  — A. C. Duddleston

Duddleston was at one time the editor of the *Saturday Spectator*. His wish for the return of the "Prairie City" nickname did not come true. Logos and slogans based on the "crossroads" and "banks of the Wabash" themes have come and gone as well as "Pride City" and "Terre Haute Gets My Vaute."

we're excited about terre haute!
  ...the pride city!

CHAPTER 3
City Government

Mayor P. Pete Chalos was assisted by Lisa Williamson, Terre Hautean and Miss Indiana, 1989, in lighting the Christmas tree at The Meadows as a part of the American Cancer Society's program. *Tribune-Star Publishing Co. photo*

> **"***It was divine nature which gave us the country, and man's skill that built the cities.***"**
>
> Marcus Terentius Varro (116- 27 B.C.)

The responsibilities of local government are a challenge to the electorate and to the officials they elect.

The verbs used in specifying the powers given to the government of the Town of Terre Haute in its charter in 1838 give the reader a sense of the magnitude of these responsibilities. Each power is introduced with words such as prevent, restrain, prohibit, punish, suppress, compel, direct, regulate, determine, abate, remove, provide, and establish.

True, local officials are no longer required to prevent horse-racing in the streets, to regulate the times and places of swimming in the river, to establish market houses, to direct the location of slaughter houses, or to prohibit the rolling of hoops which annoy other persons, but in a sense these officials have the same types of activities with which to deal. Now we call them traffic control, recreation programs, economic development, zoning and, perhaps we might say skate boards have replaced hoops.

However, the emphasis has changed. The powers in 1838 were mostly "restraining" with very little "providing;" now the city government is much more involved in creating a better life for its citizens through such departments as parks and recreation, redevelopment and the housing authority.

The growth and decline of population, a changing tax base, economic conditions in the country, mandates and appropriations from the state and federal governments and improved technology all have played a role in the history of city government in Terre Haute. Equally important are the people of the city with contentment, politics, and reform efforts alternating in intricate patterns through the years.

Looking over the list of city departments today, it is not difficult to see why the budget has increased. Historian C. C. Oakey wrote: *No stated salary was paid the mayor up to 1842. The Express said "it is generally understood that our city fathers have to work for prosperity and receive their pay, if any, from the same source," and the hope was expressed that there were men patriotic enough to take the positions for which few were anxious.*

This changed in 1842 when Mayor Harrison explained how much time the services he rendered to the city had taken and how he believed the council should allow him $100.

The city government also has come a long way from rented meeting places to the beautiful city hall of today; more importantly, it has survived and even flourished through "ups and downs" experienced by governments everywhere.

Elijah Tillotson
City of Terre Haute collection

William K. Edwards
City of Terre Haute collection

The Mayors

Indiana cities are granted charters by the Indiana General Assembly according to set classes based on their population. Terre Haute is a second class city and must have a mayor-council form of city government. Any change must come by action of the General Assembly.

It wasn't always this way. Terre Haute was incorporated as a town in 1832. Citizens met and divided the town into five wards with a trustee elected from each ward and the trustees, in turn, elected the town's first municipal officers. The trustees were: James Warren, James B. McCall, Thomas Houghton, James Ross and William Herrington. Officers elected were: James B. McCall, president; James T. Moffatt, clerk; Charles G. Taylor, assessor; Samuel Crawford, treasurer; and William Mars, constable and collector. The trustees were to pass ordinances for the governing of the town and elect executive officers.

In 1838 the state legislature provided a charter for the town which called for the election of a mayor and councilmen. The charter was approved by a majority of 63 votes and in May, 1838, a mayor and two councilmen from each of the five wards were elected.

The occupations or professions given for the mayors are their primary means of livelihood. Most of these individuals were on the City Council at one time or another or were elected to other city and county offices. Many of the mayors, particularly the attorneys, also served as state legislators.

ELIJAH TILLOTSON 1838
  jeweler, watchmaker
  (resigned after four months)
MARCUS HITCHCOCK 1838-1839
  medical doctor
  (resigned after 10 months)
BRITTON M. HARRISON 1839-1843
  soap & candle factory owner

The office of mayor was abolished in February, 1843 by the state legislature. The president of the Common Council (Board of Trustees) took over mayoral duties until April, 1853, when the town was incorporated as a city.

The last council of the town met on January 4, 1853. In April the citizens voted 139 in favor, 18 against, to have the town incorporated as a city. The first election of officers was May 30, 1853, and the Common Council for the city of Terre Haute first met on June 6, 1853.

WILLIAM K. EDWARDS 1853-1855
  Whig, later a Republican
  attorney
JAMES HOOK 1855-1856
  Whig, later a Republican
  building contractor
CHAMBERS Y. PATTERSON 1856-1860
  Democrat
  attorney (resigned to accept
  judicial appointment)
WILLIAM H. STEWART 1860-1863
  Democrat
  sheriff, hotel operator

This building at the northwest corner of Fourth and Walnut streets was built in 1874 as the City Market house and used as the City Hall from 1877 to 1936. *Saratoga Restaurant collection*

ALBERT LANGE 1863-1867
  Republican Union
  attorney
GRAFTON F. COOKERLY 1867-1871
  Whig, later a Democrat
  attorney, newspaper publisher
ALEXANDER THOMAS 1871-1875
  Republican
  blacksmith, farmer
JAMES B. EDMUNDS 1875-1877
  Democrat
  newspaper publisher
  (died while in office)
HENRY FAIRBANKS 1877-1878
  Republican
  farm owner (died while in office)
JOSEPH M. WILDY 1878-1879
  Nationalist (Greenback)
  carriage manufacturer
BENJAMIN F. HAVENS 1879-1881
  Democrat as mayor,
  later a Republican
  attorney
JAMES B. LYNE 1881-1883
  Republican
  wine and liquor business
WILLIAM H. ARMSTRONG 1883-1885
  Republican
  druggist
JACOB C. KOLSEM 1885-1889
  Democrat
  clothing store manager
FRANK C. DANALDSON 1889-1891
  Republican
  attorney
JAMES M. ALLEN 1891-1892
  Democrat
  attorney   (died while in office)

HENRY GRISWOLD 1892
  Republican
  grocery/drugstore owner
FRED A. ROSS 1892-1898
  Republican
  hardware/general store owner
HENRY STEEG 1898-1904
  Democrat
  general contractor
EDWIN BIDAMAN 1904-1906
  Republican
  police officer (removed from office)
FRANK M. BUCKINGHAM 1906
  Republican
  bookkeeper
JAMES LYONS 1906-1910
  Democrat
  police officer
LOUIS GERHARDT 1910-1914
  Democrat
  baker/bakery owner
DONN M. ROBERTS 1914-1915
  Democrat
  civil engineer   (removed from office)
JAMES GOSSOM 1915-1918
  Democrat
  feed mill foreman
CHARLES R. HUNTER 1918-1922
  Republican
  dry goods dealer
ORA D. DAVIS 1922-1930
  Republican
  attorney
In 1929 the voters rejected a referendum for a city manager form of city government. The vote was 8,401 to 7,248.
WOOD POSEY 1930-1935
  Democrat
  shoe store owner

The Indiana General Assembly enacted legislation providing for mayoral elections to be held on odd number years rather than in the same years of elections for the governor of the state.
SAMUEL BEECHER, SR. 1936-1940
  Republican
  attorney
JOSEPH DUFFY 1940-1944
  Democrat
  teacher/attorney
VERNON R. McMILLAN 1944-1948
  Republican
  sporting goods store owner
RALPH TUCKER 1948-1968
  Democrat
  radio commentator/salesman
Mayor Tucker served five terms, more years than any other Terre Haute mayor.
LELAND LARRISON 1968-1972
  Republican
  pharmacist
WILLIAM BRIGHTON 1972-1980
  Democrat
  printer
P. PETE CHALOS 1980-
  Democrat
  teacher/coach

As the chief executive of the city, the mayor is elected for a term of four years and serves as the supervisor and representative of the city government.

The present Terre Haute City Hall at 17 Harding Avenue was designed by Miller and Yeager and occupied by the city government in 1937. The fountain in front of the building was designed by Robert L. Payne and Keith A. Hennecke and installed in 1974.
Artie Harbaugh photo

Police Department

Harvey E. Jones, Superintendent of Police, 1908. ... *Mr. Jones has run the gamut of service from patrolman to Chief of Police (1898-1932). For thirty-four years he saw the personnel of the department grow from 39 to 76 members, the horse and wagon transformed into the radio-equipped automobile... The Wabash Valley Remembers, 1787-1938*

A few of a long list of rules and regulations governing Terre Haute police officers and patrolmen on duty in 1904 were: prompt obedience to orders and conformity to rules; carry a club, whistle and revolver; no use of vulgar language toward any member of the force or any citizen; no use of intoxicating liquor or smoking or loitering about saloons, houses of ill fame or any public places; no membership in a political organization.

Terre Haute police officers who have died in the line of duty:
William E. Dwyer, 1908
Mathew Dorley, 1919
Hurbert Long, 1922
Stephen Kendall, 1924
Harry Borum, 1924
Herman Harms, 1925
Walter Lanfair, 1934
Wayne E. Jones, 1951
C. D. Thompson, 1964
James Utz, 1981
Harold Lee Rogers, 1984

Other law enforcement officers who have died in the line of duty include these members of the Vigo County Sheriff's Department:
John M. Cleary, 1877
Peter Feiler, 1914
Paul Mankin, 1936
W. Kevin Artz, 1987

Members of the Terre Haute Police Department posed in the early 1920s in front of their headquarters on the first floor of the former City Hall. In 1922 Superintendent of Police John B. Smock headed a force of 75 members including 11 "bicycle and motorcycle" police. Bicycles were removed from the list by 1924. *Terre Haute Police Department collection*

Officers appear here in the late 1940s outside the present City Hall. In 1949 the Superintendent of Police Cleon R. Reely, 82 men and two matrons worked under the direction of the Board of Public Works and Safety. Law enforcement in the city had grown since the appointment of William Mars as the first constable and collector in 1838. *Terre Haute Police Department collection*

Fire Department

... an ordinance of the Town Board required that every householder should keep on hand at all times filled with water one leather bucket for each male in his family over the age of 18 and under 45 years. When there was an alarm of fire each person as above was required to go to the scene of the fire with this bucket of water.
—from "Recollections of an Old Terre Haute Fire Fighter" by John E. Wilkins.

John Kennedy, Chief of Fire Force, 1907. The volunteer system had ended in the 1870s. Chief Kennedy reported the 1907 payroll for 66 men at $55,573. He also listed 36 head of horses; the first motorized equipment was not put into use until 1910.

Terre Haute firemen who have died in the line of duty:

Dan Roper, 1897	William Sholton, 1921
John Osterloo, 1898	Robert Day, 1935
John Boland, 1917	Olie C. Reed, 1945
Aberham Brown, 1921	Richard Gray, 1951
Remis Hicks, 1935	John O'Brien, 1963
John W. Blunk, 1936	

The lists of police and fire personnel who have died in action were compiled by Tom Champion, a retired fireman. Through his leadership and effort, the Retired Policeman and Fireman's Association preserved Fire Station No. 9 at Eighth and Idaho Streets and maintains a museum there to preserve the story of the individuals who have protected lives and property in the city.

Members of Hose Company #5 (above) are pictured in front of the department headquarters at 28 South Ninth Street on July 23, 1923. Left to right: Captain Ralph Dinkel, Edward Seeburger, Richard Gray, Edwin Yeakle, Ross McLaughlin, Vance Day, Lt. Joseph Davern, Thomas Stevenson. *Ralph R. Dinkel collection*

October 8, 1940—The *Terre Haute Tribune* reported on page one: "Terre Haute's New Long Range Weapon against the Menace of Fire Demonstrated to City at Fire Headquarters." This headline referred to Terre Haute's first 100-foot aerial truck shown here. *Martin photo*

Terre Haute Parks

Most Terre Hauteans will agree that their parks are the green jewels in the city's crown. The number has grown from one park in the last century to the 22 parks listed below:

ANACONDA (.5 acre) -1979- North Fourteenth and Elizabeth streets - The land and playground equipment were a gift of the Anaconda Aluminum Company.

BOY SCOUT (.3 acre) -1914- Lafayette and Barbour avenues - The trees were planted by members of the Boy Scouts in honor of President Theodore Roosevelt.

BRITTLEBANK (7 acres) -1975- North Twentieth and Grant streets - The park was funded by a bequest from Julius Brittlebank.

COLLETT (21 acres) - 1883- North Seventh Street and Maple Avenue - The oldest park in the city, its land, once a part of the C. Barbour farm, was the gift of Josephus Collett (1831-1893), successful coal

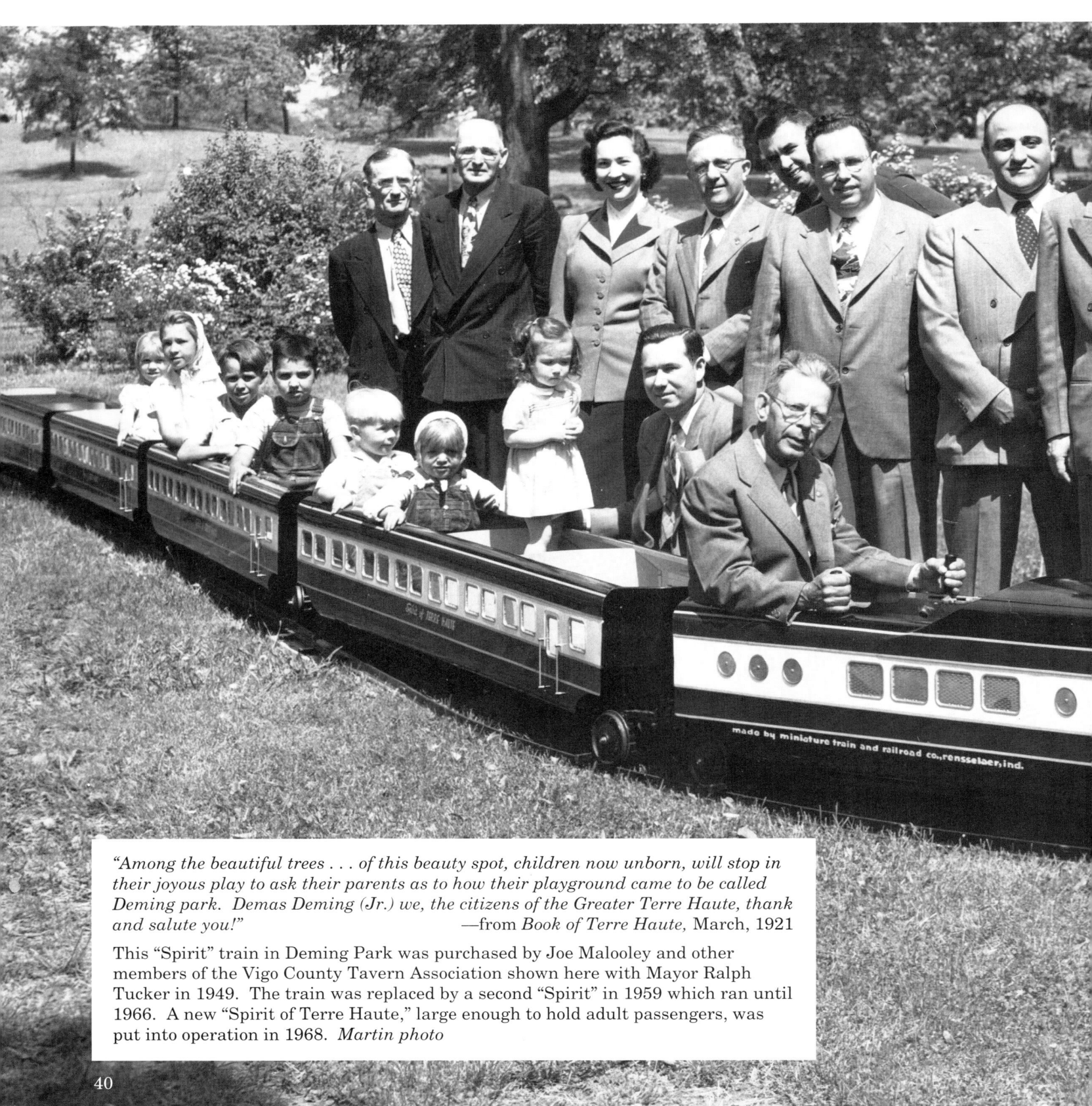

"Among the beautiful trees . . . of this beauty spot, children now unborn, will stop in their joyous play to ask their parents as to how their playground came to be called Deming park. Demas Deming (Jr.) we, the citizens of the Greater Terre Haute, thank and salute you!"
—from *Book of Terre Haute*, March, 1921

This "Spirit" train in Deming Park was purchased by Joe Malooley and other members of the Vigo County Tavern Association shown here with Mayor Ralph Tucker in 1949. The train was replaced by a second "Spirit" in 1959 which ran until 1966. A new "Spirit of Terre Haute," large enough to hold adult passengers, was put into operation in 1968. *Martin photo*

and railroad businessman.

COY (8 acres) -1987- North Sixteenth Street and Barbour Avenue - The park was named for Kenneth Coy, president of the Terre Haute Park Board.

CURTIS GILBERT (4 acres) -1919- South Sixteenth Street and Wabash Avenue - First named Steeg Park in honor of Mayor Henry Steeg, the park is located on land contributed in part by the Beach and Gilbert families.

DEMING (177 acres) -1921- Fruitridge Avenue and Ohio Boulevard - The Park Board accepted the offer of the Deming Land Company to buy the ground for park purposes for $155,000, of which $100,000 would be given to the Rose Polytechnic Institute, and the balance spent in opening Ohio Boulevard from South Twenty-fifth Street to the park. Torner Center was constructed in the park in 1984.

DOBBS MEMORIAL (105 acres) -1944- East Poplar Street - Effie Frances Dobbs and Mary Hollis Call donated the land as a memorial to Miss Dobb's

continued

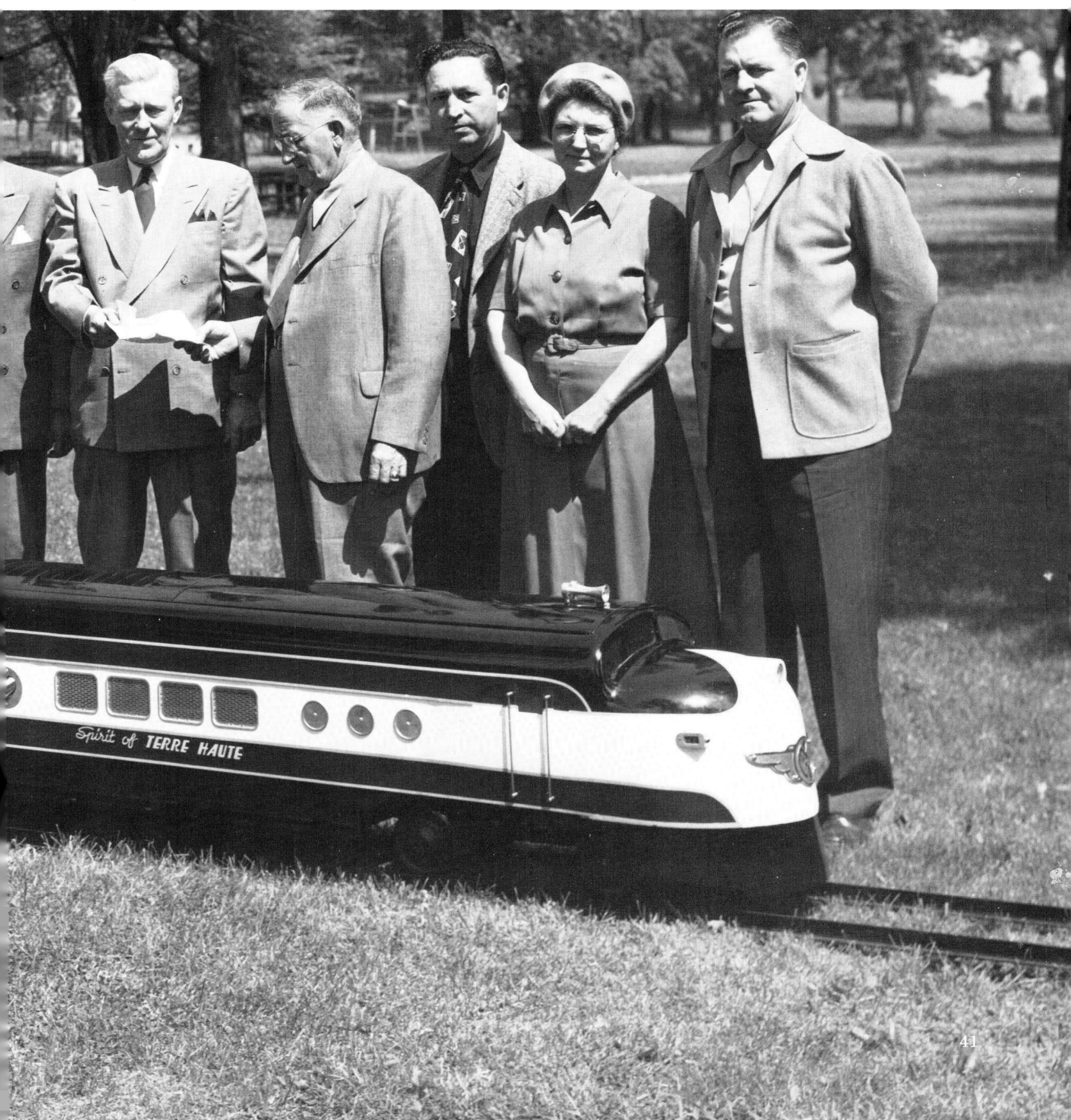

father, John G. Dobbs. The popular Nature Center was established on the park grounds in 1976.

DRESSER (6 acres) -1940- U.S. 40 west - This park was a gift of the Paul Dresser Memorial Association.

FAIRBANKS (145 acres) -1916- South First Street - The original 38 acres of land for this riverside park was donated by Crawford Fairbanks and Mr. and Mrs. Edward Fairbanks in memory of Henry Fairbanks, mayor of the city from 1877 to 1878.

GRAHAM (1 acre) -1921- 1400 South Seventeenth Street - Henry Graham was superintendent of parks in 1921.

HERZ-ROSE (5 acres) 1909- North Fifteenth and Locust streets - The land was purchased from Anna Pflaging and the park named for Chauncey Rose and Adolf Herz, owner of the A. Herz Department Store on Wabash Avenue.

HULMAN LINKS (230 acres) -1978- U.S. 40 East - This challenging 18 hole golf course was developed with funds donated by the Anton Hulman, Jr. family.

MEMORIAL (10 acres) -1936- Eighth Avenue and North Fourth Street - A Works Progress Administration (WPA) project helped convert this site from a dump to a beautiful park with a sunken athletic field popular for softball games.

OAKLEY (.5 acres) -1981- College Avenue and South Eighth Street - The park was a gift of the Hollie and Anna Oakley Foundation.

Street cars of the Terre Haute Electric Railroad Company, crowded with folks who have enjoyed "a day in the park," leave Collett Park in 1895.

No matter what the season, the Collett Pavilion is a beautiful site. It is the city's oldest park structure; a recent addition to the park is a gazebo which was built in 1988.

Lawrence King, assistant park superintendent, and his crew were responsible for the maintenance of the city's parks in the 1970s.

all photos Terre Haute Parks & Recreation Department collection

REA GOLF COURSE (160 acres) -1925- South Seventh Street and East Davis Drive - The land was given by W. S. Rea and funds for the clubhouse by his wife, Geraldine Rea.

SHERIDAN (6.5 acres) -1922- North Twenty-eighth and Beech streets - The donors of the land were Frank Miller, Albert Owen and Felix Blankenbaker.

SPENCER F. BALL (10 acres) -1920- North Fifteenth Street and Eighth Avenue - Ball, editor of the *Terre Haute Tribune*, left income from $25,000 for use by the Park Department. The land was purchased from Loriette Z. Hulman.

THOMPSON (5 acres) -1909- South Seventeenth and Oak streets - Purchased from Indiana State Normal School, the park was named in honor of Col. Richard W. Thompson.

TWELVE POINTS (.12 acres) -1993- Maple and Lafayette avenues - Formerly the site of a gas station, this patch of green is the newest and smallest park in the city.

VOORHEES (11 acres) -1910- Voorhees Street and State Road 63 - Named in honor of Senator Daniel W. Voorhees, the park is located on land purchased by the city from Benjamin F. Boring for $900.

WASHINGTON (5 acres) -1921- South Thirteenth Street and College Avenue - Named for Booker T. Washington, this park has been the site of Hyte Community Center since 1972.

Named one of the top 50 municipally-owned golf courses in the country, Hulman Links has hosted numerous championship tournaments.

This beautiful fountain, designed by Indiana State University student Tom Dubois in 1983, welcomes visitors to Fairbanks Park. It is located not far from the site of the first municipal swimming pool which was removed in 1966.

These youngsters were paying strict attention to their swim instructor at the Deming Park pool in the 1980s. Other municipal pools are located at Sheridan and Voorhees Parks.

CEMETERIES

Mary Grover, assistant city cemetery superintendent, was commended in 1973 by the U. S. Army National Cemetery Supervising Office for her work in keeping the Civil War Memorial in Woodlawn Cemetery. The monument honors 11 unknown Confederate soldiers who died in Terre Haute as prisoners of war.

INDIAN ORCHARD, One Sycamore Street, is the site of graves of members of the Wea tribe and early settlers. It was the first burying ground in the city. The second was located on the east side of Sixth Street between Wabash Avenue and Ohio Street.

WOODLAWN, 1230 North Third Street, was established in 1839 as the "City Cemetery." The north part was set aside for the Catholic burial ground (St. Joseph Cemetery) and immediately west was the Hebrew Cemetery.

HIGHLAND LAWN, 4520 East Wabash Avenue, was purchased in 1884 from Ray and Grace Jenckes. Woodlawn and Highland Lawn are the two municipal cemeteries operated under the board of cemetery regents.

CALVARY, opened in 1912, at 4425 East Wabash Avenue, was purchased and given to the Catholic community by the Herman Hulman, Sr. family.

GRANDVIEW, 1601 Lockport Road, was founded by the Order of Red Men and was first known as Lone Tree.

ROSELAWN MEMORIAL PARK, opened in 1929, and many smaller cemeteries are located outside of the city limits in Vigo County.

This 1897 photo shows the entrance gate to Highland Lawn Cemetery, the second cemetery in the State of Indiana to be accepted to the National Register of Historic Places. The chapel on the hill was designed by Jesse A. Vrydagh and completed in 1893. Its renovation was a 1987-88 project of the city.

U. S. Senator Daniel Voorhees, the "Tall Sycamore of the Wabash," was influential in building the present Library of Congress and served longer in the U.S. Senate than anyone from Indiana before or since. His funeral procession on April 15, 1897, pictured here, proceeded from St. Stephen's Episcopal Church to Highland Lawn Cemetery. The procession was described as one of the longest ever observed in the city—three cars of floral arrangements, 511 marching men; 36 carriages; and 20 buggies.

Historic Places

The Williams-Warren-Zimmerman House was constructed about 1849. This photo, taken about 1939, shows the tin roof installed by George S. Zimmerman, owner of the home from 1899 until 1938. *Vigo County Public Library collection*

Built in 1860 for Lucien Houriet, the Condit House was the home of the Blackford Condit family from 1863 until 1962 when Helen Condit bequeathed the house to Indiana State College. *Indiana State University archives*

NATIONAL REGISTER OF HISTORIC PLACES IN TERRE HAUTE:

Allen Chapel African Methodist Episcopal Church, 1913,
  224 Crawford Street
Collett Park, 1890-1904, North Seventh Street and Maple Avenue
Condit House, 1860, Indiana State University campus
Eugene V. Debs House, c.1890, 451 North Eighth Street
Downtown Terre Haute Multiple Resource Area
  building 23-27 South Sixth Street, 1882
  building 509-511 Wabash Avenue, 1893
  building 510-516 Ohio Street, 1892
  building 810 Wabash Avenue, 1870
Chamber of Commerce Building, 1925,
  687 Cherry Street
Citizen's Trust Company Building, 1921,
  19-21 South Sixth Street
First Congregational Church, 1903,
  630 Ohio Street
Hippodrome Theater, 1915,
  727 Ohio Street
house 209-11 South Ninth Street, c.1880
house 823 Ohio Street, c.1880
Star Building, 1912,
  601-603 Ohio Street
Terminal Arcade, 1911,
  822 Wabash Avenue
Terre Haute Post Office and Federal Building, 1934,
  Seventh and Cherry streets
Vigo County Courthouse, 1888,
  Courthouse Square
Wabash Avenue-East Historic District, 1816-1926,
  bounded by Wabash Avenue, Seventh and Eighth streets
Wabash Avenue-West Historic District, 1876-1940,
  bounded by Wabash Avenue and Sixth Street
Paul Dresser Birthplace, 1859,
  First and Farrington streets
Farrington's Grove Historic District, c.1850-1935,
  roughly bounded by Poplar and South Fourth streets,
  Hulman and South Seventh streets
Fire Station #9, 1906,
  1728 South Eighth Street
Highland Lawn Cemetery, 1884,
  4520 East Wabash Avenue
Ohio Boulevard-Deming Park Historic District, 1919-1939,
  Ohio Boulevard from Nineteenth Street to Keane Lane
Old State Bank of Indiana (Memorial Hall), 1834,
  219 Ohio Street
Sage-Robinson-Nagel House, 1868,
  1411 South Sixth Street
Williams-Warren-Zimmerman House, 1849,
  904 South Fourth Street
The Markle House and Mill Site, 1817, 1849, is located just north of the city in Otter Creek Township.

The Hippodrome Theater opened for vaudeville performances in 1915. It was the home of the Community Theater from 1931 to 1947, then remodeled into the Wabash Movie House before it was purchased by the Scottish Rite, Valley of Terre Haute, in 1956. *Jane Hazledine collection*

FEDERAL BUILDINGS

This Federal Building, pictured at the left, was the first building in the city to house both the post office and other federal agencies. It was completed in 1887 at North Seventh and Cherry streets and razed to make space for the present Federal Building shown below which opened in 1935.

The picture at right was signed by Guy T. Kuntz, construction engineer, to certify the completion of work on December 1, 1934. The local firms who had contracts for its construction were Glenn W. North Construction Co.; Raymond Kintz Lumber Co.; J. W. Dennis Trucking Co.; Terre Haute Vitrified Brick; and Vigo American Clay. Miller and Yeager were the architects.

The Banks of the Wabash Association acquired the columns from the first Federal Building for use in building the Chauncey Rose Memorial at Fairbanks Park.

An Open House at the U. S. Penitentiary, south of Terre Haute, on October 4, 1940, was in progress when this photograph was taken. The event marked the dedication of the $2.25 million WPA project, a welcome addition to the local economy. Designed to house 1,016 inmates, the institution has increased its number of inmates and employees through addition of the federal prison camp in 1960 and expansion of the main facility. The area became a part of the city in 1989 through annexation.
U.S. Penitentiary, Terre Haute, collection

CHAPTER 4

The City, the Nation, the World

Harold Friend, a Marine veteran of World War II, played taps at the end of the 50th anniversary of Pearl Harbor ceremony in 1991 on the roof of the U. S. Naval Reserve Center in Terre Haute. *Tribune-Star Publishing Company photo*

> "I believe in the United States of America as a Government of the people, by the people, for the people; whose just powers are derived from the consent of the governed . . ."
>
> —from *The American's Creed,* by William Tyler Page

The phrase "the city, the nation, the world" might well be expanded to include "the individual, the family, the city, the state, the nation, the world." Whatever affects one, eventually affects all.

Wars often brought prosperity and higher employment to the city, but these economic advantages could not make up for the tragic loss of loved ones fighting away from home.

Each action of the federal and state governments to pass and ratify an amendment to the U. S. Constitution found its way to the city, too. The 19th gave voting power and opened the political system to women in 1920, before employment opportunities were opened to them during World War II.

The 18th amendment, which also went into effect in 1920, helped cause the city to suffer hard times before the stock market crash of 1929 launched the Great Depression throughout the country. A local headline, "Terre Haute Saloons Pass into History," was a victory for the Anti-Saloon League, but it also brought about the unemployment of an estimated 3,500 local workers. It is no wonder that Virginia Jenckes ran for the U. S. Congress on a platform which favored Repeal, not on moral grounds, but as a way to increase employment.

The 21st amendment, which was ratified in 1933 to repeal the 19th, did bring back some jobs, but by then hard times had arrived. No place in the country was spared.

On the positive side, the federal government in 1935 recognized the need to help aged and dependent citizens through the Social Security Act and established the Works Progress Administration to provide jobs for unemployed workers. Among the local WPA construction projects were Laboratory School and three other buildings at Indiana State Teachers College, City Hall, a fire station and the Vigo County Infirmary. In addition, sewer construction, road and street improvements, and projects such as sewing, school lunches, nursery schools, recreation, library and adult education were funded with WPA money.

While events and actions of a national and international nature affect the residents of the city, a number of Terre Hauteans noteworthy in government, education, entertainment, sports and the arts have influenced the nation and, in some cases, the world.

No one has brought more international recognition to the city during the past 100 years than Eugene V. Debs. Yet it was Debs who wrote to the *Terre Haute Tribune* in 1925 to say, *Chauncey Rose did more for Terre Haute than any other man living or dead. Rose built the first railroad into Terre Haute and devoted his entire fortune to the growth and development of the city and the prosperity and welfare of the people.*

Greatness appreciates greatness in the city or in the world.

AMERICAN REVOLUTION 1775-1783

Known to have some direct connection with the early years of Vigo County, Indiana are 38 veterans of the American Revolution. Of this group it is known where 27 are buried within the county.
—Dorothy J. Fox Clark, Vigo County Historian

WAR OF 1812-1814

William Henry Harrison in command of the Army of the Northwest Territory and Zachary Taylor, commander of Fort Harrison in 1812, are remembered for their victories over the British and Native Americans who were allies in the War of 1812.

MEXICAN WAR 1846-1848

Two companies went to Mexico from Vigo County. Arriving there in 1846, the first group had enlisted under Philip Kearny and is said to have drilled on Strawberry Hill. The Fort Harrison Guards, under Landon Cochran, a Terre Haute gunsmith, reached Mexico in 1847.

CIVIL WAR SOLDIERS

Charles Cruft 1826-1883
Cruft was born in Terre Haute. After his graduation from Wabash College, he returned to the city to teach and study law. In 1861 he organized and was chosen colonel of the 31st Indiana Regiment, Indiana Volunteer Infantry. Later he was named commander of a brigade. Noted for his bravery and leadership skills, Cruft was given the rank of major general by President Lincoln in 1865. He was the only officer from Vigo County to have attained this rank during the Civil War.
After returning home, Cruft continued as owner of the *Terre Haute Express* newspaper and resumed his practice of law with John P. Baird. *Vigo County Public Library collection*

John J. P. Blinn 1840-1863
John J. P. Blinn was born at the Blinn home which would now be at the site of 433 North Third Street. After his student days at Wabash College, he helped organize and was made adjutant of Company F, 14th Regiment, Indiana Volunteer Infantry. He was later commissioned captain. Wounded at the Battle of Gettysburg, he died three days later in the field hospital there.

William E. McLean 1832-1906
A native of Maryland, McLean moved to Terre Haute as a young boy. He was a graduate of Indiana University and became editor of the *Terre Haute Journal*. He founded the 43rd Regiment, Indiana Volunteer Infantry, and was appointed lieutenant colonel and later brigadier general. In addition to his Civil War career, McLean was an orator, attorney, county prosecuting attorney, state legislator and Commissioner of Pensions under President Grover Cleveland.

Peter J. Ryan 1844-1908
Private Peter J. Ryan, Company D, 11th Regiment, Indiana Volunteer Infantry, was awarded the Congressional Medal of Honor for capturing, with one companion, 14 Confederate soldiers "in the severest part of battle" during the Civil War. He returned home to Terre Haute to open a harness shop, a livery stable and the first Ryan family funeral home. *Mary Frances Smith collection*

CIVIL WAR 1861-1865

The historian C. C. Oakey wrote, *The news of the assault upon Fort Sumter fell like a bomb upon Terre Haute, causing intense agitation and excitement . . . Isaac M. Brown claimed the honor of being the first three years' volunteer from Vigo County.*

A number of companies and six regiments were organized in the city. William F. Cronin wrote that the grand total of troops from Vigo County in all enlistments reached 4,445, of which 2,003 were from Harrison Township (including Terre Haute).

Camp Vigo was located on North Seventh Street across from the present site of Collett Park and Camp Dick Thompson on the Bloomington Road (now Poplar Street). Confederate prisoners were housed at the Williams and Farrington Pork House on First Street.

In 1909 the Soldiers and Sailors Monument on the courthouse lawn was erected in memory of those who served in the Civil War from Vigo County.

SPANISH-AMERICAN WAR 1898

Vigo County was represented by one company of infantry in the Spanish-American War . . . The war had been of such short duration that the Terre Haute Boys did not get into any engagements, but a number of them re-enlisted for service in the Philippines.

There was no other military unit from Vigo County, but there were numerous . . . enlistments. In fact, the Spanish War veterans camp at Terre Haute has more than 200 members today.

– William F. Cronin, 1922

Company B of the First Indiana National Guard Regiment (later the 159th Indiana Volunteer Infantry) is shown leaving the city for the Spanish-American War. They served nine months and 23 days. *Vigo County Public Library collection*

This interior view of Memorial Hall "with a group of the boys in blue" appeared in *Terre Haute Today*, in 1915. The local Civil War veterans had purchased the building in 1910. The Kesler and Kesler law office now occupies the former bank building.

WORLD WAR I 1914-1918

A. C. Duddleston reported that Terre Haute had furnished two volunteer infantry companies, a company of engineers, a machine gun company and approximately 7,000 selective draft men to this war. Of these men, 83 died in the service of the United States and Allied Nations from 1914 to 1918. Their names are listed on the Gold Star Honor Roll published by the Indiana Historical Commission in 1921.

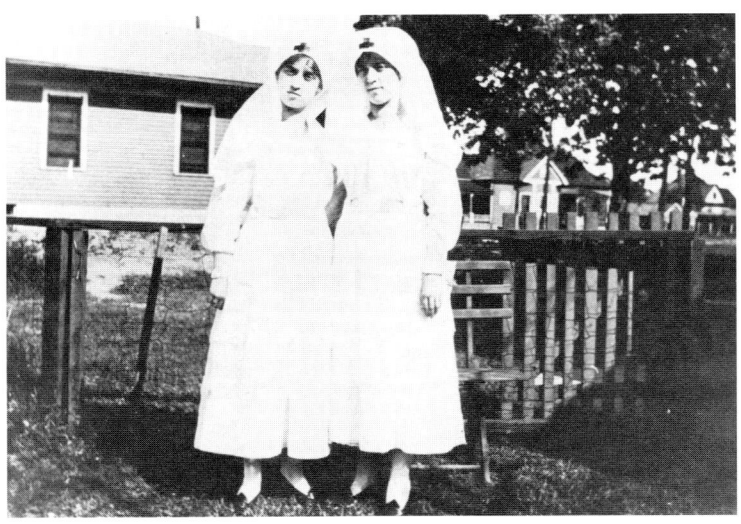

Twin sisters Reba and Ruth Hayworth were nurses in the service of the American Red Cross. The Terre Haute Chapter had been organized in 1916.

The Third Liberty Loan drive in April, 1918, passed by Patsy Mahaney's Candy Shop on Wabash Avenue. Local citizens sponsored four Liberty Loan drives and one Victory Loan drive to help finance the war.

Some of the members of Company H, First Infantry, posed with Captain A. C. Duddleston (front row, fourth from left) in front of the courthouse after the war.

Eugene V. Debs, 1855-1926, Pioneer Labor Leader—Champion of Social Justice

"... while there is a lower class, I am in it; while there is a criminal element, I am of it; while there is a soul in prison, I am not free..."
—Eugene Debs

"One of the 100 most important Americans of the century—a fiery spokesman for social change...eloquently calling for such unheard-of-reforms as social security, the eight-hour day, workmen's compensation and sick leave."
—Life magazine (Fall, 1990)

Eugene Debs, age 14 years, appears on the far left in this 1870 photo of a railroad painting crew. In 1874 he became an employee of the wholesale grocery firm of Hulman & Cox. The following year he was elected secretary of the local Brotherhood of Locomotive Firemen lodge and in 1893 he founded the American Railway Union. He had been elected city clerk (1879) and a member of the Indiana legislature (1885). His leadership role in the Pullman Strike of 1894 brought him into national prominence.

Founder of the American Socialist Party in the late 1890s, Debs is shown in this 1904 poster in one of his five campaigns for the U. S. presidency. Imprisoned under the 1917 Espionage Act for a speech against World War I, he ran his last campaign for the presidency in 1920 from prison. Petitions circulated for his release received more than 21,000 signatures from the citizens of Terre Haute. Debs returned home after his sentence was commuted to time served by President Warren G. Harding.

The family posed in 1925 on the porch of the Debs home, 451 North Eighth Street. Left to right: Howard Debs Selby, Theodore and Gertrude Debs, and Katherine and Eugene Debs. Constructed in 1890 and named a National Historic Landmark in 1966, the home is maintained as a museum by the Eugene V. Debs Foundation.

all photos Eugene V. Debs Foundation collection

19th Constitutional Amendment Woman's Sufferage, 1920

Ida Husted Harper 1851-1931
Ida Husted Harper, a columnist for the (Terre Haute) *Saturday Evening Mail* from 1878 until 1890, went on to speak and write for the woman's suffrage cause in this country and in Europe. One of her Terre Haute columns reads: *... let me tell you that we, women, do not ask the ballot on the ground of our goodness, intelligence, morality or any other quality. We claim it as an abstract Right, and as such, we mean to have it.*

She was no longer in the city when a parade celebrated the passage of the woman's suffrage amendment or when the local League of Women Voters became the successor to the old suffrage league. *Vigo County Public Library collection*

Virginia E. Jenckes 1878-1975
The right to vote opened the political door to women. In 1932, Virginia E. Jenckes of Terre Haute was elected to her first term as U. S. Representative. The first woman elected to Congress from Indiana, she served until 1938.

Jenckes was a proponent of flood control, the anti-lynching bill, and the American Flag Act and she was responsible for many of the WPA building projects in her district. *Vigo County Public Library collection*

This cartoon by Bushnell appeared in the *Terre Haute Tribune* on August 28, 1920 at the time the 19th Amendment became law. An article about voter registration in the *Tribune* on September 4, 1920 reads: *Woman, that is Terre Haute woman, did not quite accept her privilege as an equal in politics with men, in quite the proportion expected today ... However, there were some who were on hand early. Captain Mary Brown (Volunteers of America) was the first to register.*

18th & 21st Constitutional Amendments
Prohibition & Repeal, 1919 & 1933

Indiana was a jump ahead of the federal government when it adopted statewide prohibition against the sale of alcoholic beverages during World War I. Ready to operate again at the end of the war, brewery production was destroyed and the distilleries were left with only commercial alcohol and solvent manufacture after nationwide Prohibition went into effect in 1920. Related container, printing, coal and shipping industries and agribusiness were also affected.

Julius Lederer Liquor Store, 20 South Sixth Street, in the 1930s after the repeal of Prohibition.

These workers were employees of the Terre Haute Brewing Company at South Ninth and Poplar streets. Incorporated in 1889, the company was in business until 1958 and was best known for its "Champagne Velvet" brand. In 1915, the company was producing 400,000 barrels of beer per year. *Doris Dicus collection*

One of the first shipments of beer into the city after Repeal arrived by air to Paul E. Pfeifer, Inc., wholesalers in April 1933. The Charles W. Bauermeister Company, local distributor for Anheuser-Busch used this text in a 1933 Budweiser advertisement: *Beer is back . . . hands long idle find new jobs . . . thousands upon thousands find honorable livelihood. And with it, a new fountain head of tax revenue arises to add its dollars gladly to a nation in need.* Martin photo

THE GREAT DEPRESSION, 1929-1942

The Stock Market Crash of 1929 ushered in the Great Depression. Fortunes accumulated during a lifetime were swept away within a few hours as stocks and bonds lost their value. Banks and Building and Loan companies closed their doors, spreading fear and eventually panic among the people.

. . . Their debts were far beyond their ability to pay . . . Their creditors began to repossess their furniture, their homes, their cars. Soon they could not buy food. Bread and soup lines formed all over the nation. Rent could not be paid. Families moved in together. Landlords could not pay taxes.

. . . Several hundred people in Terre Haute had organized an Unemployment Council. H. N. Oakley, a man of compassion, permitted the council to use a vacant building he owned, located on North Fourth Street at Cherry . . The Harrison Township Trustee gave out relief food a few doors away.

The spirit of sharing, of consideration for others was in evidence everywhere among the poor. Many upper class people shared in the desires to do something in the early stages of the Depression . . . Greed seldom raised its ugly head.

. . . Rabbi Taxay and several ministers offered to cooperate with leaders of the Unemployment Council . . . Members of the business community called a meeting. Ben Blumberg became active in urging that no more people be evicted for non-payment of rent . . . and it became known that it was better to take a half a loaf than to get none at all.

—Shubert Sebree in *Better Times*, June 15, 1947

A pediment and some of the columns from the first Federal Building at North Seventh and Cherry streets were moved to Fairbanks Park to use in the construction of the Chauncey Rose Memorial. Dedicated in 1936, it was one of the many WPA projects in the area which reduced the relief rolls by providing work to employable persons. *Martin photo*

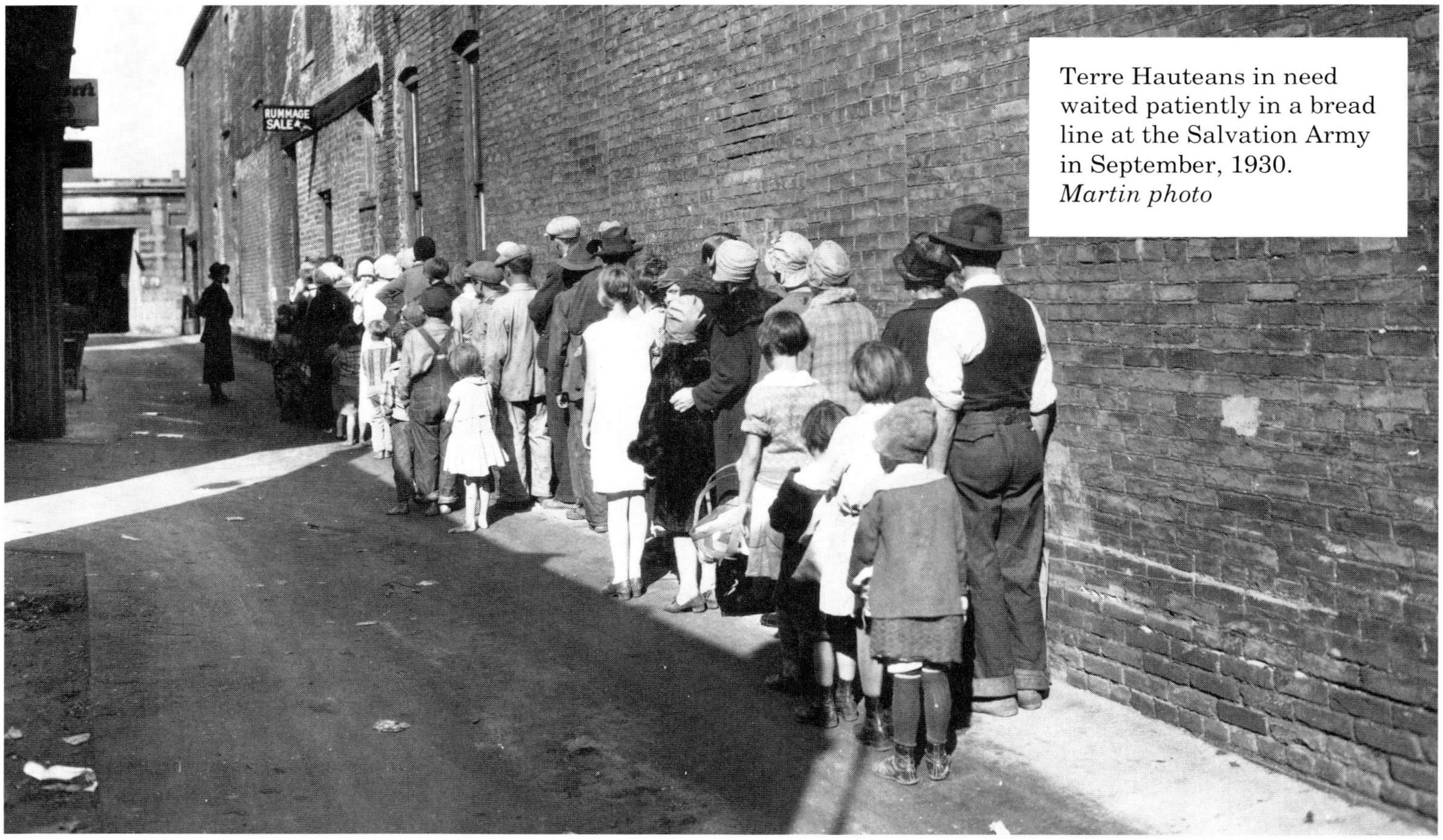

Terre Hauteans in need waited patiently in a bread line at the Salvation Army in September, 1930. *Martin photo*

WORLD WAR II
1939-1945

"Terre Haute teemed with workers during the World War II years. Buses, restaurants, bars, shops and streets were crowded at all hours . . . for Terre Haute was the focal point of three large ordnance facilities. Not only were thousands of civilians and military personnel needed for actual production but an equal number of construction workers built and maintained roads, buildings and railroad spurs. The area was remote from both coasts and considered 'attack proof' . . . and the community played an important part in winning the war."
—Susie Dewey in the *Terre Haute Tribune-Star*, 1983

These Selective Service Board No. 1 draftees were sent to Evansville for U. S. Army physical examinations in November, 1942. Those who passed were inducted into the service and given a two-week furlough before beginning training.

Vigo County families suffered the loss of loved ones:

Honor List of Dead and Missing, U.S. Army	211
Casualties, U.S. Navy, Marine Corps, Coast Guard	44

The Julia Lambert WAVE platoon departed for training at Hunter College, New York City, in November, 1943. The following year Governor Schricker recognized Terre Haute for leading the state in WAVE enlistments. Indiana in turn led the nation in this recruiting campaign. The letters WAVE stood for "Women Appointed for Voluntary Emergency Service in the Navy." *Helen Hanley Pollara collection*

Plans for a local USO campaign to raise $40,000 were announced in 1942 by Benjamin Blumberg, R. F. Nitsche and Senator Charles Kolsem. This USO center on Cherry Street, the 100th in the nation to open, served service personnel traveling by bus. The USO lounge at Union Station served those traveling by rail. The eleven young men pictured here in 1945 were leaving for Indianapolis to be inducted into the armed forces.

World War II – The Home Front

The Girl Scouts at Sarah Scott Junior High School did their bit in 1943 by collecting fat for Uncle Sam's war effort. The 40 local Girl Scout troops had exceeded the goal set for this program designed to help provide glycerine needed for the manufacture of munitions and medicines.

It was said the national goal would be achieved if every housewife would salvage one tablespoon of kitchen fat and grease every day. *Martin photo*

These National Youth Administration (NYA) workers deposited the first aluminum items in this collection bin which they had constructed for Wabash Avenue. This 1941 "Old Aluminum for Defense" campaign was co-sponsored by the American Legion, Boy Scouts, and the Terre Haute Fire and Police Departments.
Martin photo

Members of the Terre Haute Chapter of "Bundles for Britain" met on a regular basis to make items for British war relief. Note the bundles to the right ready for shipping overseas in this 1941 photograph.
Martin photo

Terre Haute was the first Indiana city to be organized for the 1943 "Clean-Your-Plate" campaign. "Pledge now, a clean plate at every meal. Wasted food sabotages victory." These young girls posed by this milk wagon at Borden's Pure Milk & Ice Cream Company, 531-35 North Fifth Street.
Martin photo

Women Ordnance Workers (W.O.W.) took over the work formerly assumed by men during these war years. They are shown here in 1943 operating the fork-lift trucks at the Terre Haute Ordnance Depot, the site of the present Industrial Park on North Fruitridge Avenue.

The Wabash River Ordnance Works was located two miles south of Newport on Indiana 63; the Vigo Ordnance Plant was in operation south of Terre Haute, now the site of Pfizer, Inc. *Judith Calvert collection*

Members of the auxiliaries of the three local American Legion Posts sold war bonds and stamps in front of the Montgomery Wards store on Wabash Avenue in 1943. The "Molly Pitchers" on the left are Mrs. L. Lewis, Mrs. Bessie Close, Mrs. Rachel Joslyn and Mrs. Ethel Maxwell. *Martin photo*

The "horse who came to dinner" in the Mayflower Room of the Terre Haute House was a special guest at the opening of the Sixth War Loan drive in 1944. By January, 1945, Vigo County had oversubscribed its quota of $6,239,400 by purchasing $9,9311,226 of war bonds and government securities. This was the sixth time Vigo County had come through with its war loan quota, passing each one well ahead of schedule. *Martin photo*

The "S.S. Terre Haute Victory" was launched February 2, 1945, at Portland, Oregon. Mrs. J. P. Pfister of Terre Haute, mother of six sons serving in the armed forces, had the honor of christening the ship with champagne at the ceremony.

The "Terre Haute Tornado" flew 114 combat missions in the European Theater from March 9, 1944 to April 5, 1945. The July 19, 1944 mission, rated as the most accurate bombing of a bridge for the entire 9th Air Force, was featured in a "March of Time" movie short show in a Paramount newsreel. Captain R. E. Wilson of Terre Haute is shown here standing center, back row.
J. K. Havener collection

Emergency housing for veterans in Fairbanks Park was in use when this photograph was made in January, 1945. The units were constructed to help house the large number of returning veterans who had enrolled at Indiana State Teachers College under the GI Bill of Rights.
Martin photo

KOREA - VIET NAM - THE PERSIAN GULF

KOREAN WAR 1950-1953
The bridge located on Indiana 63 across the Wabash River was dedicated to Charles Abrell, one of the 22 men from Vigo County who were killed in action during the Korean War. The marker reads: *"This bridge commemorates the memory of Charles Gene Abrell, Corporal, First Marines of the United States First Marine Division, posthumous holder of the Congressional Medal of Honor. Born August 12, 1931; died June 10, 1951."* Mary Abrell collection

Cpl. Charles Gene Abrell

VIET NAM WAR 1961-1973
Casualties incurred by U.S. military personnel from Vigo County from January 1, 1961 through March 3, 1973, numbered 28. The memorial shown here was placed on the southwest corner of the courthouse lawn in 1991. The inscription, written by Marla J. Ferguson, reads: *"For the veterans of Viet Nam, for the MIAs, for your fallen comrades, for those who came home; for your heroic efforts abroad, for your greater efforts at home. With belated acknowledgement of your duties performed, for God and country, we offer our heart-felt gratitude, in saying — at long last: Welcome home."* Artie Harbaugh photo

The Viet Nam Veterans Memorial

PERSIAN GULF WAR 1990-1991
A number of local reservists were called to join active duty forces; yellow ribbons and a renewed sense of patriotism were evident in the city. In this photograph (March, 1991) more than 2,500 persons gathered at Hulman Regional Airport to greet the men of the 35th Tactical Fighter Wing on their way from Spain to their home base in California. *Tribune-Star Publishing Company photo*

SERVICE REMEMBERED

Veterans and other patriotic organizations have always played a large part in the life of the city. Each war has been remembered and its service personnel honored by groups from the Fort Harrison Chapter of the Daughters of the American Revolution to the local Viet Nam Veterans of America.

Following the Civil War, the Grand Army of the Republic, the Sons of Veterans, the Women's Relief Corps and the Ladies' Aid Society organized to consecrate the principles on which the nation remained one. The turn-of-the-century veterans organized as the Claude Herbert Camp No. 38, United Spanish-American War Veterans. The American Legion and Veterans of Foreign Wars posts formed after World War I.

Groups and their auxiliaries who meet and sponsor many worthy projects in the city of Terre Haute and who are members of the Vigo County United War Veterans Council include: American Legion Posts #40 (Fort Harrison); #104 (Krietenstein), #340 (Pioneer) and #346 (Wayne Newton); Veterans of Foreign Wars #972 (Lawton-Byrum); 40/8, Voiture 21; Disabled American Veterans (Leon Von Schepper, Chapter 9); and Viet Nam Veterans of Terre Haute, Inc.

November 11, 1948
Terre Hauteans jammed the sidewalks downtown today to see veterans of three wars parade in celebration of the World War I armistice 30 years ago . . This afternoon thousands of persons are expected for the annual Wiley-Gerstmeyer High School football game at Memorial Stadium.
Terre Haute Tribune
Martin photo

The Korean War era jet fighter plane on the courthouse lawn honors Vigo County veterans. The plaque read: *In dedication to those of Vigo County who faithfully served their country during times of national peril, the Hulman Field units of the Indiana Air National Guard upon this Veterans Day Eleventh Day of November, Nineteen Hundred Fifty Nine, hereby dedicate to the County of Vigo, State of Indiana, this F-84F Thunderstreak to be so displayed as a tribute from the Air National Guard to the men and women of our armed forces past and present.*

CHAPTER 5

Terre Haute in the Headlines

Terre Hauteans check the headlines at the *Tribune* office at the turn of the century.

> "Terre Haute is:
> a) the sin capital east of the Mississippi River
> b) 'the most nowhere place in America'
> c) The Crossroads of America
> d) All of the above
>
> The answer is d."
>
> —Abe Aamidor, *The Indianapolis News,* October 20, 1989

The news media can only choose so many subjects at any one time. Therefore, they often choose the "unusual" or the "sensational" because these stories draw readers upon whom their very existence depends.

There is a certain fascination to stories of disasters, disagreements and corruption. Even today residents will mention the General Strike and the *Saturday Evening Post* article about Terre Haute more often than the awards and accomplishments of the city.

In September, 1903, Col. William E. McLean wrote, "It is gratifying to know Terre Haute has never been the victim of mal-administration, inefficient or mischievous corporate government . . ."

McLean did not have a crystal ball which might have helped him predict the impeachment of Mayor Edwin Bidaman in 1906 for non-enforcement of laws regarding saloons and prostitution or the conviction of Mayor Donn Roberts in 1915.

The January 15, 1916, issue of *Literary Digest* reads: *The wholesale arrest of practically its entire city government and many of its leading politicians would be enough to draw outside attention to the busy city of Terre Haute even if the Mayor . . . had not started for Washington to arouse Southern Democrats against Federal interference with local elections.*

. . . And to cut off premature rejoicing in more righteous communities, the District Attorney hints of investigations in Indianapolis, Evansville, and over the line, in Paris, Illinois.

A few months later, the April 26, 1915, issue of *The Independent* reported: *Of the 126 men indicted, eighty-nine pleaded guilty and the twenty-seven who went to trial were found guilty by a jury. Donn M. Roberts, mayor of the city . . . was sentenced to be imprisoned . . . for six years and to pay a fine of $2000.*

News of a positive nature in the January 1928, issue of *The American City* received much less attention. R. I. Pierce wrote: *Terre Haute's $400,000 stadium has . . become the recreation center of the Wabash Valley. . . . The stadium stands on the old Terre Haute fair grounds . . . In the memorial arch are bronze tablets containing the names of nearly seven thousand men and women whose services Terre Haute contributed to the World War.*

Every city has its ups and downs and a number of Terre Haute's events made news in national magazines and out-of-town newspapers. Whether or not residents agreed with the content of the articles, they are a part of the history of the city. Excerpts from a sampling of these releases and articles are included on the following pages.

TERRE HAUTE NO. 3 GENERAL-STRIKE CITY

"The two-day cessation of normal activity, designated by the unions as a 'labor holiday' followed the pattern of its predecessors in Seattle in 1919, which lasted five days, and in San Francisco in 1934, which lasted three days.

The Columbian Enameling and Stamping Company made an arbitration agreement with the Federal Labor Union at its Terre Haute mill. Then, contrary to the agreement, according to labor leaders, preference was shown to unorganized workers.

The union called a strike . . . Peaceful picketing continued until the city deputized special guards for duty at the plant. Equipment was damaged in a subsequent raid on the building.

Later 58 men were imported from Chicago. In protest against the 'invasion of strike-breakers,' 48 organizations, mostly American Federation of Labor affiliates, called a 'labor holiday.' About 23,000 responded to the call.

Street-cars, buses, and trucks halted; restaurants, gasoline filling-stations, barbershops and stores closed; moving-picture theaters were dark; the morning and evening newspapers elected to miss an issue for the first time in their history . . .

Gov. Paul V. McNutt ordered martial law, and 2,000 National Guardsmen moved into the county."

The Literary Digest, August 3, 1935

The strike at the mill and unrest continued for three days before peace returned. Martial law was in effect until February, 1936.

OH, THE MOONLIGHT'S FAIR TONIGHT ALONG THE WABASH

Reviewing the General Strike of 1935, a subsequent article reads:

"But no one could claim victory. Conservative industrialists were confirmed in their belief that organized labor in Terre Haute was unreasonable and 'radical.' Organized labor, embittered by the calling in of the militia, was more than ever convinced that local industrialists were unscrupulous and 'fascistic.'

Yet today, four years later, Terre Haute is prosperous, thriving, and peaceful . . . The principal factor had its beginning on the night of April 4, 1938. . . the Junior Chamber of Commerce . . . first annual 'Bosses Night Banquet.' Out of it came a program known as the Greater Terre Haute Movement, whose principal end product was a plan for dealing with capital-labor relations in Terre Haute."

—FORTUNE, May, 1939

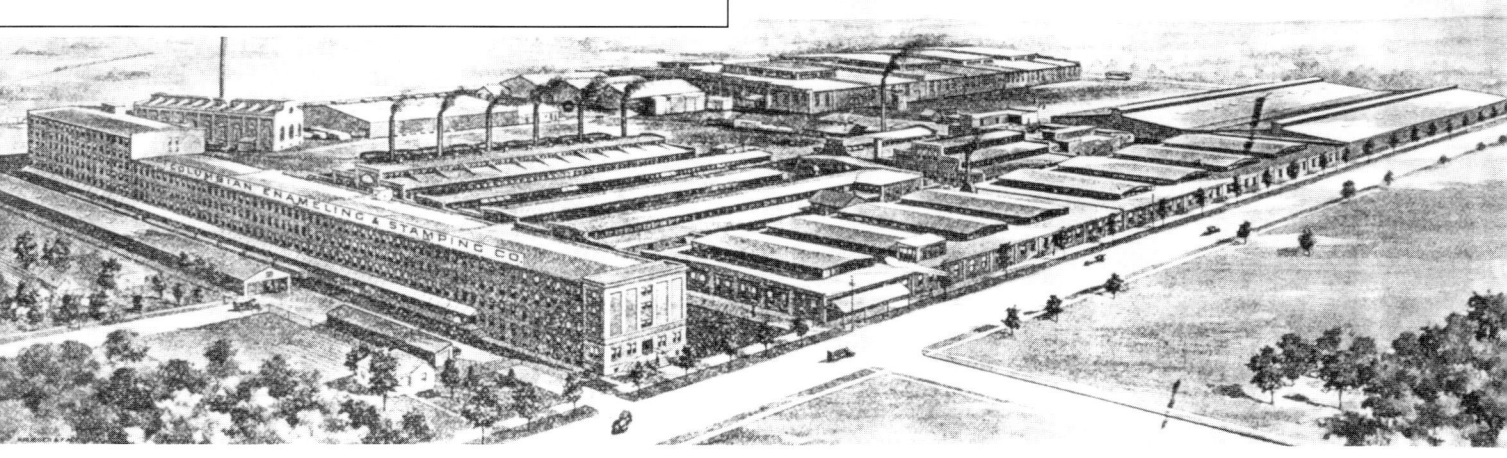

Columbian Enameling & Stamping Company, Beech Street, between Fifteenth and One-Half and Nineteenth streets.

THE POSITIVE VIEW

TERRE HAUTE TREASURE
"Sheldon Swope was a Civil War veteran, an eccentric bachelor, and a prosperous jewelry merchant of Terre Haute, who lived modestly and few knew just how much he had stowed away.... When Swope's will was probated, its provisions amazed and pleased the citizens of Terre Haute; he had left them his substantial fortune — in the form of an art gallery."
NEWSWEEK, April 13, 1942

CLEANUP ON THE WABASH
A post card promoting the sale of the September 2, 1944 issue of the Saturday Evening Post reads: "How Terre Haute rallying behind a businessman mayor, regained its long-lost self-respect and got back on the beam... 'Cleanup on the Wabash' (by Rufus Jarman) tells of Mayor Vernon R. McMillan's successful battle to reform city departments, lower taxes and attract new industries."

THE NEW TERRE HAUTE
"An article on Terre Haute in the February issue of the Kiplinger Magazine has centered the country's attention on what a run-down city can do to raise its business above average.
... What Terre Haute has done any other decaying city can do if it can find a few McMillans and Hulmans."
INDIANAPOLIS NEWS, February 25, 1947

THE FORTUNE SURVEY
"The people of Terre Haute, Indiana, decide which of the leading industrial companies in town are good neighbors — and why.
The chief reason for choosing Terre Haute was because it is far from being a one-industry or one-company town.
The 'best' company (Commercial Solvents Corporation) actually turned out not to pay the highest wages or to build the most playgrounds, but it did create the greatest number of opportunities and, therefore 'did the most for the town.'"
FORTUNE, March, 1950

Mayor Vernon McMillan
Vigo County Public Library collection

The Commercial Solvents Corporation, shown here in the 1940s, merged with International Minerals & Chemical Corporation in 1975. The plant was renamed Pitman-Moore in July, 1987.

Terre Haute "Sizzles"

TERRE HAUTE SIZZLES OVER MAGAZINE 'RED LIGHT' STORY

"Terre Haute, says a racy magazine that devotes much space to sin, is 'as hot as a depot stove.' And the author of the article isn't talking about the temperature along Wabash Avenue at high noon. But if he visited the city again he'd find out that most of the heat is coming from tempers boiling since the November issue of Stag magazine reached the local stands.
The Terre Haute article on bawdy houses and gambling joints is entitled 'Nightime Girlies of Terre Haute' and is written by Stephen Hull. . . . Last year about this time Hull, in the same magazine, called Indianapolis the 'hottest Saturday night town' east of the Canadian Rockies."
THE INDIANAPOLIS NEWS, September 21, 1955

THE BIG, BIG BETTORS HIDE, HIDE AND HIDE

"When U. S. Treasury agents moved in on a third-floor office in Terre Haute, Ind. last fall they seized six surprised bookies, a large quantity of betting records and called it a good day's work. Last week they realized that they had bagged a major U. S. gambling center and had made the biggest haul of big-name gamblers and customers ever cornered in the U. S."
LIFE, September 1, 1958

OPEN HOUSE IN TERRE HAUTE

"Mayor Leland Larrison, 53, appeared on a local TV news show to protect his reputation. Indignantly, he denied a wire service story that he had vowed to rid Terre Haute of prostitution and gambling . . . Though the town seemed happy with the mayor's decision, the gown was not. Alan C. Rankin, president of Indiana State University . . . declared, 'My position is, let's enforce the law . . .'"
TIME, February 21, 1969

Madame Edith Brown opened her first house in 1901 at 213 Mulberry Street. Her later addresses included 318 Eagle Street and 206 North Second Street.

In 1915, the *Tribune* reported that President W. W. Parsons of Indiana State Normal School asked that the red light district be removed totally, but Mayor James Gossom saw no reason to do this. However, the houses of ill fame in the city were restricted to the area between the river, Chestnut Street, Wabash Avenue and the alley between North Third and Fourth streets. *Robert E. Johnson, Sr. collection*

A Story Remembered

INDIANA'S DELINQUENT CITY
by Peter Wyden

"I had spent less than a day in Terre Haute, Indiana, when it became apparent to me that the town was—well, let's say unusual. In a decorous little night club on the main street, which is also U.S. Highway 40, I watched customers straining in concentration over a whirling roulette wheel. Farther downtown I climbed a short flight of steps right into a booming bookie joint. At other stops utterly respectable citizens assured me that there weren't 'over a dozen' brothels operating any more. They were convinced that Terre Haute (pop. 71,851), the somber, tranquil-appearing seat of Vigo County . . . really was a fine city—except for just a few flaws.

High water, unemployment—these are hardships which can be met, other cities have done so. but what can be done for a city enfeebled by apathy . . . Bluntly speaking, folks there don't give a hoot."

SATURDAY EVENING POST, February 11, 1961

INDIANA'S EXPANDING CITIES: TERRE HAUTE AREA . . .
By Paul M. Doherty

". . . the movers and shakers in Terre Haute believe that their city, which grew prodigiously with industries like mining and brewing that now have dwindled or disappeared, has a good start on a secure life."

THE INDIANAPOLIS STAR MAGAZINE, September 17, 1961

TUCKER PLANS REPLY TO "SIN CITY" CHARGES

"Mayor Ralph Tucker called a conference of educational, religious and civic leaders today to reply to what he termed a 'dastardly' magazine article that labels Terre Haute as 'Indiana's delinquent city.'

John Lamb, executive vice-president of the city Chamber of Commerce, said the article 'avoided everything constructive that we've done in the last 10 to 12 years.'"

THE INDIANAPOLIS NEWS, February 7, 1961

Doherty contrasts the portrait of Terre Haute, painted in the *Saturday Evening Post* just seven months before, with the words, accomplishments and future plans of businessmen George F. Johnson, Anton Hulman, Jr., and Morris Landsbaum, Mayor Ralph Tucker, Chamber of Commerce executive secretary John K. Lamb, redevelopment director Emanuel Gorland and Indiana State College president Dr. Raleigh Holmstedt.

Housewives Effort for Local Progress

H.E.L.P. headquarters at 661 Wabash Avenue.
Vigo County Public Library Collection

"HELP's Answer to Peter Wyden and the Post: In February, 1961, Terre Haute was described as 'Indiana's Delinquent City'... What's the picture in 'Sin City' now? Well, some things we had then, we don't have now! One addition to the Terre Haute scene has been H.E.L.P.—Housewives Effort for Local Progress— which was created as a direct result of Mr. Wyden's story. Hundreds of women have become increasingly interested and active in issues ranging from schools to sewers, from rabies to recreation and from garbage to government. We have spent endless hours investigating complaints..., pursuing public and private authorities with questions, digging up local and state laws, attending meetings of public bodies... We have met with occasional cooperation, frequent misunderstanding, and infinite frustration— we have had some defeats and some victories—but most of all, we have learned a great deal about what really goes on in Terre Haute!"
THE SIN CITY SPECIAL, October, 1962

"The efforts of four housewives to spur Terre Haute to progress and dispel apathy has mushroomed into an organization of more than 1,500 persons.
They have organized under the name of HELP (Housewives Effort for Local Progress), but the group also includes many men and residents of surrounding communities whose lives are affected by Terre Haute's economic and social growth....
Mrs. Jacqueline L. Becker described the purpose: It will serve as a recruiting agency for volunteer workers, including many existing organizations, and as a clearing house for problems besetting the city.... The other three founders of HELP are Mrs. Jane C. Hazledine, Mrs. Elvira Carle and Mrs. Joan L. Marx."
THE INDIANAPOLIS STAR, February 15, 1961

**HELP DISBANDS;
MEMBERS TO CONTINUE WORKING**
"Terre Haute's Housewives Efforts for Local Progress (HELP), after 14 years of work throughout the community will disband formally as a result of a vote taken during a May 15 meeting.
HELP members will continue to focus their attention on finding solutions facing local citizens."
TERRE HAUTE TRIBUNE, June 25, 1975

Plus & Minus

A JURY OF PEERS
"Quietly the jurors filed last week into the small, gray-walled Terre Haute courtroom and heard a simple case: a defendant admitted shoplifting a 98-cent key chain in a department store. With the evidence and instructions from the court in hand, the panel repaired to an adjoining room to decide what punishment to recommend . . . the trial was a milestone in Terre haute's fight against juvenile delinquency. Each juror was only 17 years old, the same age as the defendant.

The idea of letting teen-agers be judged by their peers was the nub of an all-out campaign by Vigo County Judge Harold Ralph Johnston to hold down teen-age miscreancy . . . The decision (of the jury)—which under the law could be no more than a recommendation—was accepted and enforced by Juvenile Referee Herbert R. Gerdink."

NEWSWEEK, January 20, 1964

TERRE HAUTE WINS RELIGIOUS AWARD
"Mayor Ralph Tucker yesterday answered 'those who would call Terre Haute a sin city' as he announced that the community-of-the-year award will be presented to municipal officials . . . by Religion in American Life.

It is presented for the best worship program in the U. S. during 1963-64. RIAL is a public service program conducted by an interfaith group composed of 30 religious organizations and 24 service clubs."

THE INDIANAPOLIS NEWS, September 11, 1964

FROM NOWHERE TO SOMEWHERE, STEVE MARTIN RETURNS TO TERRE HAUTE
"Terre Haute had not received so much publicity since the Saturday Evening Post dubbed us 'Sin City' nearly 20 years ago. This time it was another magazine, Playboy, which was responsible for bringing our city to public attention, but it was almost the exact opposite of the prior charges against us.

Steve Martin called Terre Haute 'the most nowhere city' he had ever played in. The noted comedian's remark drew immediate and good-natured responses from local leaders, primarily Mayor William Brighton.

The upshot was a quickly-put-together media event that featured Martin's return to Terre Haute.

. . . it's all in good fun, and most of the local citizenry seemed to take it that way. That in itself says something about Terre Haute. If we can laugh at ourselves, we ought to be in pretty good company."

Fred J. Nation, Editor;
THE SPECTATOR, December 15, 1979

The Spectator reported that 150 reporters and photographers from 35 news organizations covered Martin's return to Terre Haute. These included representatives from CBS, *Newsweek* and *Time* magazines, as well as Playboy Enterprises and Universal Studio who promoted the day in behalf of Martin's new film, "The Jerk." *The Spectator* photo

THE 1913 TORNADO

The Indianapolis News headlines on Monday, March 24, 1913, reads: "Terre Haute Hospital Scene of Sorrow; Mothers Cry for Children." A deadly tornado and severe electrical storm had brought death and ruin to the city on Easter Sunday about 9:30 p.m. Adding to the disaster, the rising waters of the Wabash River flooded part of the city after the tornado.

A second article in this issue commented that the 1913 storm destroyed the old Terre Haute theory which held that the bluffs on each side of the river deflected such storms. It also reported that tornadoes were known to have swept through the same section of the city in 1861 and 1893.

In 1949, the eastern edge of Terre Haute was hit by another tornado; two men were killed at Deming Park.

The floods of 1913 and 1943 are well remembered by many Terre Hauteans. A massive sandbagging effort in May, 1943, saved the Conover levee which extended diagonally from North Third Street in the Collett Park area. Seepage water stood in the residential area as far south as North Fifth and Linden streets.

It had to have been a "blue Monday" for this woman after the Easter Sunday tornado. Citizens cared for the homeless and set up a relief fund.

This postcard photograph shows the tangled wires and trees damaged by the force of the tornado.

Residents look over the remains of these homes in the southwestern part of the city. The death toll was 17.

The 1913 and 1943 Floods

These views of the flood waters, which followed the 1913 tornado, are looking west over the Wabash River (above) and the neighborhood of North Sixth and One-half and Linden streets (left).

Waters of the 1943 flood are shown here rushing under the Pennsylvania Railroad Bridge (right) and looking south from the courthouse over Dresser Drive (left). The Wabash River crested at 30.5 feet, just short of the 31.4 high water mark in 1913. *Kenneth and Jane Hazledine collection*

TERRE HAUTE FIRE LEVELS FIVE DOWNTOWN BUILDINGS

"A wind-swept fire which burned out of control for seven hours in downtown Terre Haute was checked today after it had destroyed 10 business places in five buildings . . . on the north side of Wabash Avenue between Sixth and Seventh streets. Thirty pumper trucks were at the scene, pouring thousands of gallons of water onto the flames . . . Six firemen were injured."

THE INDIANAPOLIS NEWS, March 20, 1963

Martin photo

Claude L. Herbert, a Spanish-American War veteran, perished in the flames of this Havens and Geddes store fire on December 19, 1898, after saving the lives of many people who were in the store. A memorial water fountain commemorating his bravery was erected at Fifth Street and Wabash Avenue. The city bus transfer station now occupies this corner and the fountain stands in front of City Hall.

FIRE AND EXPLOSION

"The 16th body—believed to be the last casualty—was removed today from the blast-shattered rubble of the Home Packing Co. (First and Chestnut streets at the west edge of the city.)

... Workers sifted through the debris of the plant throughout the night in search of victims caught under tons of building materials and equipment after the blast at about 7:05 a.m. yesterday."
January 3, 1963,
THE INDIANAPOLIS NEWS
Martin photo

74

THE 1980s AND THE 1990s

THE MOOD IS GRIM IN WEATHER-VANE COUNTIES
"Terre Haute, Ind. Their city's name means 'high ground' in French, but people living here on bluffs overlooking the Wabash River are anything but high on the 1980 race for the Presidency.

What residents of Terre Haute and the rest of Vigo County think could be important. The county not only has voted for the winner in every presidential election since 1960 but by very close to the percentages that prevailed nationwide."
U.S. NEWS & WORLD REPORT, May 26, 1980

SHOOTING TO KILL IN INDIANA
"Gerald Loudermilk is an unabashedly old-fashioned lawman. SHOOT BACK, says a sign on his desk . . . His town was once infamous as a city of sin, but that has changed in recent years, and Loudermilk, 53, likes to boast that in his two-year tenure as police chief Terre Haute's crime rate has dropped by 13 percent.

'Most people feel more protected by his policies,' says Ken Davidson of the city's chamber of commerce. 'And crime IS down.'"
NEWSWEEK, December 6, 1982

WHERE THE GROWTH IS
The *Inc.* Metro Report
"If you know which signs to follow, you'll find thriving markets all over America . . ."
—John Case

The report ranked Terre Haute/Bloomington, Indiana fifth in a list of cities for having "the most high-growth companies, 1988-1990."

THE TOP 300
Money magazine chose the top 300 places as "The Best Place to Live Now" in their fifth annual survey. Terre Haute ranked 70th, having moved up from its 188th spot in 1990.
MONEY, September, 1991

BASF Corporation announced it was considering Vigo county's industrial park as a site for a new manufacturing plant in March, 1988. Citizens for A Clean County, a local community action group, organized in September to campaign against BASF's plan to build a hazardous-waste incinerator and landfill along with a paint manufacturing plant. With various groups actively for and against, the controversy led to lawsuits. In September, 1990, BASF announced it would not build its plant anywhere in the Wabash Valley.

A local alternative newspaper, *Window*, commented, *When the next generation of Terre Haute history books are written, the BASF controversy will go down as one of the most hotly debated issues of recent years.*

Tribune Star Publishing Company photos

Chamber of Commerce

For more than a century, Terre Haute leaders in business and industry have joined together to improve the local economy. The Board of Trade was organized in 1884; it was followed by the Citizens' Manufacturing Association in 1887 and the Business Men's Association in 1889 with Herman Hulman as president.

Ten years later in 1899, the Commercial Club was founded to take an active role in promoting the city. This successful group, with Adolf Herz as president from 1905 to 1913, was responsible for the relocation or establishment of more than 50 companies.

The successor to the Commercial Club was the Terre Haute Chamber of Commerce. By 1915 it claimed more memberships, in proportion to population, than any other business organization in Indiana.

Governor Evan Bayh addressed the 75th annual meeting of the Terre Haute Chamber of Commerce in 1989.

His father, Birch Bayh, was born in Terre Haute and served in the United States Senate from 1963 to 1981. Governor Bayh's grandfather, Birch Evan Bayh, was on the faculty at Indiana State Teachers College and later was an administrator in the Terre Haute public school system. *Tribune-Star Publishing Company photo*

At one time, the Terre Haute Chamber of Commerce had its own band. The date of this photo is unknown.

CHAPTER 6
At Work in the City

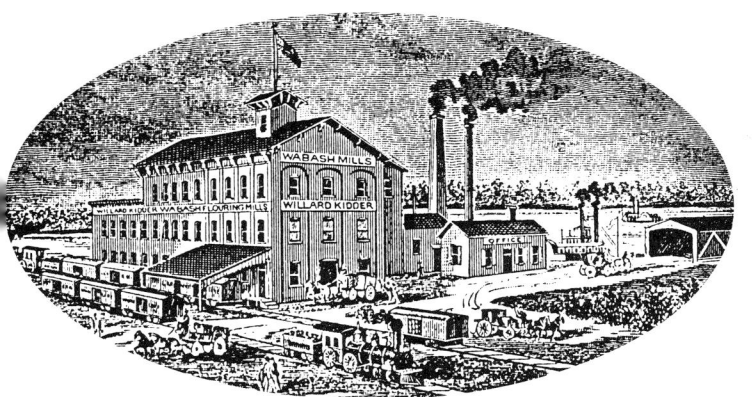

The Wabash Mills of Willard Kidder at the foot of Wabash Avenue produced 800 barrels of flour daily in 1890. The flour was shipped without any re-handling once the wheat was unloaded directly into the mill by a steam shovel at the side track which entered one side of the structure.

> *"It is not an easy matter to define Terre Haute's commerce . . . its reputation does not hinge upon the manufacture of a certain kind of watch, wagon or reaper . . . it possesses a wide fame and influence for diversified industries."*
>
> Illustrated Industrial Souvenir of Greater Terre Haute, 1904

"Diversity" is the key word in the history of business and industry in Terre Haute. The records of every decade from its settlement until now indicate that the economy has been made up of a variety of jobs producing a diversity of products.

At first Terre Haute was an agricultural settlement; there was opportunity for millers, pork packers, blacksmiths, coopers, and harness and wagon makers to name a few. Once the railroads offered transportation to other markets in the 1850s, business and industry related to coal and the railroads opened and prospered.

Loren Hassam, the author of *A Historical Sketch of Terre Haute*, quoted the *Indianapolis Journal* to indicate the standing of the city within the state in 1873. The article reads: *She (Terre Haute) has less wealth than we have, but her capitalists are thoroughly identified with her interest. They are filled with city pride, and have an unbounded faith in her future . . They are, even now, in correspondence with manufacturers abroad, and within a few days, arrangements have been made to build a large rolling mill.*

A special edition of the *Terre Haute Express* listed the city's industries in 1900: *the largest hominy mills in the world, half a dozen large flouring mills, three distilleries, one of which is the largest single manufactory of whiskey in the world, a car manufactory for building freight cars, two iron mills, a new glass plant, spoke and hub factories, nine brick and tile manufacturers, clothing factories, stone works* and more. The first years of the new century were prosperous ones, but as gas, oil and automotive industries grew in the nation, the city could no longer rely on its railroad and coal economy. Reflecting on the 1920s when the breweries and distilleries were closed by Prohibition, when coal mine production slowed and the Pennsylvania Railroad moved its heavy repair shops from the city, an article in the *Indianapolis Star Magazine* (November 11, 1951) concluded: *. . . It was a time of despair. After that Terre Haute hunched on the banks of the Wabash singing the Wabash Blues, overcome by an inferiority complex and finding itself its own worst enemy.*

Still there was diversity; 123 different products were manufactured in the city in 1925 from castings to paints and from glass to enamelware to solvents.

During World War II, Vigo County secured only 59 million dollars in war supply contracts, roughly 1/10th of the amounts acquired by Vanderburgh or Allen County. However, during the last 50 years since the war, new companies have come to the city, the industrial park on North Fruitridge Street was developed and historical companies such as Gartland Foundry, Moore-Langen, Prox Company, Woodburn, and Terre Haute Engraving stayed.

Retailing is another facet of the local economy; it has remained strong through the years. The success of neighborhood stores and the downtown and later the shopping centers has proven Terre Haute to be a regional retail trade hub for the two-state area of the Wabash Valley.

LABOR

Working men organized in the Terre Haute community beginning in the 1840s. Barbers, brewery workers, meat cutters, plumbers, steamfitters and workers in other occupations joined to improve wages, hours and working conditions.

Representatives from various craft unions formed the Labor Temple Association in 1912 and located in the Phoenix Club building at Fifth and Walnut streets in 1923. This was labor headquarters until it was demolished in 1991 for expansion of the A P & S Clinic.

The Vigo County Central Labor Union established *The Advocate,* a pro-union newspaper, in 1919 and published it until the early 1970s.

Sixty-five locals were meeting in Vigo County in 1984, 42 of which were affiliated with the Wabash Valley Central Labor Council.

The idea for the American Federation of Labor, predecessor to the AFL-CIO, came about at a meeting of national labor leaders at this Empire Theater building in 1881. Located on the northeast corner of Third and Ohio Streets, the structure housed a number of businesses and was the county courthouse for a time, before it was torn down in 1984. The law offices of Anderson and Nichols occupy the site.

Tim Barton, member of Bricklayers Union Local #5 chartered in 1889, laid cinder block as part of a construction project at the Terre Haute Savings Bank in 1989. *Tribune-Star Publishing Company photo*

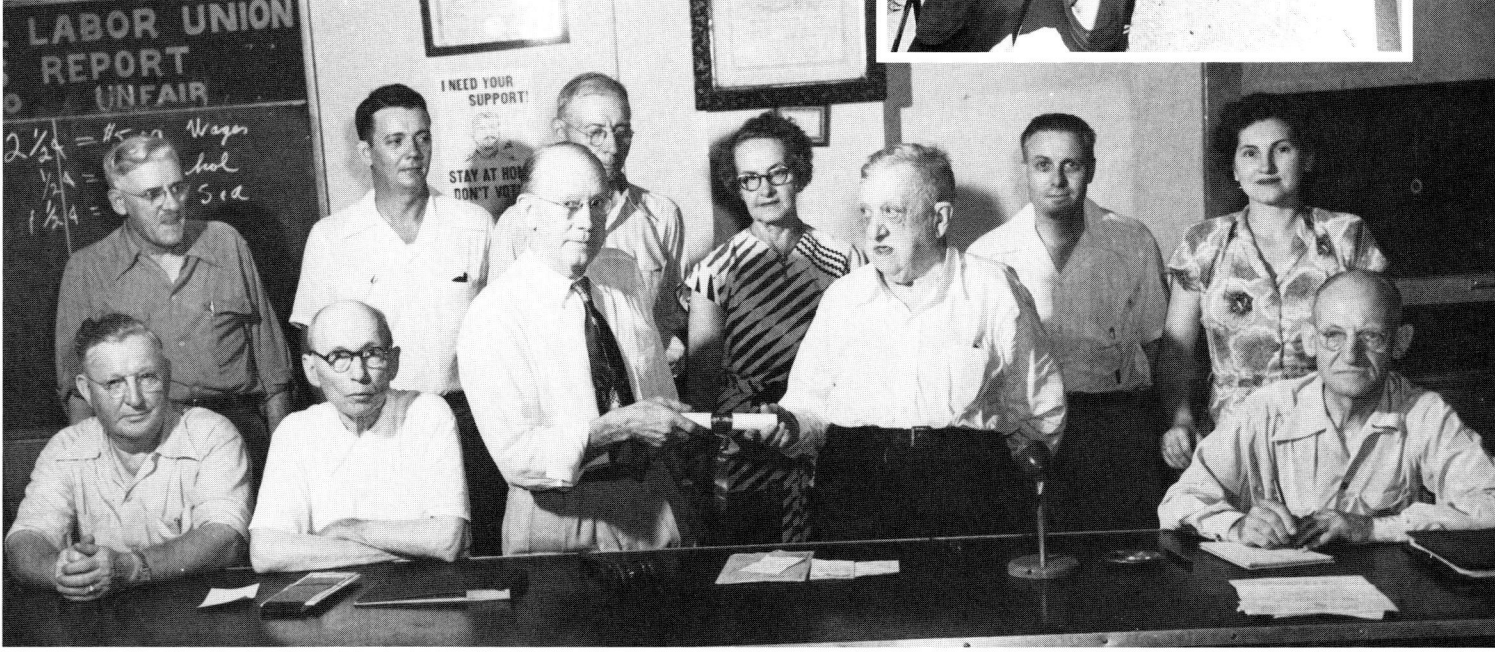

The Central Labor Union honored Edward Evinger in 1951. He and J. P. McDonagh, both members of the Typographical Union, formulated what was known as the first central labor union and sponsored the first local Labor Day celebration in 1890. *Martin photo*

COAL & OIL

From the beginning, Terre Haute blacksmiths seeking fuel for their forges brought coal from outcroppings along the river. During the 1880s railroads provided the means to ship coal to other markets. Underground mining became profitable. Commercial mines were opened in Vigo and adjacent counties and Terre Haute became the center for the operators, dealers and organized workers, as well as the location of related industries.

Production peaked in the 1920s and *The Book of Terre Haute* (September, 1920) reported there were 14 producing mines within six miles of the city. Terre Haute was by this time *the commercial and mining center of the Indiana coal field, which produces thirty million tons of fuel per year and the seat of one of the most modern by-product coke plants (Indiana Coke and Gas Company) in the country.*

Gradually, underground mining gave way to open pit mining; the last shaft mine in Vigo County closed in the 1970s.

The Indiana Coal Trade Bureau maintained this office in downtown Terre Haute in 1919. Organized in 1916, it became a part of the Indiana Bituminous Coal Operators' Association in 1924.

For a time the city hoped to become a center for oil production as well as for coal, but this dream did not come true. The Phoenix oil well on the northeast corner of Ninth and one-half and Mulberry streets, shown here in the 1940s, was one of several in the downtown area. Drilled at the Phoenix Foundry and Machine Works in 1889, it later became the property of the Frank Prox Company.

A contest to determine Indiana's oldest active miner was one of the events at the 29th annual United Mine Workers District No. 11 Picnic at Memorial Stadium in 1945. The district had been organized since 1890.

Agribusiness

The agricultural resources of the Terre Haute area attracted the early settlers who soon established flour mills, saw mills and tanneries.

The pork trade contributed to the early prosperity of the city. Ben Ives Gilman built the first pork packing plant at First and Mulberry streets in 1824. Later the river banks were lined with companies bearing names such as A. Rowe Sons (1888), Valentine (1904) and Home Packing and Ice Company (1907). The city even received a second name, "Hogapolis."

Terre Haute became a grain terminal to supply mills, breweries, distilleries and other related industries. The addition of soybeans to area farmers' crops came after World War II. In the meantime, farmers

The caption on this turn-of-the-century photograph reads "Papa Makes Them" with "Papa" being C. H. Ehrmann, owner of Ehrmann Pork Packing Company at 100-102 South Fourth Street.

Barbazette and Sparks Cattle Feeders (John Barbazette and William W. Sparks) was at 601 South First Street in 1901.

Hart's Feed Store advertised almost every one of their products on its building at 29-33 Harding Avenue. Note the National Recovery Act (NRA eagle in the center of this photograph from the early 1930s. The present City Hall is now at this location.

were replacing their horses with tractors and the farm implement business began to flourish in the city.

Baking, canning of fruits and vegetables, and dairy and poultry products became important parts of local agribusiness. Besides vegetable growers Davis and Owen mentioned below, names associated with the greenhouse floral industry included Heinl, Cowan, Weber, Henley and Smith.

The author of *Terre Haute Today* (1915) wrote, "Terre Haute is in the center of a remarkable agricultural section."

Davis Gardens, location of the world's largest greenhouse, was founded by J. W. Davis and O. Keith Owen, Sr. in 1914. Pictured here in 1939, it closed in 1974; Westminster Village retirement community is now located on the site. *Rochelle Kemp collection*

The Graham Grain Company, founded in 1930 by Carl M. Graham, operated numerous elevators for grain grown by Wabash Valley farmers. The company was purchased by ConAgra in 1987. *Vigo County Public Library collection*

Recipe Foods, Incorporated purchased the property at North Thirteenth and Plum streets in 1945. Products included the nationally advertised Bennett's prune juice and chili sauce. The Doxsee Food Corporation took over about 1972 and was in operation at the site until the late 1980s. *Vigo County Public Library collection*

Wheels

The carriage company, Wildy & Poths, established in 1867, was located on South Third Street between Ohio and Walnut. The building was demolished in the late 1980s.

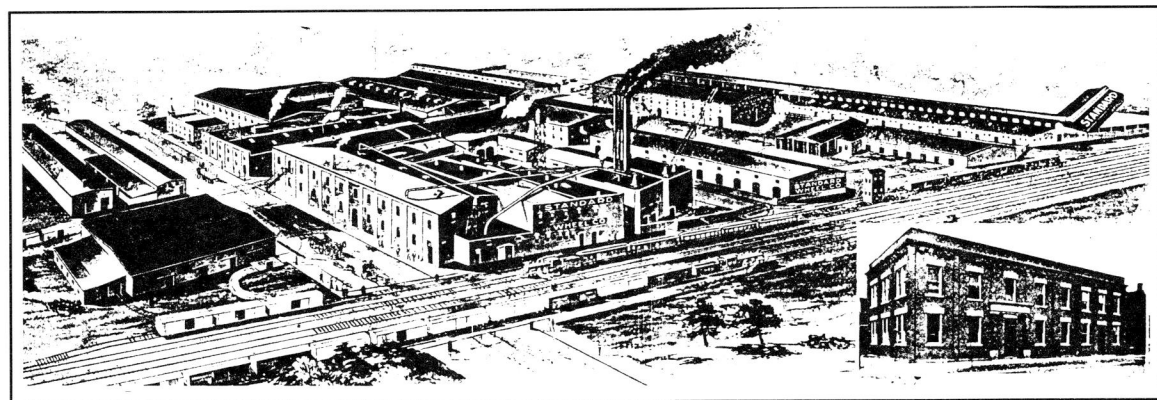

The Standard Wheel Company, established in 1892 and shown here in 1915, manufactured heavy wheels for wagons at its Terre Haute plant at North Thirteenth and Plum streets. By 1920 the company had two local subsidiaries, Standard Malleable Castings Company and Standard Machine Company. Its principal products were wooden wheels for all types of mining, rail and cross-country vehicles.

Designed by Claude Cox at the Standard Wheel Company plant in 1902, the Overland Runabout had a one-cylinder engine and solid oak frame. The 1903 model is pictured here. The operation moved to Indianapolis in 1905 and later to Toledo, Ohio. *Frank Kleptz collection*

Wilson, Clarence and Donald House were in business as House Trucking by 1935. In 1946, Wilson House founded Eastern Motors Express, Inc. and Welby Frantz joined the company as executive vice-president. By 1965 Eastern operated approximately 2,500 vehicles and 28 terminals. It was the thirteenth largest common carrier in the nation.
Martin photo

The use of trucks in transporting troops and supplies during World War I led to the growth of the industry. Hard-surfaced highways were constructed during the 1920s and railroads lost business.

For example, Harry Adams started Motor Freight Corporation in 1928 with one truck carrying goods between Terre Haute and Brazil. By 1953, the company owned and operated 166 vehicles and employed 182 persons.

In 1958, 34 companies hauled freight via the city to any point of delivery; the home office of seven of these firms was Terre Haute.

Maynard F. Niemeyer was owner and president and William Niemeyer was vice-president of Lovelace Truck Service when this photograph was taken of a Lovelace truck at the Quaker Maid plant on North Fruitridge Avenue in 1955. In business since 1937, the company merged with Commercial Motor Freight in 1976 becoming Commercial Lovelace Motor Freight, Inc.
Martin photo

Manufacturing

The Stahl-Urban Company on Ohio Street was an important garment manufacturer. It operated between 150 and 165 machines in 1920 and produced overalls, pants, shirts and mackinaws for working men. The Simplicity Pattern Company later moved into the plant.

These women were working at the Quaker Maid Company on North Fruitridge Avenue in 1948. The company, a subsidiary of the Great Atlantic & Pacific Tea Company, started manufacturing food items at the Terre Haute plant in 1930 and continued in business until 1979.
Martin photo

The Simplicity Pattern Company opened a plant at 625 Poplar Street in 1944. The operation had expanded to 400 employees by 1948 with plants at 918 Ohio Street (pictured here) and at the former Trianon Ballroom building on East Wabash Avenue. The Ohio Street building is now the home of WTHI Radio-TV.
Vigo County Public Library collection

Left: Glas-Col Apparatus Company, founded in 1939 by Dr. Glen H. and Ruth K. Morey (a division of Templeton Coal Company since 1954), produces laboratory heating and safety equipment. The plant at South Seventh and Hulman streets was constructed in 1953. Shown here is Dr. Morey with his invention — a heating mantle for laboratory flasks. *Glas-Col Apparatus Company collection*

Dr. Glen H. Morey

Right: Joseph B. Card built the Chicago Tie Preserving Company in Terre Haute in 1906. The firm became the Zinc-Creosoting Company in 1910 and the Indiana Wood Preserving Company in 1922. It merged with Western Tar Products Corporation in 1956. Both plants continue to operate on the Prairieton Road as divisions of Western Tar Products. *Vigo County Public Library collection*

The Terre Haute Malleable Manufacturing Company produced iron castings from 1906 until 1985. The men shown here are working at the 2030 North Nineteenth Street plant in 1938. Pig iron, scrap iron, and "leavings" from other moldings were melted down in huge furnaces, then poured and cooled. *Martin photo*

The Root Glass Company, the North Baltimore Glass Company and Turner Brothers Glass Company together made glass production an important Terre Haute industry. Pictured here is a 1920 advertisement of the Root Glass Company at South Third and Voorhees streets and a 1923 company delivery wagon. The Coca-Cola bottle was designed in Terre Haute in 1915 by Alex Samuelson, a Root employee. Established in 1901, the Root Glass Company was sold to Owens-Illinois Glass Company in 1932.

Merchants Distilling Corporation, manufacturers and producers of high quality whiskey, on South First Street, operated from 1898 to the 1950s except during Prohibition. Production required 5,000 bushels of corn per day in 1900 and resulted in 25,000 gallons of spirits.
Vigo County Public Library collection

Columbia Records, Inc. opened its plant on North Fruitridge Avenue in 1953 to produce records. The Columbia Record Club, now a part of Columbia House Company, was created in 1956. In 1982 record and tape manufacturing operations were moved to other CBS facilities. Digital Audio Disc Corporation, a subsidiary of Sony, U.S.A. and the nation's first manufacturer of compact discs, purchased the facilities, enlarged them and began production in 1984. *Martin photo*

The Bemis Bag Company opened its plant, pictured above, on North Fruitridge Avenue in 1956. Ten years later, *Indiana Business and Industry* (October, 1966) named Bemis, American Can, Visqueen and Weston Paper the "Big Four" in Terre Haute's packaging industry. The Alliance for Growth and Progress, a group coordinating community resources to generate economic strength, lists the Bemis Company as one of ten local industries in its promotion of Terre Haute as "Plastic Center U.S.A."
Tribune-Star Publishing Company photo

The Weston Paper and Manufacturing Company was formed in 1949; however, operations had begun in Terre Haute in 1899 at the Terre Haute Mill and in 1924 at the Wabash Fibre Box Company. This 1953 photograph of the mill on Prairieton Road shows straw stacks ready for conversion to pulp for the production of corrugating medium. *The Weston Paper and Manufacturing Company collection*

Herman Hulman, Sr.
1831-1913

Anton Hulman, Sr.,
1864-1942

Anton Hulman, Jr.
and Mary Fendrich
Hulman in 1969.

Northeast corner, Fifth Street and Wabash Avenue

The Hulman Family

Herman Hulman emigrated from Lingen, Germany to Terre Haute to join his brother, Francis Hulman, in the wholesale grocery business which opened in 1850 as Ludowici & Hulman.

In 1858 Francis Hulman and his family perished when the ship *Austria* burned at sea on their return from a visit to Germany and Herman Hulman took over the business. For a time his partner was R. S. Cox.

The business outgrew its building at Fifth Street and Wabash Avenue and plans were made for a new structure. It was a proud day for Herman Hulman and his family on September 28, 1893 when 3,500 quests attended the dedication ceremony of their present building at Ninth Street and Wabash Avenue.

Herman's eldest son, Anton Hulman, Sr. and later his grandson, Anton Hulman, Jr., (1901-1977) continued the business. Mari Hulman George, Herman's great-granddaughter, now serves as president and chair of the board of directors.

Its best known product is Clabber Girl Baking Powder. Through the years the Hulman interests have diversified to include ownership of the Indianapolis Motor Speedway. Tony George, Mari's son, is president of that enterprise.

Opening Day – September 28, 1893

On the occasion of this, the 100th Anniversary of the Hulman & Company Building, we of the fourth and fifth generation Hulman family are very proud of the continued use of "The House that Hulman Built."

. . . Certainly after 100 years of continuous use, durability is not in question. As for beauty, after 100 years, this cannot only be measured by the structure, but should also be measured to reflect the manner in which the Building has served as a nucleus for events that have touched the lives of the thousands of friends, customers and employees of Hulman & Company throughout the years.

Mari H. George,
Board Chairman/President
April 12, 1992

Indiana Historical Society Library, Martin Collection (negative #35871)

Utilities

At the turn of the century, the *Terre Haute Express* reported the city was lighted with electricity to the remotest suburb. The Citizens Gas Company supplied gas to consumers, the water works provided residents and industry with a supply of pure water, and two telegraph companies and two telephone exchanges made local and long distance communication available.

The Citizens Gas & Fuel Company advertised in the *Up-To-Date Cookbook,* published by the Terre Haute YWCA in 1905. Stores, businesses and streets were first lighted by gas in 1856 by the Terre Haute Gas Light Company, which consolidated with Citizens Gas and Fuel Company in 1895.

This horse-powered "high rise" vehicle of the Terre Haute Traction & Light Company was being used to repair electric power lines on Poplar Street about 1913. *Thelma Lamb collection*

July 16, 1921
... Don Gwinn, manager of the Terre Haute Waterworks Company, took his official family up the river for a boat ride ... brought them before a wonderful feed and in more ways than one provided an excellent half day jollification for his 'gang.'
—*Terre Haute Tribune*

City businesses began listing two phone numbers after the Citizens' Telephone Company incorporated in 1886 and began competing for customers with Central Union. The women pictured above are working in a Central Union "operating room" on the second floor of the Kaufman Building at 681 1/2 Wabash Avenue.

Terry McIntyre and Jack Ridge, PSI Energy employees, were hard at work repairing a street light at Ninth Street and Wabash Avenue in April, 1992. *Tribune-Star Publishing Company photo*

Citizens' Independent bought out Central Union in 1920. Their building at South Seventh and Poplar streets, which opened in 1926 and is now occupied by GTE, is shown here. *Vigo County Public Library collection*

THE PRESS

The staff took a minute to pose for this photograph in the editorial room of the newspaper office at 719-725 Wabash Avenue in 1940. The managing editors were William F. Cronin *(Tribune)* and James R. Benham *(Star)*. In May, 1983, the evening *Tribune* merged with the morning *Star* to produce a seven-mornings-a-week newspaper known as the *Tribune-Star*. *Indiana Historical Society Library, Martin Collection (negative #35871)*

Red Skelton is one of the many famous individuals photographed by Ken Martin who appears in this photograph with Skelton. The Martin family, in business as Martin's Photo Shop, photographed the people, places and events of the city and county from 1906 to 1976. Their photographs are now a part of the Indiana Historical Society Library collection in Indianapolis. Many Martin photos appeared in the popular rotogravure section, a part of the *Sunday Tribune-Star* from 1928 until 1979. This "roto" or "brown section" was the last one of its kind in the nation.

Over 60 different newspapers have been published in Vigo County, the majority of them within the city of Terre Haute. Their pages document the history of this county. In fact, at times these pages hold the only known history of an event or person, all other traces have vanished.

—David M. Buchanan, 1988

TERRE HAUTE NEWSPAPERS

-1860-	-1890-	-1940-
Terre Haute Journal	Terre Haute Daily News	Indiana Republic
Terre Haute Zeitung (German)	Terre Haute Express	Saturday Spectator
Wabash Express	Terre Haute Gazette	Terre Haute Star
	Saturday Evening Mail	Terre Haute Tribune
	Terre Haute Journal (German)	The Advocate

RADIO AND TELEVISION

Broadcasting in Terre Haute had its beginning at Rose Polytechnic Institute in 1927. The station was WRTI. One year later it became WBOW; the only station in the city until WTHI opened on January 13, 1948.

Local television came to the city on July 22, 1954 when WTHI-TV went on the air. WTWO-TV followed in 1965 and WIIL-TV in 1973. WIIL-TV became WBAK-TV in 1977.

By 1985 the city was the media center for the Wabash Valley with three television and ten radio stations, more than most cities of the same or larger size.

Harry Frey began his broadcasting career at WBOW radio in 1942. After additional radio experience at WTHI and WMFT, he joined the television news staff at WTHI-TV in 1962. Twenty years later, he retired from his position as anchor on the 6 p.m. newscast and became the administrative assistant to Mayor P. Pete Chalos. Other local persons who began their media careers at WBOW radio include Ralph Tucker, Johnny Palmer, Martin Plascak, Wayne Jenkins, Bob Forbes, and Jim Underwood. *WBOW Radio collection*

RADIO STATIONS

1950	1970	1985	1992
WBOW	WAAC-AM	WBOW-AM	WBOW-AM
WTHI	WBOW-AM	WISU-AM	WCBH-FM
	WTHI-AM-FM	WMHD-FM	WISU-FM
	WVTS-FM	WPFR-AM-FM	WJSH-AM
		WTHI-AM-FM	WMGI-FM
		WVTS-FM	WMHD-FM
		WWVR-FM	WPFR-FM
		WZZQ-FM	WTHI-AM-FM
			WWVR-FM
			WZZQ-FM

Beginning as a photographer for the *Brazil Times* in neighboring Clay County, Betty Chadwick Sullivan was hired at television station WTHI in 1958 and became the first female news photographer in the United States. *Wabash Valley Broadcasting Company collection*

Our History Is Our Heritage

The ancestors of Terre Haute First National Bank, wrote A. R. Markle in 1939, "furnished the money that built the National Road, the railroads and the canal, that financed the freight of the steamboats from here to New Orleans and the Eastern markets.

"The building of the streets, the gravel roads of the county, the building and operating of the old pork-packing houses, the purchase of the salt and barrels, the cooper shops that made the latter for both pork and whiskey and the distilleries and breweries that used the grain, the very buildings all were financed by these old institutions that were the backbone of commercial activities that helped to make Terre Haute."

Terre Haute First's earliest ancestor came into being in November 1834 as the Terre Haute branch of the State Bank of Indiana. The state was divided into ten banking districts; the Terre Haute branch served the ninth district, which included Vigo, Clay, Owen, Putnam, Parke and Vermillion counties.

The earliest document of record for the new bank was dated November 13, 1834, and was the bond for $20,000 given by James Farrington, first cashier, signed by himself; the bank's president, Demas Deming; its secretary, Chauncey Warren; and John D. Early, Curtis Gilbert and Chauncey Rose.

Although there is no record of where the bank was located, Markle wrote that it was "in all probability on the west side of the public square, the main commercial business center of the village."

Wherever the State Bank of Indiana stood in its earliest days, the structure it built in 1836 still stands today as the GAR Memorial Hall, now the law offices of Kesler & Kesler, on the south side of Ohio Street across from the Vigo County Courthouse.

In 1855, a new bank was chartered under the name of the Bank of the State of Indiana. While it was closely patterned after the old bank, the state had no stock in this one, would have little control over it and would derive no profit from it.

The State Bank sold its branches to the Bank of the State, and the Terre Haute branch was transferred on January 17, 1857. Meanwhile, the Indiana General Assembly passed the free banking law in response to popular clamor for more banks and more currency.

"Under this act almost anyone could, and many did, start a bank with almost no effort or capital, much less any experience," Markle wrote.

When the National Currency Act establishing the National Banking System was signed into law by President Abraham Lincoln on February 25, 1863, the Bank of the State was reorganized as the First National Bank of Terre Haute. It received National Charter No. 47 on August 3, 1863. That number is held today by its descendant, Terre Haute First National Bank.

A 1963 centennial issue of *Hoosier Banker*, the official publication of the Indiana Bankers Association, noted that only one other bank in the state—The First National Bank of Richmond with Charter No. 17 —holds an earlier number.

In 1865 the former State Bank was reorganized to become the National State Bank. In 1868 it moved from its quarters on Ohio Street to a building at the southwest corner of Fifth Street and Wabash Avenue, which now houses the Saratoga Restaurant.

GAR Memorial Hall, the city's oldest building, once housed the State Bank of Indiana, the earliest ancestor of Terre Haute First.

We always have time for you… and temperature, too! This art deco neon sign graced the entrance of the main office banking center at 643 Wabash Avenue for many years. The number 47 at the bottom of the shield refers to the National Charter number issued to the bank in 1863.

The building that was home to the bank from 1868 to 1905 still stands at the corner of Fifth Street and Wabash Avenue.

Always Close to Home

It stayed at that location until 1905, when it was reorganized into the Terre Haute National Bank.

Also in 1905, another of Terre Haute First's ancestors, McKeen National Bank, was organized. In 1928, it would merge with the Terre Haute National Bank and Trust Co. to become First-McKeen National Bank. Terre Haute National Bank and Trust Co. was the product of a merger the previous year between Terre Haute National Bank and the United States Trust Co.

Organized in 1902, the United States Trust Co. had constructed a building at 643-645 Wabash Avenue, which it first occupied in 1904. It was in that building that the newly merged banks made their home.

Following the merger, the building that until 1988 housed Terre Haute First's main office underwent an extensive renovation that included the painting of the Vincent Aderante murals that grace the high domed ceiling of the building's lobby.

Much ado was made of the murals when the refurbished building had its formal opening on June 18, 1928—the same day Amelia Earhart became the first "girl," as the newspapers referred to her, to successfully fly an airplane across the Atlantic.

On November 15, 1932, First-McKeen National Bank and Trust Co. merged with the Terre Haute National Bank and Trust Co. The two banks were consolidated under the charter of First-McKeen National Bank and Trust Co. and under the corporate title of Terre Haute First National Bank. That was the final merger until 1980, when Terre Haute First acquired the State Bank of West Terre Haute.

Anticipating passage of a state law that would allow multi-bank holding companies, the bank applied for approval from the Federal Reserve Board to establish such an entity. It received that approval in February 1983, and First Financial Corporation became the holding company for Terre Haute First National Bank.

First Financial Corporation became the first multi-bank holding company in the state of Indiana in August 1984—nearly a year before the General Assembly passed a law in July 1985 allowing the practice.

Under an earlier law, a bank that failed could be bought and operated as a newly chartered bank. That's what First Financial Corporation did when People's State Bank of Clay County failed. It now operates as First State Bank.

Four more affiliate banks have been added since the passage of the 1985 law: First Citizens State Bank of Vermillion County in December 1985; First Farmers State Bank of Sullivan and Greene counties in December 1987; First Ridge Farm State Bank of Vermilion County, Illinois, in November 1990; and First Parke State Bank of Parke County in August 1993.

But don't look for that to be the end. According to First Financial Corporation's president and chairman of the board, Donald E. Smith, "We are continuing to look for expansion opportunities in our market areas. Our goal is to remain a financially strong group of community banks."

(above left) "Industry" is the title of this Vincent Aderante mural from the building at 643 Wabash (lower left), which served as the bank's main office for 60 years. (above) For its formal opening in 1928, the renovated lobby of 643 Wabash was decorated with flowers.

Banking

The growth of industry and business in Terre Haute, resulted in part from the activity of local banks and savings and loan associations. Banks listed in the city directories include:

1880: First National, McKeen & Company's National State, Prairie City, Shannon's, and Terre Haute Savings banks.

1925: Terre Haute National, McKeen National, First National, United States Trust Company, People's State, Indiana State, Citizens Trust, Twelve Points State, Terre Haute Trust Company and Terre Haute Savings banks.

1980: Indiana State, Merchants National, Terre Haute First National, Terre Haute Savings banks.

This advertisement appeared in the September, 1921, issue of *The Book of Terre Haute* which reported the existence of 15 associations in the city. Charles M. Trout wrote, *One of, if not the largest, factor in the encouragement of home building and owning in Terre Haute has been and is the Building and Loan Associations. Seventy-five to eighty percent of the homes in the city have been bought, built, or remodeled with assistance of these institutions.*

Money to Loan

Ready money to loan on good improved city real estate or farms

Interest compounded semi-annually on savings accounts

The Wabash Savings, Loan and Building Association

ROSS HARRIOTT, Secretary

Northeast Corner Sixth and Ohio Sts.

The Terre Haute Savings Bank, founded in 1869, moved to its present location at the corner of South Sixth and Ohio streets in 1884. The building is shown above in the 1890s. The present building was constructed on the same site in 1910-1911. The top floors, which had been occupied by Levin Brothers, dry goods wholesalers, were removed in 1972.

The Citizens Trust Company originated in 1913 at 612-614 Wabash Avenue. The company built Terre Haute's only "skyscraper," the twelve-story building now known as the Sycamore Building, at 19-21 South Sixth Street in 1922. Charles Newlin, shown second from left in this photograph, founded the C. C. Newlin Company in 1932. It became the Newlin-Johnson Company, Inc. one year later.

The Central Eastside

No more active 'pep' developing organization exists in Terre Haute than the East Side Boosters Club made up of the merchants and other business men of East Wabash Avenue. The Book of Terre Haute, March, 1921

The Eastside Businessman's Association was founded in the early 1930s and reorganized in 1955 under its current name - the Central Eastside Association. The boundaries are from Ninth Street east to Twenty-fifth Street and from Poplar Street north to Chestnut Street.

The J. D. King drug store was at 1241 Wabash Avenue in 1898. Next door was the Quong Lung Chinese Laundry. On the Thirteenth Street and Wabash Avenue corners were the Samuel Smith Saloon, Gerdink and French (grocers and saloon) and Frederick Hoff (grocer and feed store.) *Jane King collection*

Rhyan & Goodman funeral directors, shown here at South Fourteenth and Poplar streets, advertised their establishment as being "out of the high rent district." They were one of nine undertakers in business in the city in 1915.

Diners could choose "curb service" at Frank's Restaurant & Drive Inn during the late 1950s. This central eastside dining spot was located at 1229 Wabash Avenue. *Martin photo*

Barbers and Beauticians

Hermann Lang advertised in the 1860 city directory. Other barbers in business that year included P. Ackerly, K. Brooks, S. Bonds, H. Ehrenhardt, T. O'Niel, C. Perry and M. Stewart.

Barbers were in demand before hair dressers, later called beauticians. Indeed, the 1901 city directory listed 72 barbershops and only two hair dressers — Agnes Johnson and Agnes Talburt. The so-called "roaring twenties" changed this ratio rather drastically.

An article in a 1925 issue of the *Terre Haute Tribune* declared "Beauty Culture Now A Profession" and described the classes at the Smart Appearance Beauty College. By 1952, there were 78 beauty shops as well as 72 barbershops in business in the city.

Elmer Evans operated a barbershop at 110 South Fourth Street from 1925 until the early 1940s. Evans, second barber "Jake" Van Gilder and shoe shiner Tyree Gordon are shown here in about 1930.

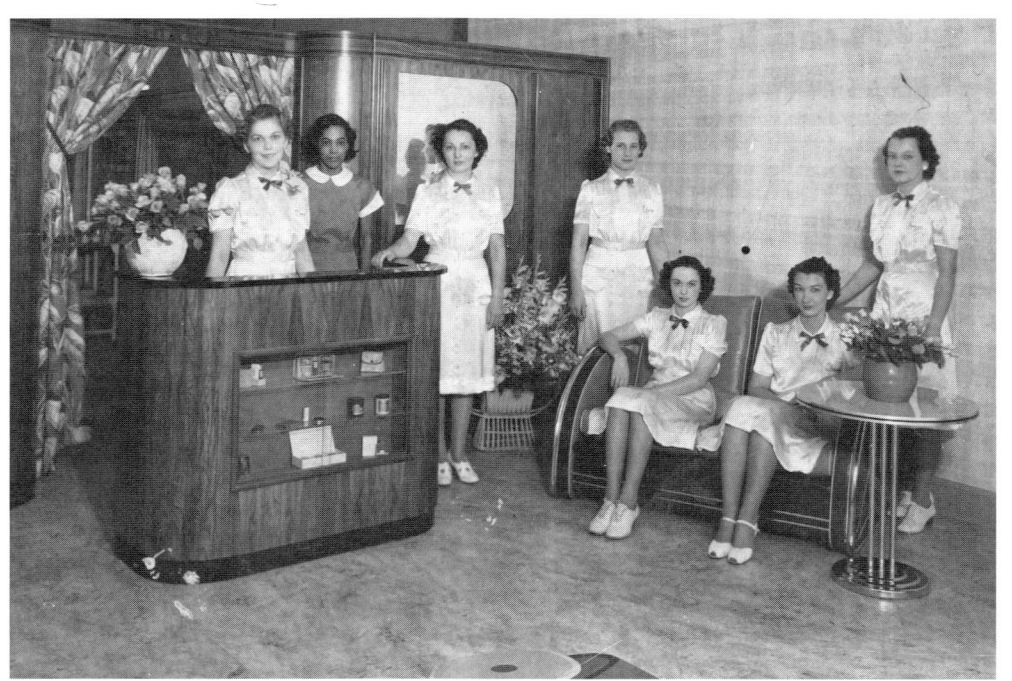

Vera Diel Baesler opened her Charm Beauty Salon in 1935 at 1105 Wabash Avenue. This photograph shows her business in 1936 after a move to 907 Wabash Avenue. A 1956 newspaper advertisement described the salon as "Terre Haute's oldest." *Vera Baesler collection*

Ohio Street

Ohio Street was in importance second only to Wabash Avenue just one block north. However, Spencer F. Ball's advertisement in a 1907 issue of *The Saturday Spectator* announced, "Ohio Street will soon rival Wabash Avenue," revealing a healthy competitive spirit in downtown.

John Foulkes advertised insurance, loans and real estate on the front door of his office at 511 Ohio Street about 1900. His business was between the law offices of Adrian Beecher and Ben Henderson and those of William Hice and George O. Dix.

The Terre Haute Decorating Company at 415 Ohio Street carried 60,000 rolls of wallpaper, window shades, room moulding and hardware, paints, oils and varnishes in stock in 1900.

Jerry's Bakery at 207-213 Ohio Street was directly opposite the courthouse. Other major bakeries in 1922 included the Ideal and the Miller-Parrott baking companies. The 213 Ohio Street location was the site of the Milks Emulsion Company plant from 1903 to 1916.

Kivits Brothers (William H. and Albert F.) sold wholesale produce, both fruits and vegetables, at 428 North Third Street. The horse-drawn wagon of H. Richey appears in this early 1920s photograph.

Third Street

Once known as Market Street, Third Street (U.S. 41) now carries the largest share of traffic through the city. Businesses line the street from Maple Avenue on the north to the junction of U.S. 41 and Seventh Street on the south. The historic courthouse and Woodlawn Cemetery along its west side lend a sense of history to this thoroughfare.

The Temple Laundry on the northwest corner of North Third and Chestnut streets was in business from about 1914, the date of this photograph showing both the plant and stables. A 1915 advertisement stated the company had 2,800 square feet of floor space devoted exclusively to laundry work. *Anne Temple Lambert collection*

Just off Third Street at 311 Walnut, was the site of Motor Springs Service Company, established about 1921 by Harvey W. Ford and Alfred L. Fischer. The Wabash Electric Company was next door at 313 Walnut, and the David Baughman grocery was on the corner at 301 Walnut.

C. C. Smith on the southeast corner of Third Street and Wabash Avenue advertised stoves, kitchen furnishings, hardware, furnaces, wagons, buggies, bicycles and plows in 1901. Established in 1842, Smith Hardware remained one of the oldest retail stores in the city until it closed in the late 1970s. A modern strip mall now houses MAB Paints, Manpower Temporary Services and Systems House on this corner.

Third & Wabash, 1900

Fourth & Wabash, 1930

On the north side of Wabash Avenue from the corner of Fourth Street (right to left) toward Third Street in the 1930s, businesses include Charles Hanley's Terre Haute Shoe Repair, Jacob Hulman men's furnishings, the men's clothing store of Abraham Schultz, and David Becker's Peoples Pawn Shop.

Downtown Hotels

At first, taverns accommodated travelers along the National Road. Later taverns became hotels and travelers' transportation changed from stagecoach and boats to trains and finally buses and automobiles.

Eleven hotels were listed in the 1858 city directory with the Clark House at First and Ohio streets charging one dollar per day. In 1890, downtown Terre Haute was the site of 19 hotels, and in 1930, the city directory reported a dozen hotels with a total of 1,081 rooms.

After railroad traffic declined, the number of downtown hotels decreased. The Terre Haute House closed its doors in the 1970s giving way to the plethora of hotels and motels around the junction of U.S. 41 and Interstate 70.

Chauncey Rose opened the Prairie House, the forerunner of the Terre Haute House, in 1838 at the corner of Seventh Street and Wabash Avenue. Terre Haute architect Juliet Peddle later wrote, ". . . people thought Mr. Rose was rather optimistic to think any business would come to a hotel located way out on the prairie." They were, of course, mistaken.

The name Prairie House was changed to Terre Haute House in 1853. Later the structure was improved and rebuilt with three prominent turrets and a fire escape. By 1900 the five-story hotel advertised accommodations for 550 people and was the site of almost every public event. The present Terre Haute House opened in 1928.

The eight-story, fireproof Hotel Deming was constructed by Demas Deming in 1913 at the corner of Sixth and Cherry streets. A 1915 advertisement read "250 rooms, 250 baths, every room an outside room." The hotel became Deming Center, a residence for older citizens, in 1979.

Looking west on Wabash Avenue from Eighth Street in 1904, one can see Bement, Rea & Company (wholesale grocers), George Ehrenhardt Barber Supplies Company, George C. Rossell (bicycles), Logical Dress, and Lease Brothers Billiards and Bowling Parlor. It also rained on May 30 causing the Memorial Day parade to be cancelled and Colonel W. E. McLean's speech to be given in the courthouse rather than at Woodlawn Cemetery.

Two Rainy Days in Downtown Terre Haute, 1904 and 1936

The same view 32 years later shows Wabash Avenue decorated in red, white and blue for "Elks Week" in 1936. The Gillis Drug Store, shown here across from the Terre Haute House, was one of six Gillis stores in the downtown area. Gillis Drugs' seasonal specials included "Flying Scot" golf balls with liquid centers at 39 cents each. The public was invited "to come in and let us show you how these balls are constructed."

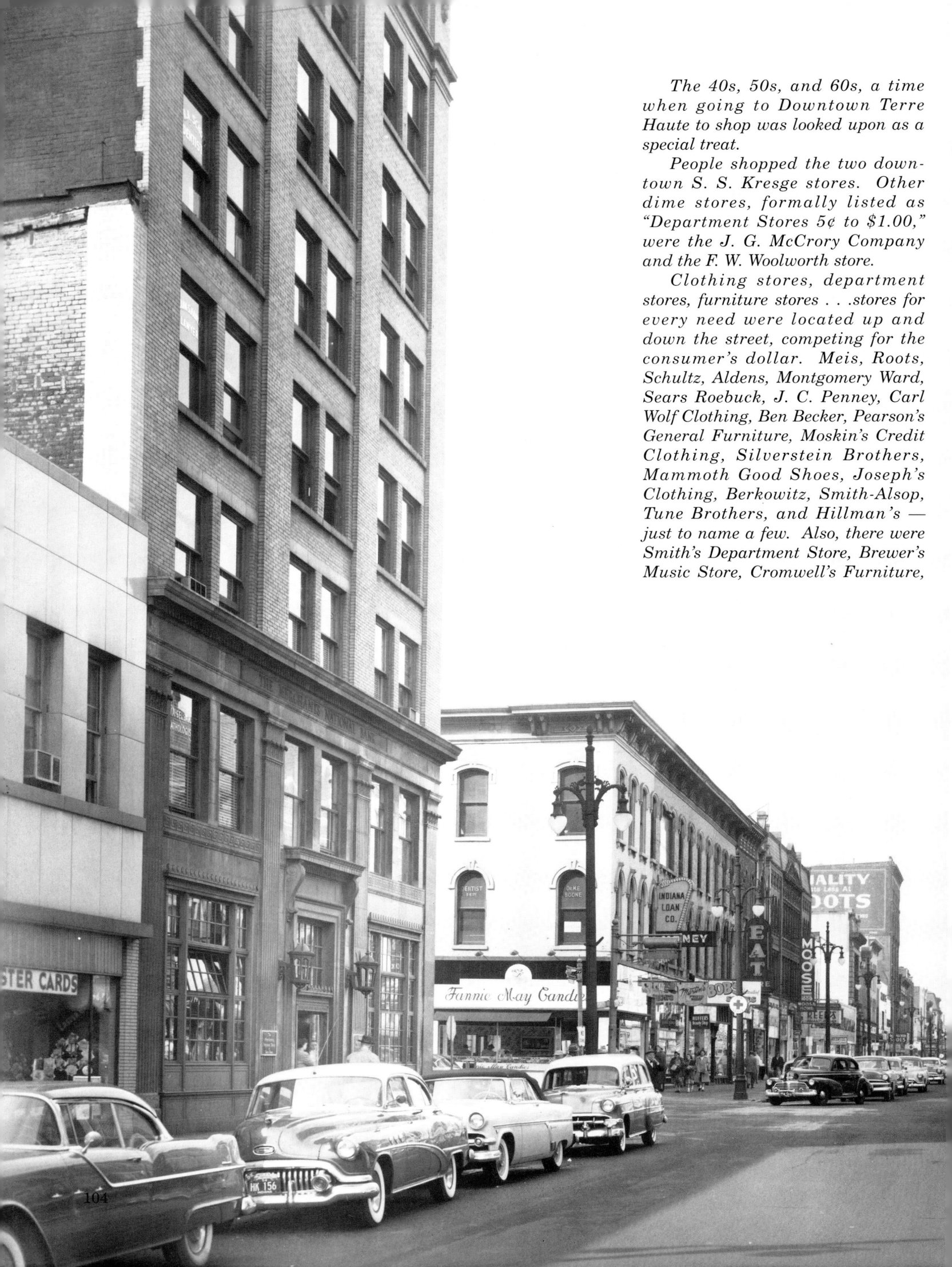

The 40s, 50s, and 60s, a time when going to Downtown Terre Haute to shop was looked upon as a special treat.

People shopped the two downtown S. S. Kresge stores. Other dime stores, formally listed as "Department Stores 5¢ to $1.00," were the J. G. McCrory Company and the F. W. Woolworth store.

Clothing stores, department stores, furniture stores . . .stores for every need were located up and down the street, competing for the consumer's dollar. Meis, Roots, Schultz, Aldens, Montgomery Ward, Sears Roebuck, J. C. Penney, Carl Wolf Clothing, Ben Becker, Pearson's General Furniture, Moskin's Credit Clothing, Silverstein Brothers, Mammoth Good Shoes, Joseph's Clothing, Berkowitz, Smith-Alsop, Tune Brothers, and Hillman's — just to name a few. Also, there were Smith's Department Store, Brewer's Music Store, Cromwell's Furniture,

King's Mens Shop, The Holly Shop, Anchor Stove & Furniture, Bigwood's Jewelry, E. J. Rogers & Company, Levinson's, Stewart & Foulke, Brinkman's Apparel, The Shoe Box, KayBee, Two Legs, Morris Pawn Shop, — the list could go on and on.

. . . During the late 60s and early 70s, the entire nation saw a swing from downtown shopping districts to strip shopping centers and enclosed, climate-controlled malls. It became clear that in order to survive, the downtowns in many cities must change. The same held true for Terre Haute.

. . . Shops, restaurants and offices have taken the place of abandoned stores.

—Terry Tevlin
Terre Haute Tribune-Star,
December 21, 1984
Martin Photo, 1955

Dime Stores

... as the five-and-ten became the heartbeat of downtowns from coast to coast, all of the chains enjoyed steady expansion. ... not only did the five-and-ten chains adopt common signage, they located together — often side by side on the same street — so that if customers didn't find what they wanted in one store, they could easily walk to another.
—Bernice L. Thomas, in *Historic Preservation,* Jan/Feb, 1993

This S. S. Kresge Company store was located at 635-637 Wabash Avenue in 1915. The F. W. Woolworth dime store was close by at 613 Wabash Avenue. In 1925 a second Kresge store (25¢ to $1.00) opened at 607-609 Wabash Avenue, and by 1949 J. G. McCrory Company as well as the Woolworth and two Kresge stores were all located in the 600 block of Wabash Avenue.

635-637 Wabash Avenue: It was January sale time in the late 1940s; Kresge store manager Donald R. Foster and food manager Helen E. Moore posed with other store employees for this photograph. The occasion was the opening of the newly remodeled soda fountain and lunch counter, one of the downtown's popular meeting and eating places. *Helen E. Moore collection*

Shopping Centers

The site of the Edward Hein Dairy on the northeast corner of Twenty-Fifth and Poplar streets became a part of The Meadows complex. *William and Jean Farr collection*

The official dedication of Meadows Center, the first shopping center in Terre Haute, in 1956 attracted 5,000 persons. The mall was enclosed in 1982-83 as part of a renovation project and was renamed The Meadows. *Tribune-Star Publishing Company photo*

Race horses had been trained and bred on Warren Park farm. The property was purchased from F. Burch Ijams and his sister, Mrs. Richard Benbridge, in 1965 for the development of Honey Creek Square.

These shoppers were part of the holiday crowds at Honey Creek Mall in November, 1990. Honey Creek Square had been enlarged and renovated and was now Honey Creek Mall. *TribuneStar Publishing Company photo*

Colonel Richard Thompson posed with his grandchildren, the children of David and Virginia Thompson Henry, in front of his home at 1214 South Sixth Street.

Colonel Richard W. Thompson (1809-1900), a Virginian by birth, settled in Indiana as a young man. His distinguished career included the practice of law, election to the Indiana Legislature and United States Congress, service recruiting and training soldiers during the Civil War, and appointment as Secretary of Navy under President Rutherford B. Hayes. His last position before returning to Terre Haute was that of chairman of the American Department of the Panama Canal Company.

A memorial bust of Colonel Thompson, dedicated in 1902, stands on the Vigo County Courthouse lawn.

A tea party was another wonderful way to bridge the gap between generations in Terre Haute. The date of this photograph and the identity of these individuals is unknown.

CHAPTER 7
The People and Their Neighborhoods

J. J. Smith, a German immigrant, relaxed with his daughter, Augusta, at his home at 2701 North Seventh Street. The family continued his produce and florist business as J. J. Smith's and Sons and later as J. J. Smith Gardens following his death in 1906. *Michael Dowell collection*

> "*The people are the city.*"
>
> William Shakespeare

Population:	Terre Haute	Total Vigo County
1840	2,300	12,076
1890	30,217	50,195
1940	62,693	99,709
1990	57,483	106,107

The people of Terre Haute are not bound together by one culture; they are held together by living in the same city. Loren Hassam wrote in 1873: *"We are pleased to say that the gentlemen of southern birth, New England's hardy sons, those of Celtic and Teutonic birth, 'Abraham's children,' and those of Africa's sunny clime are all harmoniously blended and are patriotic citizens of Terre Haute. . . . a unity of purpose and general kindness and respect, is shown to each other . . .*

True there are some, who through perverted minds, or selfish motives, consider themselves individually too high above the masses to be agreeable . . . We look forward, hoping that maturer years may teach them the ways of wisdom.

Unfortunately his hope for "maturer years" did not always come about in Terre Haute or the nation. Separated from the rest of the population by language, religion or skin color, newcomers to the city established their own neighborhoods and benevolent and social societies, such as the German Maennerchor and the Friendly Sons of St. Patrick.

After World War I, the Ku Klux Klan, an organization with anti-alien, anti-Catholic and anti-African-American goals, became active in the city as it did in other parts of the Hoosier state. The *Terre Haute Tribune* (October 29, 1922) reported: *Belated citizens on Wabash Avenue at midnight Saturday night witnessed a parade of the Ku Klux Klan, consisting of approximately 50 automobiles laden with white hooded members of the organization and the machines illuminated with red torches. The cars leading the procession bore aloft the flaming cross . . . From indefinite sources it was learned that a big initiation ceremony with several hundred candidates was scheduled. . .*

Thus diversity was not always welcomed in the city, but it was accommodated by most of the residents. A positive force was the organization of many service clubs and women's groups "to do good" in the community.

A change in immigration laws in 1965 brought people from non-western countries, many of whom were in education and health care professions and came from India and the Philippines. The local India Association was organized in 1970.

Terre Haute's Vietnamese Resettlement Project was active from 1975 until 1979. The number of exchange activities with Terre Haute's sister city, Tajimi, Japan, were increased and the city sponsored its first annual Fairbanks Park Ethnic Festival in 1987 to promote understanding among the peoples of Terre Haute.

"The people are the city," whoever they are, will continue to hold true.

THE IRISH

Constructing the Wabash and Erie Canal and early railroads brought Irish laborers to the Terre Haute area during the 1840s and 1850s. A. R. Markle, local historian, described the Irish as honest, hard working and living in poverty, *but, because it was a vast improvement over what they had known overseas, they lived happily, improved their conditions, (and) grew to become some of our best citizens.*

The Hibernian Society's first annual ball attracted a crowd of 200 to Ludowici's Hall in 1856. The Ancient Order of Hibernians was organized in 1875 with P. B. O'Reilly as the first president.

The St. Patrick Catholic Church, pictured here, was built on the southeast corner of South Thirteenth and Poplar Streets in 1880. The congregation keeps the Irish tradition alive on St. Patrick's Day at their present church, dedicated in 1956, on the corner of South Nineteenth and Poplar streets. *Vigo County Public Library collection*

THE GERMANS

German immigrants, first arriving in large numbers during the 1840s, became the largest ethnic influence in the development of Terre Haute. Of the 4,799 foreign born persons accounted for in the 1880 United States census of Vigo County, 2,282 were from Germany.

Early German Protestant church congregations included the German Methodist Church (1850) and the German Evangelical Lutheran congregation (1858) which later became the Immanuel Lutheran Church. Concerned about the language barrier, the German parishioners of St. Joseph Catholic Church built St. Benedict Church in 1854.

Several newspapers were once published in the German language in Terre Haute and many German societies existed. The Germania Hall at 18 - 20 South Ninth Street was one of the largest and finest in the state.

This 1987 photograph shows members of the German Oberlandler Club, 1616 Lafayette Avenue, pointing to their home towns on a map of Germany. *Jeffrey Schrink collection*

THE JEWISH PEOPLE

The early history of Terre Haute's Jewish citizens dates back to migratory settlers in 1823. The Temple Israel was formed in 1882 and a second congregation, Temple B'nai Abraham, in 1889. The men organized the Phoenix Club; the women became a part of the National Council of Jewish Women and undertook what became a long record of service to the community.

The congregation of Temple Israel built its second temple at 540 South Sixth Street in 1911; the Temple B'nai Abraham members laid the cornerstone for their second temple in 1925 at South Fifth and Poplar Streets, now the home of the Wabash Senior Citizens Center.

The congregations consolidated in 1935 and the Temple Israel, shown here in 1915, is the location of United Hebrew Congregation.

THE SYRIANS

Kaleel Hanna, a peddler and dry goods merchant originally from the village of Ein-el Shara, was the first Syrian immigrant to settle in Terre Haute. Following his arrival in 1902, other Syrian families from his village came to the city.

At first the men were peddlers traveling through the countryside; later they opened small businesses. By 1942 there were 64 neighborhood groceries operated by Syrian families. Most members of later generations have pursued professional careers or entered into other kinds of business.

The St. George Orthodox Church was established in 1927 on North Fifth Street. The present church at 1900 South Fourth Street, pictured here, dates from 1957.
St. George Orthodox Church collection

THE AFRICAN-AMERICANS

John W. Lyda, Terre Haute educator and author of *The Negro in the History of Indiana (1953),* wrote: *There were eleven Negroes living in Terre Haute in 1820. This number had increased to 227 by 1850 . . by the rearing of large families, the immigration of emancipated slaves to the city from North Carolina and Virginia, and the movement of Negroes living in the neighboring rural communities to the city to work at such tasks as were open to them. . . .*

. . . On reaching Terre Haute most of the men readily found employment in the blast furnaces, car shops, and rolling mills; and the women desiring to work obtained it as cooks, maids and day workers in the homes of well-to-do white families of the city.

Most early congregations were located south of Wabash Avenue and included Allen Chapel A.M.E. Church (1837), Second Baptist Church (1871), Saulters M.E. Church (1879), Free Baptist Church (1880) and St. Paul Mission Church (1918). The Rising Sun Mission (1892) was located north of Wabash Avenue and later became the Spruce Street A.M.E. Church.

The Darnes Lodge No. 4, F. & A. M. was chartered in 1856 and the Bethlehem Court Order of the Eastern Star in the 1880s. Among the groups organized during the present century were the local chapter of the National Association for the Advancement of Colored People (1919), the Young Men's Civic Club (1933) and the Charles T. Hyte Community Center (1941).

Allen Chapel at South Third and Crawford streets, shown here in 1990, is the oldest African-American church in western Indiana.
Tribune-Star Publishing Company photo

This Lincoln School float was part of a parade celebrating the anniversary of the signing of the Emancipation Proclamation freeing African-Americans from slavery. The date of this photograph is unknown, but records reveal the presence of Frederick Douglass, famous leader of the anti-slavery movement, at the Emancipation Day celebration in Terre Haute on September 22, 1888.

SOUTHERN AND EASTERN EUROPEANS

After 1890, immigrants from southern and eastern European countries came to Terre Haute to work in the mines, foundries and manufacturing plants. Among the countries of birth for those living in Vigo County in 1920 were Russia, France, Austria, Italy, Hungary, Poland and Lithuania.

Many of these people lived in ethnic neighborhoods on "the avenues" north to Maple Avenue and east from North Thirteenth to Twenty-fifth streets. They attended Sacred Heart Catholic Church (1923), St. Ann Catholic Church (1876) and St. Andrew Roumanian Orthodox Church (1918).

Ethnic social groups, which include the Hungarian Lodge and the Francis Vigo American-Italian Club, remain active in the city.

These dancers participated in the 1926 Harvest Festival at Hungarian Hall at North Twenty-second and Linden streets.

NEW CITIZENS

Seven new United States citizens originally from England, Germany, Hungary, Italy and Turkey were welcomed by Judge H. DeWitt Owen and Attorney John Fitzgerald in 1949 at a ceremony in the Vigo County Courthouse. *Helen Harbaugh collection*

The Kerman Grotto received its charter in 1921. By 1925 the organization had a band of 50 pieces under the direction of H. H. Stanton and R. C. Vinsel. The date of this photograph is unknown.

Fraternal Societies

Fraternal societies offer members a "sense of belonging" to a group of individuals much like themselves and the assurance that the membership will remain that way. The Masons were among the early settlers of the new city and held their first formal meeting in 1819. In 1858 four groups of Masons, three Temples of Honor, three groups of Odd Fellows and the Daughters of Rebekah were meeting in the city. By 1910, the listing of secret organizations in the city directory numbered 109 and now included groups such as the Eagles, Improved Order of Red Men, Knights of Columbus, Independent Order of Foresters, Benevolent and Protective Order of Elks, the Tribe of Ben Hur and the Knights of Pythias.

The Masonic Temple at 224 North Eighth Street, shown here, was constructed in 1917 through the combined efforts of seven lodges. The Zorah Shrine Temple at 420 North Seventh Street was dedicated in 1927. *Martin photo*

A group of business and professional men organized the first Optimist Club in Terre Haute in 1934. Each December downtown shoppers and workers were asked to place their dimes on the line to help fund the Optimist "Clothe-a-child" program. This photograph is dated December, 1944.
Martin photo

Service Clubs

Terre Haute service clubs always have had the community's welfare at heart. Members give their time, talents and money for a variety of projects fulfilling local needs. Among a large number of service organizations, who have been active in the city are the Altrusa, Civitan, Exchange, Kiwanis, Lions, Optimist, Rotary and Sertoma clubs.

Sponsorship of the Flora Gulick Boys Club was the first project of the Terre Haute Lions Club at its beginning in 1922. Members are shown here in June, 1963, taking time off from a work session at Deming Park where they were repairing the Lions shelter. The materials were purchased with the proceeds of their "Rose Day" fund-raiser.
Terre Haute Lions Club collection

Just before and after the turn of the century, many middle and upper class women organized clubs for "culture" and socialization. The programs offered a way to enlarge the members' understanding of the world.

Cora Talley played Mr. Pickwick, Charles Dickens' adventurous character, at this meeting of the Tuesday Literary Club meeting at the home of Mary B. Greiner on North Center Street. Organized in 1899, the club was one of a number of groups which formed the Council of Women's Clubs in 1910, the predecessor to the Woman's Department Club. *Jane Hazledine collection*

Women's Clubs

Moving from one city to another became commonplace in the 1940s. Many families of United States Armed Forces personnel and workers engaged in war production moved into Terre Haute.

The Newcomers Club of Terre Haute was formed to help the women become acquainted with each other and with the city. The first meeting was held at the home of Louise Sutton on February 19, 1940. Alberta Buerkle was elected the first president, Adelaide Hahn the first vice-president. Members and their families are shown here at a picnic in Deming Park.

The Kent Avenue Women's Club

A group of neighbors organized the Kent Avenue Women's Club in 1911. They lived on the three blocks of Kent Avenue between Wabash Avenue and Liberty Street on the city's east side. The first officers were Mrs. F. E. Scott, Mrs. Ed Sparks and Mrs. Anna R. Black.

Their meetings on the third Wednesday of each month during the school year were times of friendship and service for the neighborhood and the city.

The club celebrated its 50th anniversary in 1961. Mrs. James Walsh wrote, "This club is unique in that it was the only neighborhood club surviving 50 years."

These charter members included this quotation in their first yearbook: *If you educate a man, you educate an individual. If you educate a woman, you educate a family.*

The Kent Avenue parade, consisting of costumed Sandison School children and their floats, was an annual neighborhood event. The date of this photograph is unknown.

This comfortable home was built by William White in 1912 at 500 Osborne Street. His daughter, Stella Reiman, is shown ironing in the kitchen in the 1930s.

Farrington's Grove

The children may have been celebrating the Fourth of July in the 1400 block of South Center Street. *All photos Anne Temple Lambert collection.*

The Woman's Department Club since 1931, this home at 507 South Sixth Street was built in 1867-68 for Robert N. Hudson, Terre Haute newspaper publisher.
Vigo County Public Library collection

The first homes in the city were located near the river in what is now the downtown area. As the city expanded, the residents of the emerging middle and upper classes chose lots for building homes south of the central business district. The first homes, constructed as country homes, became city residences as the city grew to encompass them. This is the area which has been designated as Farrington's Grove Historical District. The name was that of James Farrington's farm, which in the 1840s made up a large portion of the district.

The south end became known as Strawberry Hill, near the mansion of Judge Samuel Barnes Gookins. Like Farrington's Grove, "it was a place for celebrations, orations, and, in 1844, the first of the city's two legal hangings."

Farrington's Grove Historical District is located in an area bounded roughly by Poplar (N) and Hulman (S) streets and South Fourth (W) and Seventh (E) streets.

The Washington Avenue Presbyterian Church, 1400 South Sixth Street, was dedicated in 1894. It is one of seven Christian, Jewish and Islamic houses of worship in Farrington's Grove.
Washington Avenue Presbyterian Church collection

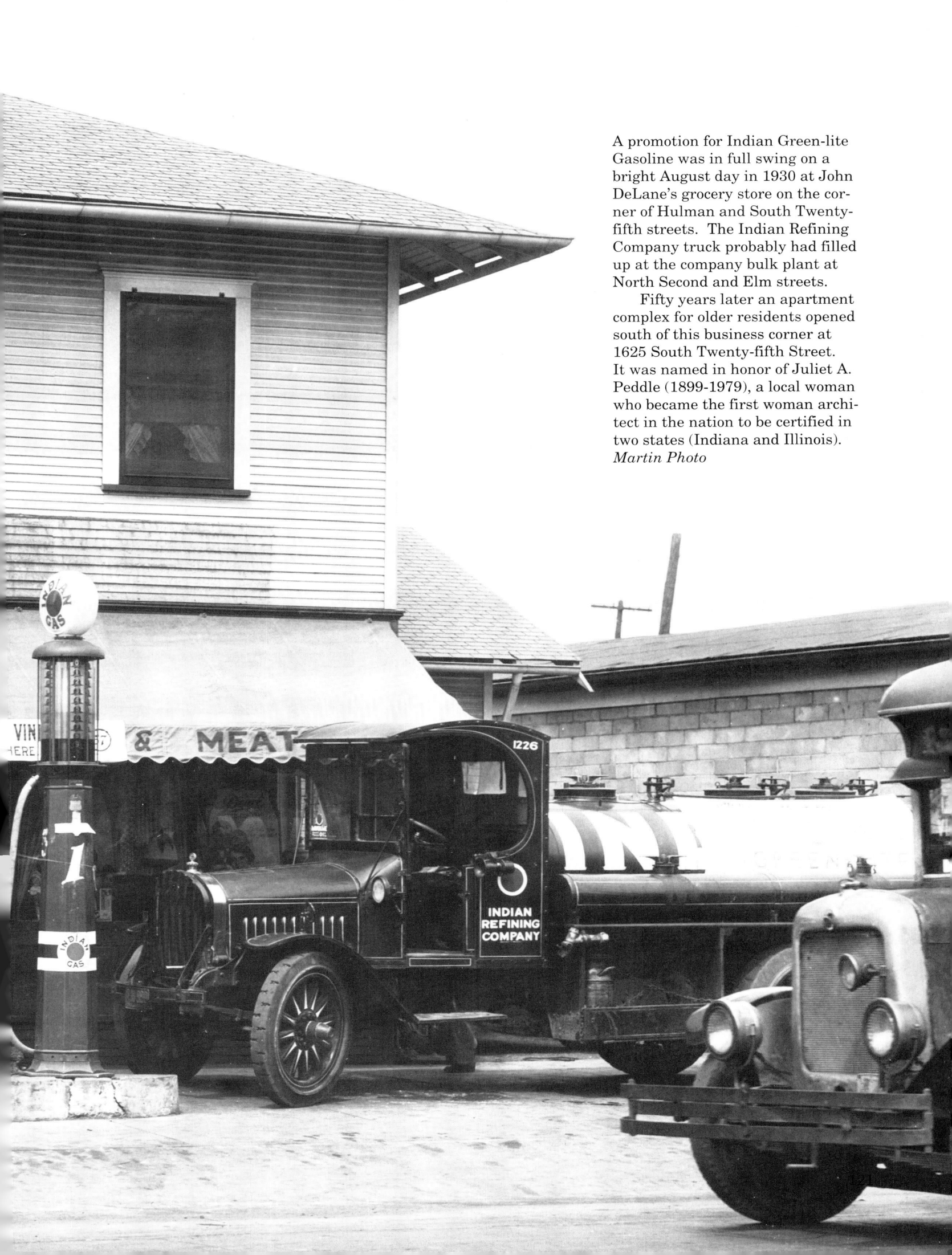

A promotion for Indian Green-lite Gasoline was in full swing on a bright August day in 1930 at John DeLane's grocery store on the corner of Hulman and South Twenty-fifth streets. The Indian Refining Company truck probably had filled up at the company bulk plant at North Second and Elm streets.

Fifty years later an apartment complex for older residents opened south of this business corner at 1625 South Twenty-fifth Street. It was named in honor of Juliet A. Peddle (1899-1979), a local woman who became the first woman architect in the nation to be certified in two states (Indiana and Illinois).
Martin Photo

Several generations of children from the Collett Park area, the second oldest neighborhood of elegant houses in the city, attended Collett School at the corner of North Tenth and Linden streets. Opened in 1896, the school operated until 1979, when Ouabache School replaced both Collett and Rea schools.

A "neighborhood" school, Collett students went home for lunch each day.

Twelve Points

The congregation of the Maple Avenue Methodist Episcopal Church moved into this building at the corner of North Twelfth Street and Maple Avenue in 1902. The rear building continues in use for educational and recreational purposes; however, a new main building in 1968 became the Maple Avenue United Methodist Church.

The Twelve Points State Bank opened in 1919 at 1267 Lafayette Avenue with most of its stock owned by northside residents. The bank moved to its present location on the northwest corner of Lafayette and Maple avenues in 1923 and became a branch of Merchants National Bank in 1934.
Vigo County Public Library collection

This filling station at the northwest corner of Lafayette Avenue and Linden Street, operated by Buford Foster in 1944, was built in 1936 and remained a service station for thirty-five years. Since 1978 Hoods Watch Shop has occupied this location. *Vigo County Public Library collection*

The Swan Theater, shown below in 1950, opened about 1915 at 1220 Lafayette Avenue. The Garfield Theater opened across the street at 1257 Lafayette Avenue in 1939. After three decades as a movie theater, the Garfield building became Harmony Hall in 1988, home of the Banks of the Wabash Chorus, a popular men's vocal group. *Martin photo*

... It is a business district which has all the charm of village life. The merchants there have grown up together and know their patrons intimately — can call them by their first names.
Terre Haute Tribune-Star, October 25, 1925

At the turn of the century Walter Phillips developed the suburban, commercial area of Twelve Points at the triangular intersection of North Thirteenth Street and Maple and Lafayette avenues. The four corners at each point of the triangle are the "twelve points."

With the Collett Park neighborhood and Garfield High School to the west and hundreds of factory workers living in the area, the community grew and prospered. By the 1930s a bank, funeral homes, churches, drugstores, grocery stores, a hotel, barber shops, a hardware store, saloons, a dime store, dry cleaners, and post office were located there.

Garfield Towers and Garfield Gardens senior housing opened at the site of Garfield High School after it was razed in the 1970s.

Sam Teal opened Sam's Popcorn Stand south of the Swan Theater in the early 1930s. The business was sold to Ralph Chappelle, pictured here behind the counter, about 1939. The stand moved into the Health Bowl bowling alley and later to 1268 Lafayette Avenue. It closed in 1961. *Martin photo*

An immigrant from Germany, John C. Vendel first worked at Hulman & Company before opening his grocery store in 1893. Vendel and his daughter posed in front of his store at the southwest corner of Eighth Street and College Avenue about 1906. There were 195 other grocery stores in business in the city at the time.

The Vendel Grocery was purchased by Paul Kelley in the 1950s. The building now houses Alex TV & Appliance Sales & Service. *Barbara Carney collection*

Neighborhood Grocery Stores

Almost every neighborhood had its grocery store; it was the neighborhood meeting place. The roll of wrapping paper, the scales, the "put it on the bill" book, and the horse-drawn delivery wagons were part of the ambiance.

Through the years neighborhood grocery stores gave way to chain stores to supermarkets; no longer did the grocer know the customer by name.

The year is 1934; Hollianna Baking Powder is 10 cents a can and do-nuts or doughnuts are 12 cents a dozen at this Oakley store at North Seventh Street and Lafayette Avenue, one of 22 Oakley stores in the city. H. N. Oakley, president of the locally-owned chain of Oakley Economy Stores had opened his first store in 1909 at 1105 Wabash Avenue. *Martin photo*

This photograph of W. R. McKeen's Edgewood Stock Farm appeared in the January 23, 1892 issue of *Industrial America*.

Edgewood Grove

Edgewood Grove, known as "The Grove," was Terre Haute's first twentieth-century subdivision. Samuel Gray and S. C. McKeen of the Edgewood Grove Realty Company subdivided the ninety acres and began selling the lots in 1911.

In 1925, the Terre Haute Trust Company listed a six-room, two-story, frame bungalow with a large brick and concrete porch and full basement on Madison Boulevard for $8,000.

Three years before, the Edgewood Grove Planning Club laid the cornerstone for the Edgewood Grove log cabin clubhouse. George Schaal was president and J. T. Simms, vice-president.

These two homes on Potomac Avenue, constructed in the 1920s, are examples of the many early twentieth century residential architectural styles in Edgewood Grove. Located just south of Wabash Avenue, early residents enjoyed the advantage of living close to both the street car line and the old Vigo County Fairgrounds.
Photo above Peter and P.J. Ekstrom collection

Southwest Area Urban Renewal Project

The Terre Haute City Council approved plans for an urban renewal project in the South Third Street area in 1960. Neighborhoods of homes, many beyond repair, and vacant lots were successfully transformed into an attractive residential and business area.

This residential neighborhood, once filled with small frame homes, like the one on South First Street pictured here, changed in the 1960s. Indiana State University constructed four family housing complexes and the Terre Haute Housing Authority built Dreiser Square units for older citizens in the area where the original houses once stood. *Vigo County Public Library collection.*

Reuben H. Donnelley erected a new office building at 600 South First Street in 1970. Other facilities built in the area after urban renewal included Commercial Solvents Corporation (now Pitman-Moore), Vigo County Farm Bureau, Inc., Moore-Langen Printing Company, and Montgomery Ward.

Montgomery Ward completed construction of its store at 333 South Third Street in 1968. The store closed in 1981 and the building became the site of Tri-Industries, Inc. *Reuben H. Donnelley collection*

The former Sheraton Inn at 555 South Third Street became Larry Bird's Boston Connection in 1987. Guests enjoy displays of awards and memorabilia from Bird's years with the Indiana State University Sycamores and the Boston Celtics basketball teams. *Larry Bird's Boston Connection collection*

CHAPTER 8
Caring for Each Other

The Rose Dispensary Building, funded with a bequest from Chauncey Rose for "an institution by which medicines shall be dispensed and advice given gratis to the poor" opened in the 1890s. Razed in 1972, the corner is now the site of Oakley Plaza, a part of Indiana State University. *Dorisann Albright collection*

> *"To pity distress is but human; to relieve it is Godlike."*
>
> Horace Mann

Caring for each other in the early days was a matter for the family and neighbors. As the population grew, community organizations, such as churches and the health professions, increasingly took responsibility for relieving distress.

By the 1970s the city had become a regional medical center with modern hospital complexes and the Terre Haute Center for Medical Education at Indiana State University.

This development began in the 1840s when the Vigo County Medical Society began to meet. Charles N. Combs, M.D. commented: *It stands to the credit of Vigo County that before the National or State Societies existed, those pioneer physicians in Terre Haute were alive to the value of medical organization and cooperative study. There were probably not over a dozen physicians in the town at that time . . .*

Physicians, community agencies and civic organizations brought about improvements in sanitary conditions and public health. The Civic League led the way for the inspection of places where food was sold beginning in 1912. At about the same time, the Terre Haute Social Hygiene Campaign brought about the adoption of a social hygiene education program and by 1919 a venereal disease clinic.

Orphanages were built in the last part of the nineteenth century to house and care for dependent children. By 1980, they had been replaced by group homes.

Care for older residents, originally the concern of charitable organizations, has been taken over by the private sector with state and federal funding.

Numerous private nursing homes and convalescent centers have been constructed in the city, including Meadows Manor which opened its doors on East Poplar Street in 1964.

Much progress has been made for the care of individuals with special needs. Two outstanding examples are the mental health work of Katherine Hamilton and the accomplishment of parents who established the United Cerebral Palsy Association (1951) and later the Beacon School for their children.

Early charitable groups included the Ladies Aid Society and later the Society for Organizing Charity. The S.O.C. was founded in 1882 at a meeting called by Dr. C. R. Henderson, pastor of the First Baptist Church, who declared, "It is better to give to ten frauds than to allow one worthy person to suffer." Organized in 1896, the Terre Haute Social Settlement served people living in the river district. The Volunteers of America came to the city in 1899. Its tabernacle at 218 North Fourth Street was one of eight missions still listed in 1963, most of which were in the downtown area. Outlying neighborhoods were served by community centers such as the Torner House and the Charles T. Hyte Center.

Perhaps the biggest change of the century was the United Way. In 1925, The *Saturday Spectator* complained how the community had fallen far short of the Welfare League drive goal putting Terre Haute "at the very bottom of the list of all cities in the United States and Canada in the support of its charitable institutions." By 1992, however, Sally Ingram Whitehurst, campaign chairperson, was proud to report $2,135,000.00 had been contributed to the United Way of the Wabash Valley, which by that time supported 33 member agencies.

St. Anthony Hospital - Terre Haute Regional Hospital

Herman Hulman, Sr. purchased the vacant St. Agnes Academy at South Sixth and Farrington streets in 1883 and presented it to the Poor Sisters of St. Francis in memory of his wife, Antonia. The academy building became St. Anthony Hospital, replacing a smaller building on the corner of North Second and Mulberry streets in which the Sisters had been caring for the sick. St. Anthony Hospital opened in 1884 and served the Terre Haute area until 1979, the last four years as Terre Haute Regional Hospital.

Antonia Hulman
1836-1883

St. Anthony Hospital established a training school for nurses in 1918. At right are the members of the first graduating class in 1921.

Bottom: After acquiring St. Anthony Hospital in 1975, the Hospital Corporation of America broke ground in 1977 for a new building at 3901 South Seventh Street. Terre Haute Regional Hospital was dedicated by Mary Fendrich Hulman on September 16, 1979. The John K. Lamb Center for treatment of alcohol and drug dependency opened in 1985, and a year later the area's first comprehensive cancer treatment center was dedicated and open heart surgery services became available. The Thelma B. Jobe Stress Center opened in 1988. The hospital is now an affiliate of Health Trust, Inc.
Terre Haute Regional Hospital collection

This is the original building. Demolished in 1982, St. Anthony Hospital had been renovated and expanded many times during 95 years of use.

Union Hospital

Dr. Benjamin Swafford and Dr. Leo Weinstein, with the help of Terre Haute's citizens, opened the Terre Haute Sanitarium in a two-story frame house at North Seventh Street and Eighth Avenue in 1892. The name was changed to Union Home for Invalids in 1895 and two years later became Union Hospital.

The brick North Wing had been completed in 1902; the hospital as it appeared in 1906 is shown above. The original sanitarium building was torn down and a new building erected in 1909. Later construction included the South Wing (1922) and the North Wing on the site of the original brick building (1953).
Union Hospital collection

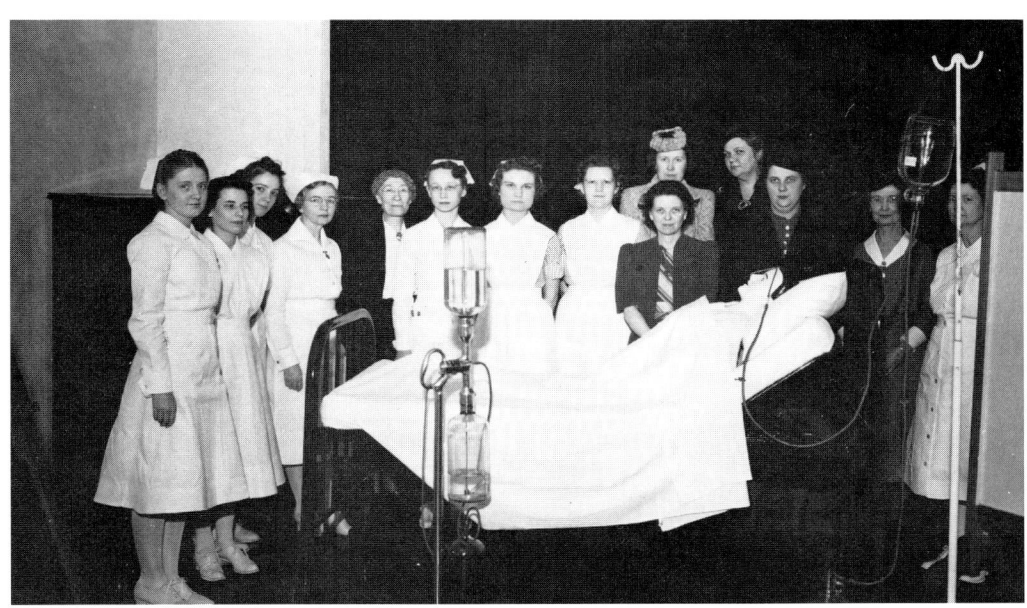

Student nurses attended a demonstration of a new procedure in the auditorium of the nurses' quarters in 1939. Organized by Sister Johanna M. Baur in 1900, the Training School for Nurses continued in operation until 1965. The Indiana State University School of Nursing Clinical Education Building was opened just north of the hospital in 1969.

The modern complex of Union Hospital is shown here in 1992. The Hook Rehabilitation Center and the Hux Cardiovascular Center opened in 1988 and the Hux Cancer Center a year later. A Center for Occupational Health and HealthCheck of Union Hospital at 4001 Wabash Avenue were 1992 additions to the facilities.
Union Hospital collection

The Friendly Inn

Built in 1921 through the generosity of Charles and Helen Minshall in memory of their father, Deloss Wesley Minshall, The Friendly Inn replaced an old station house which the Society for Organizing Charity had used as a transient shelter since 1883.

The Society became the Family Welfare Society in 1934 and the Family Service Association in 1956. At various times the Friendly Inn was also the site of the Central Index clearing house, the Fresh Air Camp, the Vigo County Tuberculosis Society and the Vigo County Association for Mental Health. The building became Olis G. Jamison Hall, a part of Indiana State University, in 1972.
Vigo County Public Library collection

Hamilton Center

Katherine Hamilton (1902-1961) devoted 33 years of her life to the mentally ill. She was one of the persons who organized the Vigo County Mental Hygiene Association in 1950; it was renamed the Vigo County Association for Mental Health in 1955. Active at the local, state and national levels, Hamilton's accomplishments included the elimination of patient jailing, provision for transportation to state hospitals, development of the Adopt-a-Patient program and the establishment of the Vigo County Adult and Child Guidance Clinic.
Mental Health Association in Vigo County collection

A committee representing Vigo and six surrounding counties began planning for a comprehensive mental health center in 1964; construction started in 1970, just west of Union Hospital at 620 Eighth Avenue. Named in memory of Katherine Hamilton, the center was dedicated in December, 1971. The Community Support Services Center at 1420 Lafayette Avenue opened in 1986 and a new building to house Spectrum Industries and the Children's Learning Center in 1988. *Hamilton Center, Inc. collection*

Associated Physicians & Surgeons Clinic

After a visit to the Mayo clinic in Rochester, Minnesota, in 1911, Dr. J. H. Weinstein and Dr. C. N. Combs returned to the city with the idea of establishing a clinic in Terre Haute. In 1916 the organization was formed by Drs. J. H. Weinstein, J. R. Gillum, F. H. Jett, C. N. Combs and H. J. Pierce with Edith Reinking as secretary.

World War I interrupted plans because four of the doctors were called to military service. After their return, a corporation was formed in 1920 by the original five organizers plus Drs. W. G. Crawford and O. O. Alexander for *the purpose of owning and operating an institution for the practice of better medicine through cooperation of specialties and the supply of laboratory and other equipment not at that time available in Terre Haute.*

This First Baptist Church building served its congregation from 1916 until 1968 when the construction of a new church building was completed at 4701 East Poplar Street. This corner is now part of the A P & S Clinic complex. *Vigo County Public Library collection*

The physicians and surgeons purchased and remodeled the Riley McKeen home at 221 South Sixth Street and opened the clinic there in 1920. Additions to the building were made in 1924 and 1950. *A P & S Clinic, Inc. collection*

Growth of the clinic led to the decision to erect a new building in back of the original clinic building on South Sixth Street. After the new clinic building was opened in 1959, shown here one year later, the old structure was razed to make space for a parking lot. Since that time A P & S Northside (1990), A P & S Orthopaedic Surgery (1990) and the Wabash Valley Surgery Center and A P & S Eye Center (1993) have been built at other sites in the city. *A P & S Clinic, Inc. collection*

Visiting Nurse Association

Recognizing the need for public health nursing, Lillian Rose presented a resolution at a meeting of the Terre Haute Council of Women's Clubs in 1915. Following a study by the Council and a meeting at the Chamber of Commerce, the Public Health Nursing Association was organized in 1916. The office was first located in the 100 block of North Seventh Street, then the Heminway Home. It later moved to the Friendly Inn, then to the Tribune Building, and finally to property at 418 North Ninth Street. In 1939, Mr. and Mrs. Benjamin Blumberg presented the Association with their home at 328 South Fifth Street, pictured here.

The Association became the Visiting Nurse Association of Terre Haute, Indiana, Inc. in 1957, and in 1986 the offices were moved to 615 Eighth Avenue.

Dentistry

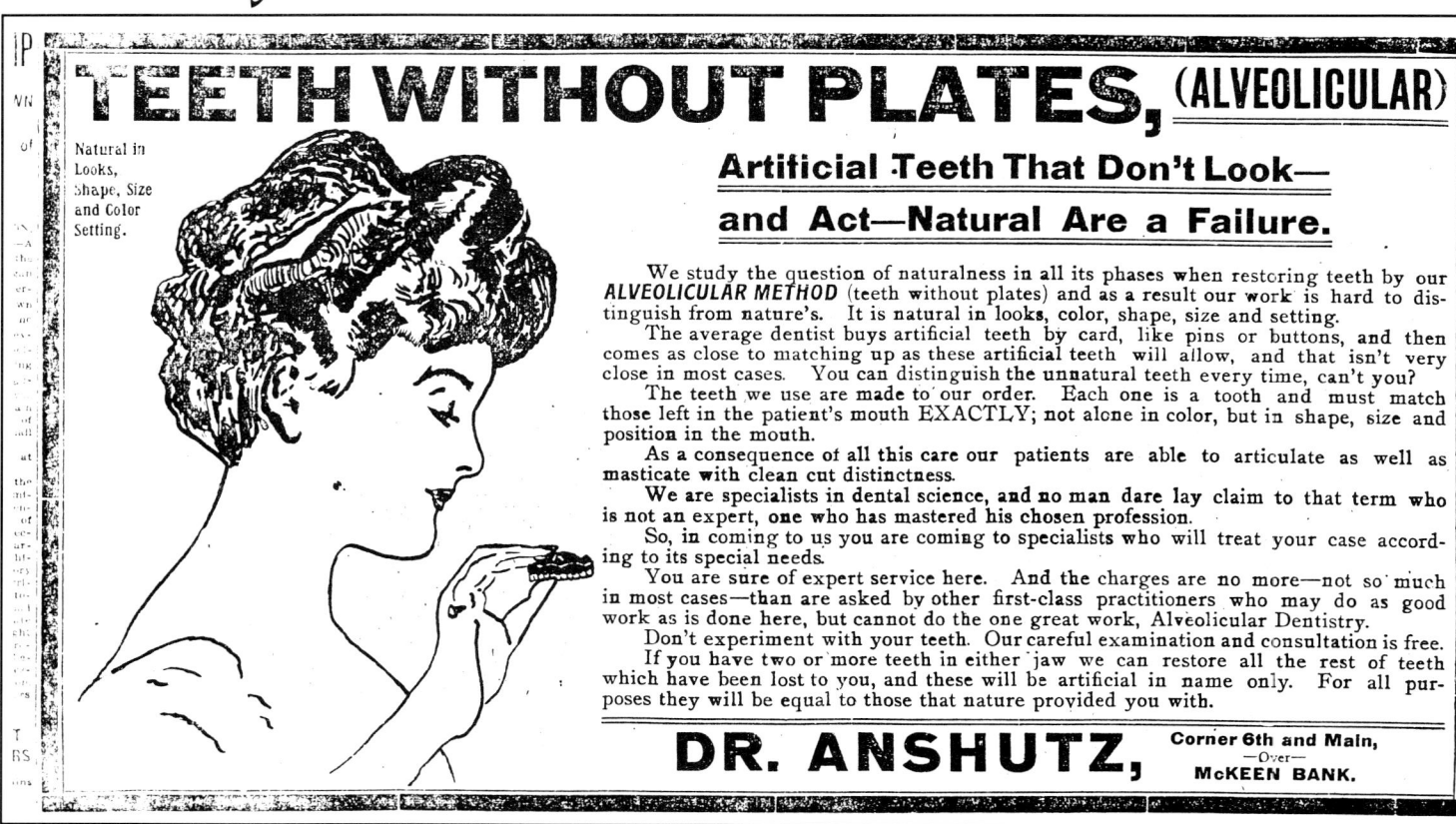

Frank P. Anshutz and his younger brother, Louis, maintained a dental office at Sixth Street and Wabash Avenue over McKeen's Bank in 1906. Their office was one of 26 dental offices listed in the 1906 directory.

Frank's son, Wade, followed in his father's profession. Now the grandsons and great grandsons of Frank P. Anshutz carry on the family tradition of dentistry in Terre Haute.

The Western Indiana Dental Society was organized 1917. Terre Haute dentist Dr. Glenn Irwin was honored in 1980 for his 61 years in the profession; he was the oldest practicing dentist in Indiana at that time.

Frank B. Anshutz collection

This 1927 advertisement promoted the sale of Bear's Jack Frost cold remedy. It was a product of Bear Manufactory Company. The plant was located on North Sixteenth Street in the city.

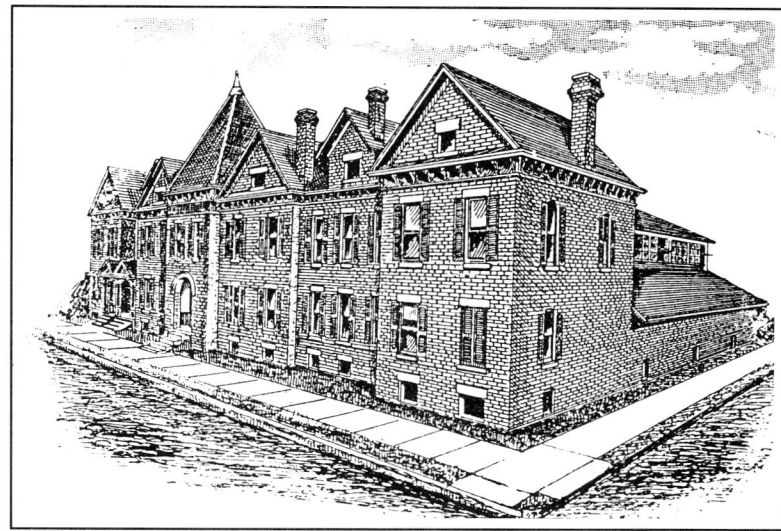

Industrial America (1892) described the Exchange Artesian Springs and Bath House located opposite Union Depot as "a fortune from misfortune" explaining: *In 1889, Terre Haute was sinking oil-wells. It chanced that one of these wells was bored on the property of Mr. David Bronson. It was sunk to the depth of 1,800 feet and struck an inexhaustible vein of magnetic artesian water chemically rich in health-giving qualities . . . this artesian water has been found a specific for rheumatism, paralysis, catarrh, dyspepsia, eczema and many forms of contagious diseases.*

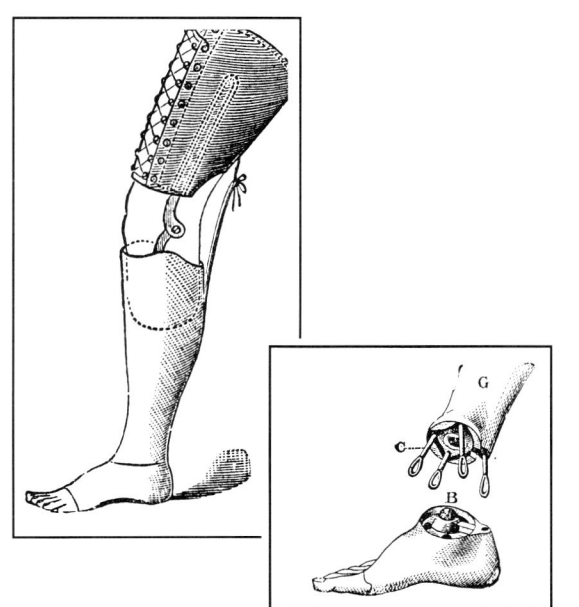

Lewis Lockwood, manufacturer of Bly artificial limbs and Lockwood patent rubber ankle legs, moved his business to Terre Haute from St. Louis in 1880. Employees who were injured on the Vandalia Railroad were provided with artificial limbs made by Lockwood.

His son, Lewis Lockwood, Jr., joined his father in the business in 1885 and continued the business at 651 1/2 Wabash Avenue.

This group posed in front of the Magnetic Mineral Springs bath house and natatorium at the foot of Walnut Street about 1900. *The Industrial Advantages of Terre Haute* (1890) reads: *The Magnetic Mineral Springs, which have acquired a national reputation for the permanent cure of many malignant diseases, were first discovered in 1871. The water is a highly saline and sulphur water, and is obtained from an artesian well at a depth of 2,000 feet from the surface . . . and reaches the air at a temperature of 85 degrees F. . . . the management has erected a modern bath house, having 46 tub bath rooms, four shower bath rooms, and eight steam rooms, all with hot and cold water, and 33 plunge bath rooms.*

Chauncey Rose

Chauncey Rose
1794-1877

Chauncey Rose came to Indiana from Connecticut in 1818. He invested in land, railroads and other businesses and accumulated a personal fortune. Yet it was his gifts to the community and not his business success which became his greatest legacy. The Rose Orphan Home, the Rose Polytechnic Institute (later Rose-Hulman Institute of Technology), the Rose Dispensary, and the Ladies' Aid Society, a group whose members assisted the poor and sick, were mentioned in the following excerpt from *The Industrial Advantages of Terre Haute,* published in 1890:

A perpetual memorial to the late Chauncey Rose is a group of four noble benefactions which will in some way benefit every tax payer and citizen of Terre Haute. Mr. Rose, the possessor of many millions, was governed by the belief that "what one saves is what he gives away"...

These children and their teacher were photographed in the nursery playroom of the Rose Orphan Home in the early 1900s. The home, later known as the Chauncey Rose School, was founded with an endowment by Rose in 1874. The buildings at 2500 Wabash Avenue were not constructed until 1883, six year's after Rose's death. It served children until about 1950 when it was reorganized into a home for the aging.

This photograph caught the "then" and "almost now" at Wabash Avenue and Twenty-fifth Street in 1965. The Chauncey Rose School in the background was awaiting demolition as construction workers were building a new Burger Chef restaurant for K-Mart Plaza. Opened just 81 years before, the school had been described as "the most complete and beautiful of its kind in the country." *Martin photo*

County Poor Farm

A home for the poor of the county was provided east of the city in 1853. Later a brick structure, shown here in 1934, was constructed on a site northeast of the city on Maple Avenue. It was known as the County Poor Farm.

The Vigo County Home, constructed on the same Maple Avenue site in 1936, was a project of the federal Public Works Administration (PWA). It was sold to Nationwide Management, Inc. of Indianapolis on December 31, 1992.

Fairbanks Home

Crawford Fairbanks, described as a capitalist and philanthropist, purchased the Scott homestead at North Seventh Street and Eighth Avenue and gave it to the Women's Order Retail Druggists in 1920 for their work on behalf of aged women.

The Clara Fairbanks Home for Aged Women, pictured here, was erected by Fairbanks in 1924 on the same grounds to meet the need for a larger facility. The home closed in 1986; a parking lot is now located on the site. *Judith Calvert collection*

Crittenton Home

The first Crittenton Home, "a place for supervisory care for unmarried girls prior to delivery and during later convalescence," was opened in 1883 in New York City by Charles N. Crittenton. The Terre Haute home at 1923 Poplar Street, pictured here, served young women from 1907 until 1972. *Vigo County Public Library collection*

Above: The Rev. Theodore Grob shared the joy of accomplishment with his son, Ted Grob, Jr., who was recognized for his 39 years of service to Goodwill Industries in 1977. Rev. Grob was the minister of the Calvary Methodist Church (German Methodist) when he started a Goodwill program in the parsonage in 1927. The workshop was constructed next door at 120-122 North Fifth Street in the 1930s and remained at that location until the operation was moved to 2702 South Third Street in 1990.

Beginning in 1947, the Terre Haute Rotary Club sponsored the annual Goodwill Good Turn Drive with the help of other community groups. Shown here ready for the 1956 drive are Ralph E. Smith and boys from the Glenn Home who joined with youngsters from the Boy Scouts, Girl Scouts, Boys Club and Gibault Home to distribute bags in Terre Haute area neighborhoods. They would return one week later to collect bags of discards which provide employment for individuals with disabilities and disadvantaging conditions.

both photos Wabash Valley Goodwill Industries collection

Day Nurseries

Lyman P. Alden, superintendent of the Rose Orphans Home, pinpointed the ongoing need for day care facilities in the city more than one century ago. On January 16, 1888, he wrote: *I know that many poor women are hindered or entirely prevented from getting employment because they cannot leave their children during the day time to work. They and their children thus frequently become entirely dependent upon the public for support.*

This letter to Mrs. D. W. Minshall from Alden inspired a group of Centenary Methodist Church women to form the Terre Haute Day Nursery Association in 1892. They rented a house at 314 North Fourth Street for $15.00 a month and opened the nursery in 1893. The nursery moved to its own house at 410 North Fourth Street in 1895.

A second facility, the Pierce Branch Nursery at 2115 Beech Street, was in use from 1917 until 1947. The Terre Haute Day Nursery moved into this building at 721 Elm Street in 1960. This photograph is dated 1961. *Terre Haute Day Nursery collection*

Under the leadership of Mrs. Melissa Bishop, a group of women organized the Colored Day Nursery Association in 1908, rented a house and hired a matron to care for their children while they worked. In 1924 the group moved the nursery from a rental house to their own building at 1320 South Thirteenth and one-half Street.

The association opened its doors to all children of working parents in 1966 and became the Southside Day Nursery. The children pictured here in 1987 are at the present Rose Southside Child Care and Development Center which was constructed in 1972 at 1438 South Thirteenth Street. *Rose Southside Child Care collection*

Organized as the North Twenty-eighth Street Day Care Center in 1969 to help working families, the United Child Care Center and Pre-School moved to its present location at 2051 Beech Street in 1971. *United Way collection*

The United Way of the Wabash Valley

- 1882 -
Formation of the Terre Haute Society for Organizing Charity as comprehensive relief agency.

- 1919 -
First unified fundraising campaign under name of Welfare League, later Community Fund.

- 1942 -
Organization of the Community Chest of Terre Haute.

- 1952 -
Community Chest changed to United Community Chest with a broader agency membership.

- 1958 -
Incorporation of United Appeal to raise funds for the Community Chest.

- 1959 -
Responsibility for fund campaigns and allocation of monies given to United Fund; Community Chest assigned the administration of trusts and bequests.

- 1976 -
The name United Fund of Terre Haute and Vigo County, Inc. changed to the United Way of the Wabash Valley.

Gordon Belles, Richard D. "Red" Newport, Paul Currin, Lucien Meis, William King and Ron Adams volunteered to work on the 1962-63 United Fund drive to benefit 25 member agencies. The slogan was "Be A People Helper and Give the United Way."

Newport, a Woodburn Printing Company employee, had earned the title "Mr. United Fund." Since his death in 1967, an award has been presented each year in his memory to an outstanding campaign volunteer. Grover C. Osborn, the business manager of Plumbers & Steamfitters Local No. 157, was the first recipient in 1968. *United Way of the Wabash Valley collection*

Girls and Boys Clubs

"The boy whom nobody else wants around is good enough for me." Flora Gulick put this thought into action when she founded the Boys Club in 1908. The club moved several times before the building formerly used by Ball Funeral Home at 220 North Third Street was purchased with help of the Lions Club in 1923. It is shown here with the gymnasium which was added in 1927.

Rebecca Torner
1864-1929

Rebecca Torner, a teacher at Wiley High School for 35 years, left one-third of her estate to the City of Terre Haute for the purchase of Torner Park at the corner of South Fourth Street and College Avenue. The Girls Club of Terre Haute was established at the community house on the site in 1945 and was active serving young girls until 1985. Later Torner Center, the activity building at Deming Park, was named in memory of Rebecca Torner. *Vigo County Public Library collection*

The present building, constructed on the original North Third Street site, was completed in 1951 and renovated and expanded in the late 1980s. *Terre Haute Boys Club collection*

Ted Moore is pictured here with some of the members of the Boys Club in 1950. Executive Director of the Boys Club from 1939 until 1971, Moore was awarded the Boys Club of America's highest honor in 1962. He was succeeded by Max E. Jones who continued in the position until his death in 1984. *Martin Photo*

The YMCA

Left: Basketball wasn't called "Hoosier Hysteria" in 1893, but this team was ready to play just one year after the organization of the Young Men's Christian Association in Terre Haute. The association used rental quarters until it moved to 644 Ohio Street in 1903, occupying the former Terre Haute Club building.

Below: A 1938 campaign, "For You, For Youth, For Terre Haute," had raised $260,000 in ten days to construct the present structure at South Sixth and Walnut streets shown here. Will Hays, president of the Motion Picture Producers and Distributors of America, Inc. and speaker at the dedication ceremony in 1940, said, "This . . . new home of the YMCA . . . is a tangible expression of this wide awake community's continued interest in youth." *Vigo County Public Library collection*

The YWCA

Left: Organized in 1902, the Young Women's Christian Association of Terre Haute first occupied the Samuel F. Early residence at 664 Ohio Street and then the Universalist Church building at 119 North Eighth Street. The 121 North Seventh Street building, shown here, was completed in 1908 with a swimming pool, gymnasium, lounges, kitchen, offices and dormitory rooms for young women. Occupied until 1976, the building was razed in 1980 to make way for an Indiana State University parking lot. *YWCA collection*

Above: The present facility in Fairbanks Park was opened in 1976, expanded in 1990, and continues to serve Wabash Valley women and their families. Active in the schools, the teen program remains the largest among the YWCAs in the state of Indiana. Teen members, now known as YW-Teens, have been active through the years, first as Girl Reserves and later as Blue-Tri and Y-teens. *Dorothy Jerse collection*

"SAVE THE EARTH" became a popular cause in the 1960s, but environmental concerns were not new to the Boy Scouts and the Girl Scouts. Appreciation and conservation of the outdoors always had played a large part in their programs.

Scouts helped with recycling in the form of salvage drives during World War II and supported later efforts such as the Terre Haute Recyclers of Waste in the 1970s and 1980s.

Application for the first Girl Scout troop in the city was made in 1918; the Terre Haute Council organized in 1930. These girls, pictured here on the porch of the Little House headquarters at 530 North Center Street in 1941, were launching the sixth annual Cookie Sale with a portion of the proceeds earmarked to fund camperships. McCormick's Creek State Park was the site of the first summer camp in 1930; Camp Na Wa Kwa near Poland, Indiana, opened in 1954.

The city council became a part of the Sycamore Council in 1957 and of the Covered Bridge Council in 1962. The present headquarters were built just south of Fairbanks Park in 1973. *Martin photo*

It was uniform inspection time at the 1989 Wabash Valley Boy Scout Council Jamboree at Camp Wildwood, contributed to the Council by Susan Ball and Mary Beach in 1931.

Boy Scouting was first organized in the city in 1912; the Wabash Valley Council was incorporated in 1926. George Krietenstein was responsible for the acquisition of Camp Krietenstein in 1921 and for the former council headquarters at South Thirteenth and Ohio Streets in 1921. Forrest Sherer presided at the dedication of the present council headquarters which were built in 1959 at 501 South Twenty-fifth Street on land contributed by H. N. Oakley. *Tribune-Star Publishing Company photo*

Terre Haute Recyclers of Waste, Inc. workers were shown here in 1989 putting glass into a crushing machine. Known as THROW, the organization incorporated in 1971 to save materials and energy, to extend the use of landfills and to help keep the environment clean. The center was sold in 1993 to Terre Haute Recycling Inc. Now THROW concentrates on research and public education about recycling. *Tribune-Star Publishing Company photo*

The Older Citizens

In 1965 Terre Haute ranked third in the nation in the percentage of older citizens. The Vigo County Council on the Aging and Aged had organized in 1960 with Dr. William G. Bannon, president, Mary Alice Banks, secretary. The group studied the needs of the older population and was successful in finding some answers.

The Wabash Senior Citizens Center, Inc., provides a drop-in activity center and Meals-on-Wheels began delivering meals to older persons in 1971. The Senior Citizens Transportation Program was initiated and the McMillan Day Care Center opened in 1975. James Conover and Otto Braunschweiger were among activists representing older citizens of the city.

Simeon House I

In 1978 St. Patrick's Convent, 1801 Poplar Street, became Simeon House I, a pilot project for the Catholic Archdiocese of Indianapolis. Operated by Catholic Charities of Terre Haute, which had been organized in 1973, it provides a congregate living program for older persons.

Among other Catholic Charities sites are Simeon House II, Bethany House (emergency housing) and Ryves Hall Youth Center.
Catholic Charities of Terre Haute collection

Wabash Senior Citizens Center

Benjamin Blumberg contributed $64,000 in 1965 for the purchase of Temple B'nai Abraham at South Fifth and Poplar streets as an activity center for older persons. It became the Wabash Senior Citizens Center, Inc. with Sidney Levin as the first president. The members soon organized their own kitchen band, shown here in 1968.
Wabash Senior Citizens Center, Inc. collection

Missions

Urban population increased rapidly in the late nineteenth century; industrialization attracted workers from rural areas and immigrants from other countries. To help relieve the problems of the growing slum areas, a number of charities were organized. Social reform became the "social gospel" at work, housing the homeless and feeding the hungry; often revivalistic preaching was combined with physical relief.

The good works of the Salvation Army in the city date back to 1888. The volunteers, pictured here, came to help with the Christmas party for children at the Salvation Army Temple, 121 South Eighth Street, in 1949. In 1972 the headquarters were moved from downtown to the former Graf & Sons Drugstore at 1670 Locust Street.
Salvation Army collection

Established in 1890 under the sponsorship of the First Congregational Church, the Light House Mission at 119 Ohio Street was described in *Terre Haute Today* (1915) as *One of the most deserving of the missions of the city, devoted under the superintendency of Benjamin E. Stahl to the help and service of the destitute poor. It is dependent entirely upon the free-will offerings of the public and personal contributions.*

The mission moved to the neighborhood of North Twelfth and Eagle streets in the 1970s and to its present location at 1450 Wabash Avenue, shown here, in 1991.

The building has been the home of Miller-Parrott Baking Company (1915-1958), Eastern Motors Express, Inc. (1959-1978), American Tredex, Inc. (1979-1981) and Patterson Equipment Company (1982-1987). Herb Patterson gave the building to Light House Mission, Inc. in 1990. *Tribune-Star Publishing Company photo*

CHAPTER 9
The Downtown Churches

A camera captured these Terre Hauteans participating in a baptism ceremony off the east bank of the Wabash River, perhaps in the late 1920s or 1930s. *Vigo County Public Library collection*

> **"***Nothing in life is more wonderful than faith - the one great moving force which we can neither weigh in the balance nor test in the crucible.* **"**
>
> William Osler

The first church service in the county is attributed to Jonathan Stanfer, the chaplain of the Kentucky troops serving at Fort Harrison in 1812. Later the circuit-riders and missionaries sought audiences in the new town of Terre Haute.

The comments of a Presbyterian missionary, who had visited Terre Haute in 1825 were retold by local historian H. C. Bradsby: *The last night I preached in Terre Haute but a few of the villagers attended . . . a very singular place; it had a population of about 200 people and much mercantile business; had no religious society of any order, but that there was at this time a great disposition to hear preaching; several gentlemen had formed a Sunday reading meeting at the court house. At these meetings they took turns in reading printed sermon.*

The booklet, *Terre Haute Today,* gave this account of the early churches: *From 1826 to 1834 there was preaching in the Court House and in the latter year the Methodists erected a "meeting house" costing $800 on a lot donated them by the town of Terre Haute. Previous to this the Gospel was expounded to the Methodists by the old circuit-riders of the pioneer days, the Protestant "soldiers of the cross" who vied with the priest-missionary of the Catholic faith in courage, tenacity, intrepidity and fidelity to convictions.*

Quakers coming from North Carolina made a picturesque feature in the early religious and secular life of the town in 1829, and for many years thereafter . . . The Baptists were here in force large enough by 1827 to acquire a lot and build a church.

In conclusion, *Terre Haute Today* reported: *In 1915, Terre Haute has over 60 churches and missions within its borders, representing the leading denominations of the religious world. The Quakers are no more to be seen, the Universalists and Unitarians have never flourished, but all the other branches of modern religious faith have notable houses of worship in the "city of the Wabash."*

The number of churches and temples in the city serving the congregations of some of these denominations in 1915 were listed: Baptist - eight; Catholic - four; Christian - four; Congregational - two; Episcopalian - two; Evangelists and Lutheran - five; Jewish - two; Methodist - four; Presbyterian - four; United Brethren - five; and Christian Science - one.

These included some of the mission churches which had been established by the downtown churches in outlying neighborhoods of the city, as the expansion of the city brought about additional needs for preaching, educating the congregation, and ministering to the sick and bereaved.

The 1858 city directory lists 13 churches, 11 of which were located in a downtown area bounded by Swan (S), Fourth (W), Eagle (N) and Sixth (E) streets. As the city grew, more churches were built near the business district, but a century later, some followed their members to suburban areas. The last to leave was the Central Christian Church in 1990.

The eight church buildings featured in the following pages remain located downtown between Fifth and Ninth streets and within four blocks north and south of Wabash Avenue.

145

Central Presbyterian Church - The Rev. David Monfort arrived in Terre Haute in 1828 and established the first organized church in the city - the First Presbyterian Church. The Baldwin Presbyterian Church was founded in 1848 and renamed the Second Presbyterian Church in 1868. Central Presbyterian Church was founded in 1879 by a union of the First and Second Presbyterian Churches.

The present building, shown here in 1889, was erected in 1863 at the corner of Seventh and Mulberry streets by the First Presbyterian Church. It was enlarged and remodeled 20 years later. The wooden manse behind the church was razed in 1954 and replaced with an education wing.

Centenary United Methodist Church - The history of Methodism in the city begins with the Asbury Chapel's log building at Fourth and Poplar streets erected in 1835. Construction of Centenary Methodist Church was completed in 1866 and restored after a disastrous fire in 1883. The name "Centenary" was inspired by the Centennial of American Methodism. The brick building was razed in 1903 and a new limestone structure, shown here in 1915, was built on the same site (301 North Seventh Street). Again in 1916 fire destroyed the building. The present building was dedicated in 1917.

St. Stephen's Episcopal Church - The Rt. Rev. Jackson Kemper visited Terre Haute in the years 1835, 1838 and 1839. The official meeting for the organization of the parish was held in 1840. The first building was erected on the west side of Fifth Street between Wabash Avenue and Cherry Street in 1845. The construction of the present building at 215 North Seventh Street began in 1862 and the first service was held there in 1863. Addition of the bell tower (1874), the great hall and cloister room (1891) and the chapel, education building, cloister porch and formal garden (1957-1958) followed. This photograph is dated 1889.

First Congregational Church - The Rev. Merrick A. Jewett, a Congregational minister, arrived in Terre Haute in 1834 and "gathered" the first congregation. Three years later, a church was built on the corner of North Sixth and Cherry streets, the present location of Deming Center. This building was extensively damaged by a tornado in 1853 and rebuilt in 1857.

The present building at 630 Ohio Street, shown here, was dedicated in 1903. The congregation is associated with the National Association of Congregational Christian Churches.

The sermon, "The Crisis, Its Causes and Cures," given in Terre Haute by Dr. Lyman Abbott in 1860, is known as one of the famous sermons of that period on the issue of slavery.

Immanuel Lutheran Church -
The Lutherans first organized in 1848 as the German Evangelical Lutheran and Reformed Church. Following the separation of the Lutheran and Reformed factions in 1857, the Lutherans formed the German Evangelical Lutheran Congregation. Later the name was changed to Immanuel Evangelical Lutheran Church and then to Immanuel Lutheran Church.

The congregation's first building at the corner of Fourth and Swan Streets was dedicated in 1860. The cornerstone of the present church at 645 Poplar Street was laid in 1886. Since the early 1940s, all services have been conducted in the English language, although services had been given in English as early as 1897. The congregation is a member of the Lutheran Church Missouri Synod.

Christian Science Church - A group of local residents began the study of the teachings of Mary Baker Eddy in 1895. Meeting in the homes of George Prescott and M. Elizabeth Wright, the Christian Science Society was organized in 1898. In 1902 the First Church of Christ, Scientist, of Terre Haute was incorporated. The congregation met in a number of rented locations, beginning with a room over Paige's Music Store, until 1913 when they moved to the former Central Christian Church on Mulberry Street. The cornerstone for their own building at the corner of South Sixth and Swan streets was laid in 1921; services were held in the completed basement until the building, shown here, was finished in 1930. Destroyed by fire in 1981, a new church building was constructed on the same site and dedicated on September 11, 1983.
Helen E. Moore collection

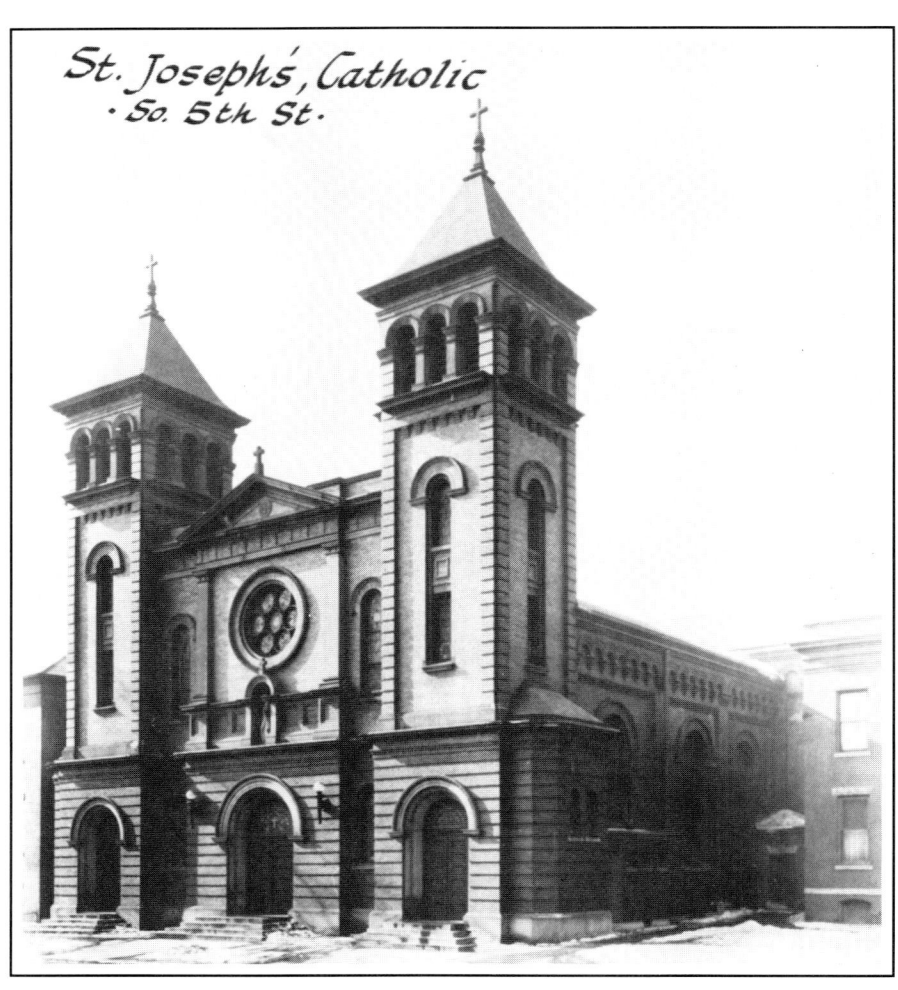

St. Joseph Catholic Church - Before the founding of St. Joseph Church, the Catholics in the area worshipped with the missionary, Father Buteux, in a log church west of the city. The first St. Joseph Church on the corner of South Fifth and Walnut streets was completed in 1838. An 1839 record of Father Buteux reported the church contained two double rows of 12 pews each, making a total of 48 pews. The present church building, which appears here, was constructed on the same site and dedicated in 1912. Following a fire in 1934, the church was rebuilt to its original splendor. St. Joseph Church became St. Joseph's University Parish Church in the early 1960s. *Vigo County Public Library collection*

St. Benedict Catholic Church - German-speaking immigrants founded St. Benedict Parish and laid the cornerstone of the first St. Benedict Church building facing Ohio Street at the corner of South Ninth Street in 1864. Final plans for a larger structure to meet the needs of a rapidly growing congregation were approved in 1895. After dedication of the present church in 1899, the *Terre Haute Express* commented: *Rising high above the surrounding churches . . . stands St. Benedict's, stately magnificent and imposing, not only the most beautiful church in the city, but in the state and the whole West.* A fire in 1930 left only the walls standing, but the parishioners rebuilt the church and it was opened for services again in 1931. *Vigo County Public Library collection*

CHAPTER 10

Private & Public Education

October 19, 1982 - *In the middle of the 1920s, the Board of Trustees of the Terre Haute City Schools and its administration designed a "dream" junior high school to be built in the near east side of the city . . . a half century later another school board and another school administration . . . decided that the original Woodrow Wilson building merited renovation rather than replacement.*
—Harmon A. Baldwin, Superintendent of Schools, 1975-1984
Tribune-Star Publishing Company photo

"Next in importance to freedom and justice is popular education, without which neither justice nor freedom can be permanently maintained."

James A. Garfield, President, United States

The Ordinance of 1787 of the Northwest Territory proclaimed, "Education shall be forever encouraged." Newspaper accounts indicate it was encouraged through the years, but citizens disagreed about the best way to do it.

The erection of a seminary building was completed in 1847. An earlier attempt in 1831 to build a two-room brick school failed when a lawsuit caused the sale of the property in 1835.

Tax-supported schools were yet to be established and the children were educated in private subscription schools. John J. Schlicher, Indiana State Normal School professor, wrote: *In 1850 education was still on a par with selling soap and bacon. Anyone with the price of an advertisement in his pocket might set up to teach . . . the city provided school buildings which were rented to teachers before it hired the teachers themselves. The seminary building is a case in point . . . Most . . held their classes in the basements of churches.*

There had been (public) schools for one year, 1853-54, but the venture was obstructed by injunctions and the like. It seems almost incredible that it was only in 1860 that schools supported by taxation came to Terre Haute to stay.

The 1860-61 city directory described the educational facilities: *There are now owned by the city four large . . brick buildings devoted to public schools. . . . In addition . . . there are many private schools, which are commanding a good patronage.*

A century later, the Indiana General Assembly passed the "School Reorganization Act." It led to the consolidation of city and township schools in all of Vigo County. Many residents opposed consolidation, but in December, 1960, the assets of the city and township schools were transferred to the new Vigo County School Corporation.

A decade later, in 1971, new high school buildings opened on the south and north sides of the city, but again only after opposition and attempts by members of the tax-paying public to stop their construction.

Both education and disagreement are parts of democracy. And, through this process, a public school system, supplemented by private schools, often church related, has come into existence in response to the changing needs of the community and nation.

Sometimes called "a college town," Terre Haute has reaped great dividends from having five colleges and universities which provide both educational and employment opportunities.

149

Public Library

Early efforts to establish a public library met with failure. In 1882, however, the Terre Haute School Board purchased a library from the Terre Haute Library Association, which had organized in 1879. Housed first in upstairs rooms on Wabash Avenue and later in the former Universalist Church, the Terre Haute Public Library became in 1906 the Emeline Fairbanks Memorial Library at 222 North Seventh Street.

The first branch library opened in 1958 at Meadows Center, the first library to be located in a shopping center in the state of Indiana. Services expanded to include all of Vigo County by 1962, including first West Terre Haute (1961) and then South and North branches (1962).

The governing body was changed from a School-Library Board to a Library Board in 1974. Under the leadership of Arch Dunbar, president, and Edward N. Howard, library director, the new board proceeded with plans for the present main library which opened in 1979.

The formal opening of the city's first public library building was August 11, 1906. The building, a gift of Crawford Fairbanks in memory of his mother, served patrons for 73 years. It now belongs to Indiana State University.

The first home of South Branch, shown here, was one-half of a store building at 3000 South Seventh Street. The branch moved across the street to a space in Southland Shopping Center, its present location, in 1968. The Cheap Frills resale clothing shop now occupies the space.

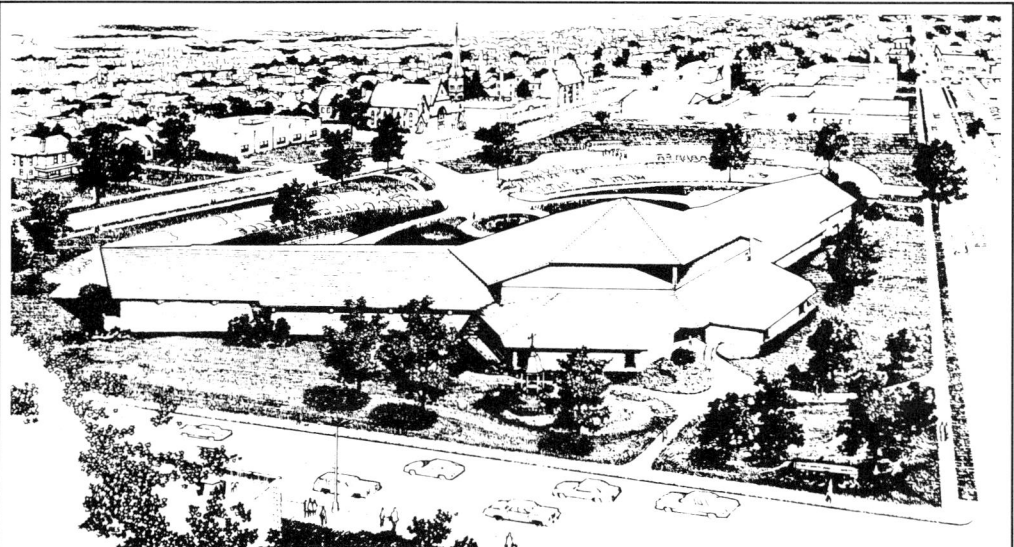

The site for the current main library was purchased in 1970. The area, earlier the location of the Methodist Temple and Wiley High School, became One Library Square in 1979.
all photos Vigo County Public Library collection

The Immanuel Lutheran Church at 645 Poplar Street founded its parochial day school in 1858. The German language was part of the instruction until World War I. Martin Braunschweiger, teacher, and students are shown here in 1925. The school closed during the World War I years, but then reopened and remained in operation until 1946.
Dorothy Braunschweiger Bilyeu collection

Private Schools

A choice in education was offered by private schools operated by individuals and by the parochial schools of the various churches. A number of these schools, most of which are affiliated with churches, continue to offer classes in the city.

Described as "the equal of the best preparatory schools in the East," the King Classical private day school was founded by Bertha Pratt King and Mary Sinclair Crawford in 1906. Located in this home at South Sixth and Park streets, it remained in service until 1945. *Vigo County Public Library collection*

Girls from the intermediate class at Coates College posed for this photograph in 1892. Jane P. Coates of Greencastle, Indiana, had funded this Presbyterian School for girls saying, "I desire that the Bible shall be the chief text book." Located on Strawberry Hill at the foot of South Sixth Street, the college opened in 1885; but financial problems caused it to close in 1897.

Members of this Rea School kindergarten class of 1945-46 were very serious about their photograph in front of their school at North Fourth Street and Fourth Avenue. The building had been constructed in 1906 and named in honor of William S. Rea of the Bement-Rea Company. The school closed in 1979 and the building has been razed.

Rea School originated as the Thirteenth District School in private houses. Later it was housed in a building at North Third Street and Scott (now Eighth Avenue) Street; that structure had been used as a pesthouse during the smallpox epidemic of the 1870s and later as a broom factory.

Public Schools

> *The year 1860 marks the re-organization of the free public schools of the city . . . The schools opened . . with 18 teachers, properly qualified under the law, for a term of five months at a cost of $2,550 for salaries, and $500 for the Superintendent . . . Of the 1,324 children of school age, within the corporation, 1,122 (624 boys and 498 girls) were enrolled . . . . The average daily attendance was 751 3/4. The term closed on the 22nd of February, 1861, . . . with a public procession (of children and teachers).*
> —William H. Wiley

The faculty of Hook School, North Fourth and Mulberry streets, is pictured above in 1894. The report to the Mayor and Common Council from the Office of Public Schools in that year reads: *. . . the teachers of the Terre Haute Public Schools, with less than half a dozen exceptions in all these years, have cheerfully and fully carried out their contracts . . . and acquitted themselves with success and honor in the school room.* Vigo County Public Library collection

Above: The Second District School, built in 1867, became the Hulman School in 1906 in honor of Herman Hulman, Sr. The school served 349 students in 1914. Located on the southeast corner of South Seventh and Swan streets, the building was razed in 1935 for a gas station. It is now the site of a B Quick convenience store.

Left: The first tax-supported school in the city for African-Americans was Dunbar School opened in 1869. Organized in 1885, Lincoln School students moved to the building, shown here, at North Sixteenth and Elm streets in 1889. A new building opened in 1922; it became the James Whitcomb Riley School in 1960 and the Benjamin Franklin School in 1961. *Vigo County Public Library collection*

This photograph was made for an extensive exhibit about the Terre Haute Public Schools at the 1904 Chicago World's Fair. William H. Wiley, school superintendent, is standing in front of the quotation on the blackboard. It reads in part: "Education is to give character rather than knowledge."

McLean Junior High School, constructed in 1917 at 961 Lafayette Avenue, was named for Colonel William E. McLean, local attorney and legislator. The administrative offices of the Vigo County School Corporation moved from 667 Walnut Street to this building in 1972. *Vigo County Public Library collection*

Fuqua School on the south side of the city and Meadows School, shown here, on the east side opened in 1957. Located at 55 South Brown Avenue, Meadows School admitted 278 pupils for the 1957-58 school year. Other schools constructed in the city during that period were Crawford (1961) and Terre Town (1962). *Vigo County Public Library collection*

Saint Mary-of-the Woods College

> ... the Church of the Immaculate Conception gathers the Sisters of Providence, and at times their relatives and friends, faculty and students of Saint Mary-of-the-Woods College and members of the Terre Haute community for moments of quiet prayer and reflection as well as celebration and ceremony.
> —Sisters of Providence, 1987

Saint Mary-of-the-Woods is home to the Congregation of the Sisters of Providence and Saint Mary-of-the-Woods College. Venerable Mother Theodore Guerin and five missionaries arrived from France to this location, west of Terre Haute, in 1840 to establish schools. Their original Female Institute, also known as the Academy, is now Saint Mary-of-the-Woods College, the oldest Catholic liberal arts college for women in the United States. Many Terre Hauteans, both women and men, received all or part of their education in schools established by the Sisters of Providence.

These Sisters of Providence had returned to campus from many teaching assignments in Terre Haute and other parts of the nation to attend summer school. They appear here in Foley Hall in 1963.

Noted for its beauty in every season, the wooded campus is shown here during a spring in the late 1930s. Foley Hall appears at the end of the drive. Dating back to 1860, the structure was razed in 1989. Providence Center, completed in 1990, now occupies the site. *all photos Saint Mary-of-the-Woods collection*

Catholic Parochial Schools

St. Joseph Academy is pictured here in 1915. The building was constructed in 1888. In 1937, it merged with **St. Patrick's High School,** which had opened in 1923, to form the new **Central Catholic High School for Girls** at South Nineteenth and Poplar streets. The academy building then became **St. Joseph School** which remained open until 1957. Central Catholic became **St. Patrick's High School for Girls** again in 1946 and remained in service until 1953 when **Schulte High School** opened for both boys and girls.

St. Benedict's School, first an out-school of St. Joseph School, opened as a separate facility in 1882. Instruction continued until 1970 in the large brick building at 128 South Ninth Street.

St. Patrick's School, also established in 1882, remains open to students. The present building was completed in 1922.

St. Ann's School was in service from 1894 until 1979 at 1412 Locust Street.

St. Margaret Mary's School at 627 Voorhees Street was ready for the opening of classes in 1921. It continued in operation until 1977.

Sacred Heart School opened in 1924 at the time the parish was formed and remains open at 1330 Lafayette Avenue.

The Gibault School for Boys, established south of the city by the Knights of Columbus of Indiana, was dedicated in 1921.

Schulte High School, named for Most Rev. Paul Schulte, Archbishop of the Indianapolis Archdiocese, opened in 1953 in a new building at 2901 Ohio Boulevard. The 1954 class was the first to graduate; the last commencement before the school closed was held in 1977. The building is now Corporate Square, an office building.

Wiley High School

Terre Haute High School opened in 1863 with six pupils at the First District School (Hook School) at North Fourth and Mulberry streets. Classes were moved to the first Indiana State Normal Building in 1869. The new Terre Haute High School building opened at South Seventh and Walnut streets in 1886 and later became Wiley High School. Its students moved to the new Terre Haute South Vigo School in 1971. Only the cupola from the Wiley building remains; it is now a part of the grounds of the Vigo County Public Library building which opened on the site in 1979.

Members of the Student Council were featured in the 1929 *Red Lantern* yearbook. Previously called the *Red Pepper,* the yearbook was renamed the *Wileyan* in 1930.

William H. Wiley 1842-1927. The name of the Terre Haute High School was changed in 1906 to Wiley High School in honor of William H. Wiley. "The father of Terre Haute's schools," Wiley was principal of the high school in 1865 and served as Superintendent of the Terre Haute City Schools from 1869 until 1906.

Students saluted the flag in front of Wiley during World War II. The 1946 *Wileyan* listed 38 "Gold Star Boys of World War II" who had lost their lives in the service of their country.

Gerstmeyer Technical High School

The beginning of Gerstmeyer Technical High School dates back to 1922 when the Boys' Vocational School students were moved to the former Rose Polytechnic Institute at 1250 Locust Street. Three years later the student body of the Girls' Vocational School also was transferred there.

A full high school curriculum was added to the vocational one after the move, but throughout its history, the school offered vocational training. In 1971 the students moved from "Tech" to Terre Haute North Vigo High School.

...Dr. Charles F. Gerstmeyer, whose sympathy and untiring efforts placed him with the foremost promoters of vocational education in Terre Haute and whose name our school bears...
The Anvil, 1929

Charles F. Gerstmeyer, M.D.
1844-1922

The "Marching Black Cats" and their director, Malcolm Scott, are shown here in 1932. The band, formed in 1922, was the first school band in the city and was led by Scott from 1926 until 1964.

Pictured here in 1959, the high school occupied this building from 1922 until 1971.

The students of Chauncey Rose Junior High School, which is located on the north side of the old campus, continue to use Gerstmeyer Memorial Gymnasium constructed in 1950. The original school building (formerly Rose Polytechnic Institute) has been demolished. *Martin photo*

Garfield High School

The Garfield High School is the culmination of the most strenuous educational contest in the history of Terre Haute. Wiley High School had become so oppressively crowded that practically everybody was advocating some plan of relief . . . It was to be an addition to Wiley High, or a new school. . . After numerous trials, changes of venue, and even State legislation, the Garfield High School building was erected on a five-acre plot of ground at Twelfth Street and Maple Avenue. . . The name given to this school was in recognition of the eminent services of (President) James A. Garfield in the cause of education.
William H. Wiley, 1924

Grace DeVaney 1897-1981
Grace DeVaney's career as an educator began in 1916 in a one-room school in Fayette Township. . . . Her career ended when she retired in 1963 from Garfield High School as the only woman to serve as a high school principal in Indiana. . . If there was a watchword in Miss DeVaney's life, it has to be "WORK." —Dorothy Becherer, Garfield High School faculty member

Jim Wittig, a member of the class of 1956, is shown here advising other students before the beginning of the 1955-56 school year. The previous year The Rhythmettes, the first group of precision marchers in the area, were organized by Bandmaster Leslie Evinger. Driver education had been introduced two years earlier. *Martin photo*

Garfield High School opened to students in 1912. The construction of the gymnasium in 1938 was one of the New Deal WPA projects in the city. After the school closed in 1971, its students entered Terre Haute North Vigo High School. The building was razed in 1973; Garfield Gardens and Towers Apartments now occupy the site.
Martin photo

The High Schools of Today

Two of the present high school buildings of the Vigo County School Corporation opened in 1971. Terre Haute North Vigo High School replaced Garfield and Gerstmeyer high schools. The students who had attended Wiley and Honey Creek high schools moved to Terre Haute South Vigo High School.

Additions were made in 1992-93 to accommodate ninth grade students when the junior high schools became middle schools offering grades six, seven, and eight.

Washington Alternative High School opened in 1977 to serve students outside the traditional school setting.

Terre Haute North Vigo High School is located at 3434 Maple Avenue, east of the Indiana National Guard facility.

Terre Haute South Vigo High School, 3737 South Seventh Street, occupies the former site of Paul Cox Airport. Also on the grounds is the Allen Memorial Planetarium, dedicated in 1971 in memory of Terre Haute physician, Dr. Orris T. Allen.

Washington Alternative High School is housed in the Booker T. Washington School building constructed in 1914 at 1201 South Thirteenth Street. The building opened as a high school in 1977 and was remodeled in 1983-84. Students with children take advantage of child care services offered by Alternatives for Living and Learning, Inc. (A.L.L.) in the building. *all photos Vigo County School Corporation collection*

Indiana State University

Indiana State Normal School with a student body of 13 women and eight men opened in an unfinished building on January 6, 1870. By the spring term of 1874, enrollment had grown to 279. These young people would teach in the fast growing public school systems across the state.

The construction of "Old Main" in 1889 to replace the original building was the beginning of more than a century of expansion and construction for the school. By 1989 enrollment totaled 12,005.

These students posed in front of "Old Main" in 1910. Three years before, the four-year college course had been added. *Vigo County Public Library collection*

The Main Building was erected on the foundation of the first Normal building destroyed by fire in 1888. The city raised $50,000 to begin construction, and classes began in the new building in 1889. The structure was razed and replaced by the Administration Building in 1950. *Ralph C. Dinkel collection*

This Student Union Building was built in 1939. Enlarged in 1959, the building was renamed in honor of former President Ralph Noble Tirey (1934-1953) in 1963. The new Hulman Memorial Student Union and Dede Plaza opened in 1991 on the other side of campus. *Indiana State University Archives collection*

The first master's degrees were awarded in 1928; the institution became Indiana State Teachers College in 1929. The following decade brought about the closing of Mulberry and Eagle streets between Sixth and Seventh streets, landscaping and the construction of several new buildings with federal WPA funding.

Many programs, in addition to teaching, were developed; academic expansion led to a new name, Indiana State College, in 1961. By 1965, one hundred years after the school was founded by an act of the Indiana General Assembly, enrollment on campus had reached 9,401 students, the college had become Indiana State University and the institution's own doctoral program had been initiated.

Since then, growth has occurred in programs, services, research and the campus itself. New buildings, the closing of portions of North Sixth and Chestnut streets, and extensive landscaping have created a scenic urban campus.

Statesman Towers, shown here, were built in 1968 near the end of a period of residence hall construction. The new halls included Burford (1959), Sandison and Erickson (1962), Gillum and Pickerl (1963), Blumberg and Cromwell (1964), Rhoads and Mills (1965), Jones and Hines (1966), and the Lincoln Quadrangles (1969). Statesman Towers, no longer needed as a dormitory, was remodeled to house the School of Education (1977) and the School of Business (1980). *Indiana State University Archives collection*

An elementary school for the training of teachers existed on the campus from 1870 until 1992. Known as Laboratory and later as University School, it moved from the Normal Training School on campus to this building which was completed in 1935 on the Heminway property, formerly the home of Chauncey Rose, at North Seventh and Chestnut streets.

Plans had been made during the 1906-07 school year to add high school grades to the school. Later known as State High School, it remained open until 1978. *Vigo County Public Library collection*

The Terre Haute School of Watchmaking opened after World War II in response to a nationwide need for journeymen in the watchmaking trade and remained in operation until the early 1950s. George W. Sims headed the school.

Established by master watch and clock makers, the school was located at 690 Chestnut Street, now the site of the Zorah Shrine Temple parking lot. Students pictured here are at the bench under the supervision of their instructors. *Clarence Hood collection*

Technical Schools

The Wabash Valley was the first region of the Indiana Vocational Technical College (Ivy Tech) to be chartered (1967) and the first to have a permanent location. C. Huston Isaacs, director, presided over the groundbreaking ceremonies in 1968.

The Indiana Vocational Technical College is a state college providing employment education through a system of regional campuses. The main campus of the Wabash Valley Region is located five miles south of Terre Haute on U.S. Highway 41. Its Technology Center, pictured here, opened in 1986. *Indiana Vocational Technical College collection*

Rose-Hulman Institute of Technology

Rose Polytechnic Institute, one of the nation's oldest engineering and science colleges, was founded and endowed by Chauncey Rose, Terre Haute philanthropist, in 1874. The school opened to students on March 7, 1883. Delivering his inaugural address on that day, President Charles O. Thompson stated: *The Rose Polytechnic Institute is a school of technology. . . . There is no good word corresponding to polytechnic or technological to apply to persons who practice the profession indicated, and so these persons are called, now as always, engineers. . .*

The school became Rose-Hulman Institute of Technology in 1971. In its annual survey of America's Best Colleges in 1990, *U.S. World News & Report* magazine ranked Rose-Hulman second among the nation's undergraduate colleges which specialize in engineering and science education.

Construction of a new campus began in 1921 east of the city at a 120-acre site on U.S. 40. The gift of Anton and Herman Hulman in 1917, it became a part of the city through annexation in 1989. *Joe Wilkinson collection*

Members of the Class of 1890 are shown here in front of the original building (later Gerstmeyer High School) at North Thirteenth and Locust streets. Twenty-five men made up the first class admitted to the institute in 1883; enrollment in 1985 totaled 1330. *Rose-Hulman Institute of Technology collection*

The Demas and Sarah C. Deming Memorial Dormitory was the first residence hall. Constructed in 1926, it is shown here overlooking one of the two small lakes on campus. *Joe Wilkinson collection*

Business Colleges

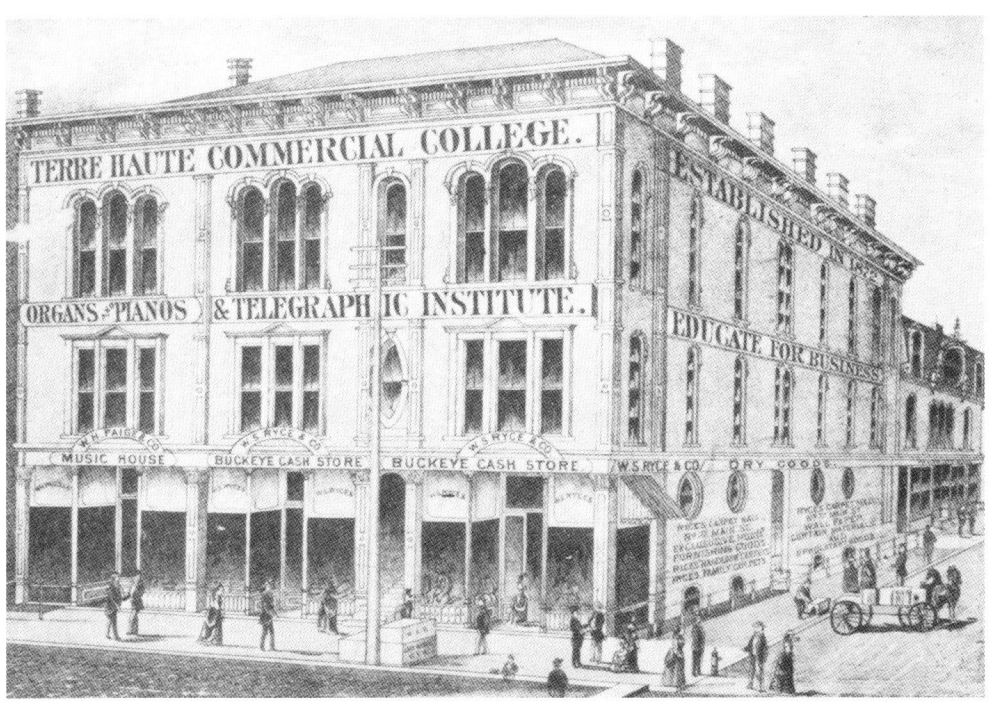

The Terre Haute Commercial College was established by Professor R. Garvin in 1862. The 1874 course included commercial arithmetic, double and single entry bookkeeping, telegraphy and phonography, shorthand reporting and business penmanship. Garvin's penmanship skills were noted as having "taken the premium in nearly all the state and local fairs for several years past."

In 1872, Garvin consolidated his Terre Haute institution with the Vincennes Commercial College to form the Terre Haute Commercial College and Telegraphic Institute, pictured here. It was located above the W. H. Paige Music House and the Buckeye Cash Store on Wabash Avenue.

Students are shown here in 1915 in the typewriting department of the Wabash Commercial College at 25 South Seventh Street. Brown's Business College, 116 South Sixth Street, was also in operation at that time. The Wabash-Brown College of Commerce later was listed in the city directories of 1934 to 1950.

The Terre Haute Commercial College, later the Indiana Business College, was located downtown from the 1930s until 1991. The emphasis had changed by the latter year from penmanship to computers and the location from downtown to a new building adjacent to Honey Creek Mall.

CHAPTER 11

The Arts & Entertainment

Benjamin "Scatman" Crothers was born in Terre Haute in 1910. A graduate of Wiley High School, he achieved success first in the musical world and later in movies and television. November 2, 1985 was proclaimed "Scatman Crothers Day" by Mayor P. Pete Chalos. *The Spectator photo*

> *" The Arts — those activities whereby man would clamber from beasts to fly among the gods. "*
>
> Bernard Iddings Bell

There was little time for activities which weren't immediately practical and useful during the early years in Terre Haute. The lack of transportation and meeting places limited entertainment options.

In 1873 Loren Hassam wrote, *Previous to 1864 the city had been much in need of a public hall of convenient size . . . to meet the growing demands and wants of the city.* In that year Thomas Dowling, newspaper publisher and Indiana legislator, built Dowling Hall with seating for 1200.

This began to change in the 1870s. The Ringgold Band, organized by Jacob Breinig and George Sickford, gave its first concert in 1876 and the Terre Haute Oratorio Society was organized in 1877. Railroad transportation allowed touring companies to travel to audiences, and cities began building facilities. The first opera house in Terre Haute, built in 1870, was known as one of the most elaborate in the state.

The *Daily Express* (February 17, 1871) commented, *Henceforth we shall have the dream of entertainments and whilst such provincial towns as Indianapolis, Cincinnati, Louisville, etc. may be ignored, managers cannot afford to omit our metropolitan city and magnificent Opera House for their routes.*

The need for an entertainment facility appeared again in 1920. That year a Chamber of Commerce publication read: *The public must be made to understand just what a coliseum will mean to Terre Haute . . . such an auditorium as every city the size of Terre Haute must have and cities smaller than Terre Haute do have.* Yet, it would be a century from the construction of the first Opera House before Hulman Civic Center was constructed by Indiana State University to house entertainment, sports and meeting events.

Many performers and artists left their native Terre Haute to achieve national recognition. Among these were a number of performers, James Farrington Gookins, nineteenth century painter, Paul Dresser and Theodore Dreiser.

Still others stayed or came to the city. William T. Turman, who headed the Indiana State Normal School art department from 1894 until the 1930s, and John Joseph Laska, who painted the murals in the Debs Home during the late 1970s, are best known for their teaching. Max Ehrmann, author of "Desiderata," who chose to stay in the city was Terre Haute's greatest celebrant.

In 1986, Nancy Metheny, writer for "Terre Haute, Indiana. The Faces. The Places." asked, "Can a lover of arts and ideas find happiness in a medium-sized midwestern city?" Her answer was "Yes! When the city is Terre Haute, the opportunities are many."

These opportunities include the collections and productions of the schools, colleges and university, Arts Illiana, the Banks of the Wabash Chorus, Community Theater, Inc., Poet's Study Club, Swope Art Museum, Terre Haute Choral Society, Terre Haute Concert Band, Terre Haute Symphony Orchestra, Terre Haute Youth Symphony and the Wabash Valley Art Guild.

Two Brothers

Paul Dresser
1858-1906

Paul Dresser was born April 22, 1858, in Terre Haute and baptized at St. Joseph Church. He was the oldest of ten children of John Paul Dreiser, a woolen mill employee, and Sarah Mary Schneppes Dreiser, a seamstress who worked for downtown tailors to supplement the family's income.

As a teenager, Paul was sent to school at St. Meinrad's Seminary but his stay was short. Running away, he joined a traveling medicine show. Changing his name from Dreiser to Dresser, he worked as an entertainer and composer for the remainder of his life.

His sentimental songs, such as "The Letter That Never Came" and "Don't Tell Her That You Love Her," made him a popular composer in New York City during the 1890s.

Dresser died January 20, 1906 and is buried with his parents in St. Boniface Cemetery, Chicago, Illinois. His death occurred before his song "My Gal Sal" became a hit and also before his "On the Banks of the Wabash" was made the state song of Indiana in 1913.

Theodore Dreiser
1871-1945

Theodore Dreiser, brother of Paul Dresser, was born August 27, 1871, the ninth child of John and Sarah Dreiser. Baptized Herman Theodore Dreiser at St. Benedict Church, he later attended St. Benedict parochial School.

The family fell into hard times and made a series of moves to Vincennes, Sullivan, Evansville and Warsaw, always looking for greener pastures. Writing to Richard Duffy in 1901, Dreiser explained: *I was raised in Warsaw, Indiana, but it would be more truthful if my early life were ascribed not so much to one place as to the whole state.*

His writing career began as a cub reporter on the *Chicago Globe* and ended as one of America's greatest novelists, best known for *Sister Carrie* and *An American Tragedy*. He died in California on December 28, 1945 and was buried in Forest Lawn Cemetery in Los Angeles.

His biographer Richard Lingeman wrote: *He had enormous influence on American literature during the first quarter of the century — and for a time he was American literature, the only writer worth talking about in the same breath with the European masters.*

In 1963, under the leadership of Dorothy J. Clark, the Vigo County Historical Society moved the birthplace of Paul Dresser from its original site at 318 South Second Street to Fairbanks Park overlooking the Wabash River. Designated as a State Shrine and Memorial by the 1967 State Legislature, the home is also significant as an example of a working man's home during the pre-Civil War period.

Max Ehrmann
1872-1945

Max Ehrmann was born to German immigrant parents in their home in the 600 block of North Fourth Street. The family attended the German Methodist Church. After his graduation from DePauw University in 1894, he studied law and philosophy at Harvard University. Returning to Terre Haute, he practiced law, always hoping he could one day devote every day to his writing, which he did in 1912.

Described as a philosopher, student of human nature and "Terre Haute's poet laureate," Max Ehrmann remains best known for "A Prayer" (1906) and "Desiderata" (1927).

Claude Bowers
1878-1958

Claude Bowers, author and diplomat, came to Terre Haute in 1903 as an editorial writer for the *Terre Haute Gazette*. Introduced into local Democratic activities by John E. Lamb, Bowers later became a Democrat of national prominence and a United States ambassador. His books were described as "popular history at its best." Two of these, *Jefferson and Hamilton* (1925) and *The Tragic Era* (1929) received Pulitzer Prize nominations.

Jane Dabney Shackelford
1895-1979

Jane Shackelford came to Terre Haute from Logansport to enroll at Indiana State Normal School and was graduated in 1919. A teacher in the Terre Haute City Schools for 43 years, she is the author of *The Child's Story of the Negro* (1938), a popular text book which was used across the nation in "both colored and white" schools. Her second book, *My Happy Days* (1944), was an immediate best seller. *Vigo County Public Library collection*

Fannie Burgheim Blumberg
1894-1964

A native of Indianapolis, Fannie Blumberg was a kindergarten teacher before she married Benjamin Blumberg, Terre Haute businessman and philanthropist, in 1916. Talented in both art and literature, she is the author of children's stories which include *The Peace Fiddler and Rowena, Teena, Tot and the Blackberries*.

Swope Art Museum

Sheldon Swope (1843-1929) was an Indiana native, born in Attica. He is an enigmatic figure. He had a long and active career as a soldier, businessman and sportsman. He never married.

. . . He came to Terre Haute in 1867 and went to work for S. P. Freeman, a local jeweler located at what is now 380 Wabash Avenue. After a time, Swope was made a partner. Later he bought an interest in the firm. Eventually the firm became Swope and Nehf. He retained an interest in it and was a respected diamond merchant until his death.

He wrote his will—a one-page document—in 1903 . . . The will provided that an art gallery be established in Terre Haute and housed in the Swope Block building. . . . Swope Gallery opened its distinguished Art Deco brass doors to the public on March 21, 1942.

          Eileen Jensen "History of the Museum" (abridged), 1987

World-renowned for its holdings, the gallery was renamed the Sheldon Swope Art Museum in 1989.

BookNation and the law firm of Sacopulos Johnson Carter and Sacopulos are also in the Swope building, constructed in 1901-02 on the northwest corner of South Seventh and Ohio streets.
Swope Art Museum collection

Janet Scudder
1874-1940

Scudder became internationally known for her figures in bronze. She and Caroline Peddle Ball had attended a private drawing class together at Rose Polytechnic Institute and were graduates of Terre Haute High School. Ball went on to win fame in her affiliation with Tiffany of New York. *Vigo County Public Library collection*

Amalia Kussner Coudert
1863-1932

Kussner Coudert was one of the most skillful and prominent miniature portrait painters of the late nineteenth and early twentieth centuries. During her childhood, the Kussner family lived above her father's Palace of Music in the building known as Memorial Hall. *Vigo County Public Library collection*

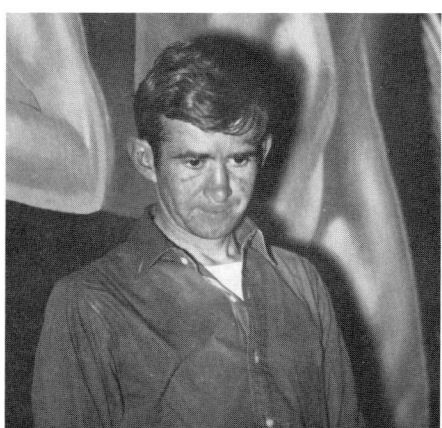

Gilbert Brown Wilson
1907-1991

Wilson is noted for his paintings of Moby Dick and his murals. His murals in Terre Haute are on the walls of Community Theater, Woodrow Wilson Junior High School and the former Laboratory School on the Indiana State University campus. A graduate of Garfield High School, he attended Indiana State Normal School before enrolling at the Chicago Art Institute.

The Terre Haute Symphony
The Terre Haute Symphony, pictured here on January 28, 1928 at the Indiana Theater, was organized in 1926 at the home of Will H. Bryant. Bryant directed the orchestra until 1949; Dr. James Barnes, 1949-1970; Dr. Victor Danek, 1970-1978; and Dr. Ramon Meyer, since 1978.
Vigo County Public Library collection

**A Century of Dance Lessons
1880 - 1980**
Oscar Duenweg, William Schomer, Rose Farrington, Ewart Twins, Reid Marlatt, Christopher Stark, Ernestine Myers, Archilene Chambers, Florence Cizek, Nancy Sauer, Betty DeLong Saberton, Elmer Watson, Roseann Callahan Claire Kincade, Jane Henry, Tamara Schaffer

---

Ernestine Myers Dance School
Students of "Miss Ernestine" posed for this photograph in the spring of 1968. At the height of her career, Myers was named one of the 12 outstanding women of the American stage by *Theater Magazine*. She returned to the midwest from Broadway to operate a dance school in Terre Haute for many years. Ernestine Myers Morrissey died in 1991 at the age of 91 years.

The City's First Opera House

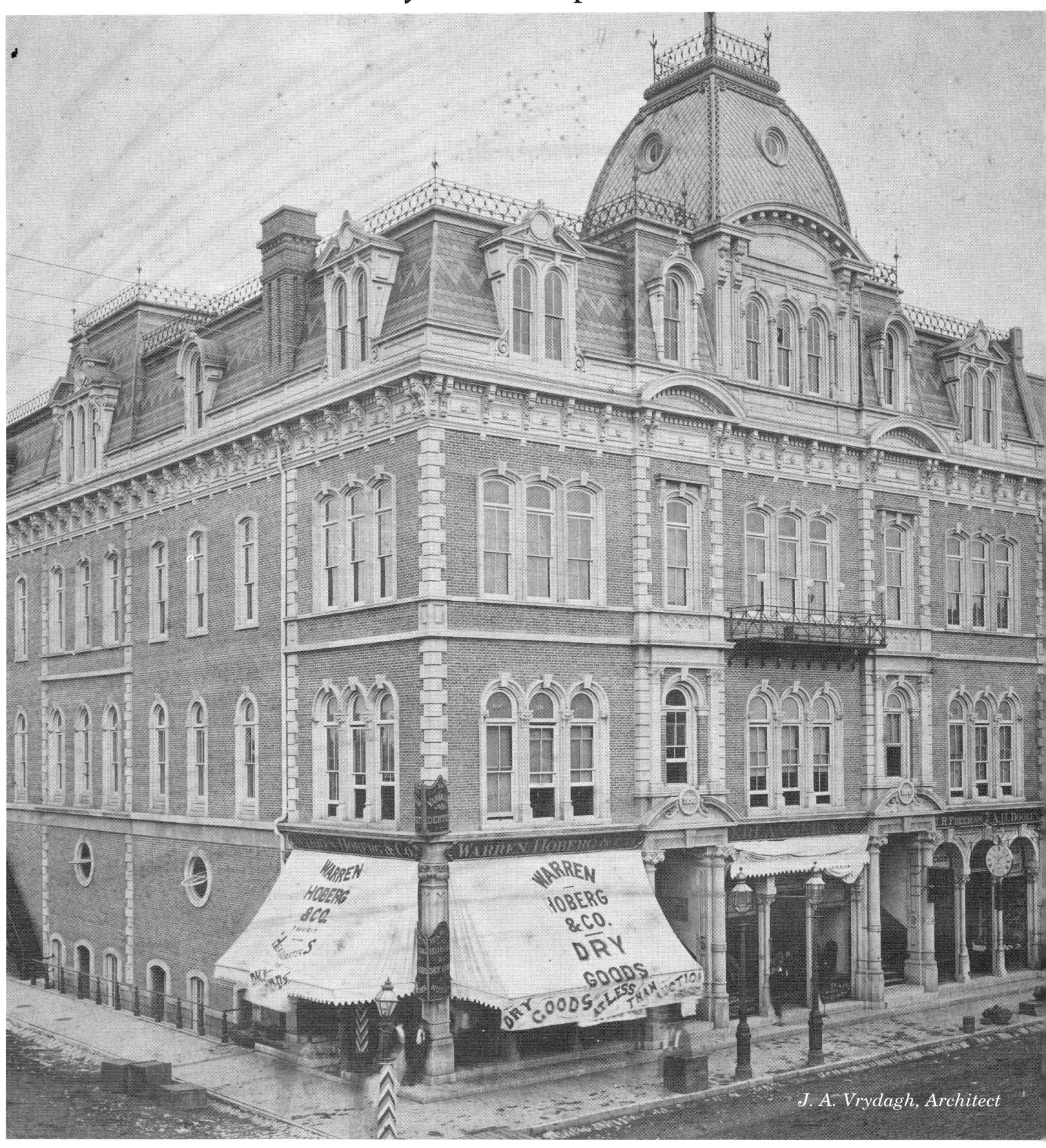

J. A. Vrydagh, Architect

The Opera House was built in 1870, by a Joint Stock Company, at a cost of $180,000 . . . It is finished throughout complete, and is the crowning ornament of our city. It is no less grand in dimensions than in architectural beauty, it being 80 feet by 150. The auditory has a capacity of seating 1400 people. . . . It is used for popular gathering of the citizens, as well as for public amusement, and is the pride of Terre Haute. —Loren Hassam, 1873

Many theatrical stars of that day, including Edwin Booth and Lily Langtry, performed on the stage. Purchased by Wilson Naylor in 1882, it became Naylor's Opera House. A fire in July, 1896, left the building in ruins; fortunately there was no audience at the time. It was located on the northeast corner of Fourth Street and Wabash Avenue.

Grand Theater

Ground was broken for the new opera house on the southeast corner of Seventh and Cherry streets on June 8, 1897. The contractor, August Fromme, had the building ready for its grand opening, planned by manager Theodore W. Barhydt, Jr., on November 2, 1897. The *Gazette* reported, *As Colonel W. E. McLean said in his dedicatory address, it was a gala night. The youth and beauty, the brains and brawn and the business of the city were all represented.*

The first production on stage was the comic opera, "The Isle of Champagne," which played to a capacity crowd of 1,600 to 1,700 persons. The management continued to feature many fine performances and famous stars on stage before the theater became a movie house in the early 1930s. The theater is shown here in 1960, the year of its demolition. The site became the parking lot for the Terre Haute House. *Martin photo*

Ethel Barrymore and other famous performers appeared on stage at the Grand Opera House, but it was especially thrilling to have native Terre Hauteans return as stars. Valeska Suratt, Rose Melville ("Sis Hopkins"), Alice Fischer Harcourt King and Rose Fehrenbach (Marie Roslyn) were among those who achieved national recognition on the stage.

FIRE NOTICE – When you enter theatre and take your seat look around and carefully note the exits and in the event of a fire keep cool and go to an exit in an orderly manner.

GRAND OPERA HOUSE
Thursday, April 17th, night only

CHARLES FROHMAN
Presents

ETHEL BARRYMORE

In the New Comedy in Four Acts

"THE OFF CHANCE"
By R. C. Carton

AFTER The PERFORMANCE VISIT The

Terre Haute House
COLLEGE INN
Noon and Evening Lunches

Popular Prices.   Sunday Dinner, $1.00.   Excellent Music
W. W. SHOOK, Manager

Play Produced by Edward Emery.
Scenery by Homer Emens.
Miss Barrymore's Gowns by Frances, Inc., N. Y.

For CHARLES FROHMAN

William Bartlett Reynolds..................Business Manager
William Frank..........................Company Manager
F. C. Butler...............................Stage Manager

The Community Theater

Jane Cunningham Hazledine, Community Theater of Terre Haute historian, wrote: *It all began in 1926 . . . Madge Polk Townsley approached the Pen and Brush Club and Woman's Department Club with the idea of sponsoring a nonprofessional civic theater group. The idea took root and prospered. In 1928, the Community Theater produced four plays.*

The group used stages at Garfield High School, the Hippodrome Theater and in various buildings on the Indiana State Teachers College campus, before they purchased the Best Theater, a neighborhood movie house at 1431 South Twenty-fifth Street. The first production opened on December 1, 1954 in the new playhouse which became the Weldin Talley Memorial Playhouse.

The international Film Series was introduced in 1954, the first Beaux Arts Ball was held in 1958 and the First Nighters were organized in 1965.

A scene from the 1977 production of "My Three Angels" appears here. *Community Theater collection*

Children's Theater

A dozen women, meeting at the home of Mrs. Oscar Baur in 1936, established the Children's Theater of Terre Haute. The women of the community have kept it an active organization to help children develop dramatic talent and an appreciation of theater. Pictured here is the cast from the 1957 production of "Aladdin." *Children's Theater collection*

The Indiana Theater

Peacocks, the mascots of Paramount Pictures, were the theme of the grand opening of the Indiana Theater on Saturday, January 28, 1922. . . T. W. Barhydt, builder and owner of the new theater on the corner of Seventh and Ohio streets, declared that the new enterprise would move Terre Haute away from being a one-street town . . referring to Wabash Avenue.
—Susie Dewey, 1992

Theater architect John Eberson had designed this movie palace in the 17th century Spanish baroque style, elegant from its marble terrazzo floors in the rotunda to the heavily ornamented ceiling in the auditorium. He wrote: *. . . Into this Indiana Theater I have put my very best efforts and endeavors . . . it is daring, but I am content to be judged by the finished structure. The best requirements for the "land of make-believe" with full comfort, refined beauty, and happy surroundings . . .*

Movie-goers had a choice of three downtown theaters in 1955, the year of this photograph. They were the Grand, the Indiana and the Liberty. At one time there had been many more with names such as American, Crescent, Fountain, Orpheum, Hippodrome, Princess and Savoy. Purchased and restored by William J. and Reta Decker in 1990, the Indiana Theater is the only theater now located in downtown Terre Haute. *Martin photo*

"Cooking Schools" brought crowds to the Indiana Theater until the early 1970s. The persons appearing here in the 1950s were stopping for a Coca-Cola before going to their seats.

Dance Bands

Dances played an important part in the entertainment world of Terre Haute. They have been held in fraternal and church social halls, school gymnasiums, at the Mayflower Room of the Terre Haute House and Deming Hotel ballroom, on the "Reliance and Reliable" riverboats and at halls specifically operated as "dance halls." Among those in the city were the Tokyo, Winter Garden, Orpheum Ballroom, Rainbow Gardens, Summer Garden and the Trianon.

A benefit dance for the Union Hospital Completion Fund opened The Trianon at 2831 Wabash Avenue on December 20, 1923 with the Bud Cromwell Orchestra. Other local groups, such as those of Jack O'Grady, Ada Campbell, Cliff Lowe, Jim Riley, Leo Baxter and Warren Henderson also played there.

Leo Baxter directed this orchestra at the Tokyo ballroom operated by the Breinig Family. It has been said that Terre Haute's "400" danced at this elite, downtown ballroom.

During his more than 50-year career, Baxter gave many young musicians a start in the music world. One of these was Claude Thornhill, Garfield High School student, whose band became nationally known during the Big Band era.

CHAPTER 12

Leisure & Sports

Ken Hazledine and Jack Thornton, Jr. prepared for a camping trip in 1927.

" He that will make a good use of any part of his life must allow a large part of it to recreation "

John Locke

Early pioneers were occupied with survival and work, but as the nineteenth century drew to a close, people found themselves with more time available for leisure activities. By the 1920s the work week had become shorter, at least for city dwellers, and housework and cooking were made easier by electrical appliances and commercially prepared foods.

At the turn of the century, leisure activities included downtown street fairs, the county fair, horse racing at the Four-Cornered Track (now the site of Memorial Stadium), amusement parks (always conveniently located on the street car line) and traveling circuses. Buffalo Bill Cody's Wild West Show performed at the fairgrounds several times and the circus big top appeared at Twenty-fifth Street and Wabash Avenue as late as 1942. Excursions by railroad took families to larger cities for special events and celebrations.

Other activities were camping, hiking and recreational hunting and fishing. These led to the establishment of Indiana's unique state park system. Organized team sports also made their appearance. Baseball began in Terre Haute as early as 1867 and from 1884 to 1956 professional baseball was played here. Football, basketball and track took place at the high schools and colleges. The interest in golf led to the creation of country clubs in the 1890s. An early tennis club played on courts at First and Locust streets, but an adequate number of tennis courts was not available in the city until the 1970s. Swimming, archery, bowling and rifle and skeet shooting have all had a strong following at one time or another in Terre Haute.

For spectators and athletes alike, the 1970s was an outstanding decade in Terre Haute. Tommy John made his phenomenal comeback in baseball; two North Vigo teams won state championships; the South Vigo boys' basketball team (led by Coach Gordon Nehf) made three consecutive trips to the Final Four; the Indiana High School Athletic Association sanctioned girls sports; and soccer came to Terre Haute. The Vigo County Youth Soccer Association was formed in 1978 with 75 boys and girls participating; in 1922, the number of youngsters involved had grown to approximately 600.

In one year - 1979 - several Indiana State athletes earned national recognition. The men's basketball team was runner-up in the NCAA tournament; Kurt Thomas received the Sullivan Award as outstanding amateur athlete; Larry Bird was named College Player of the Year for the second time; and Wally Johnson was the NCAA batting champion.

As the twentieth century ends, auto racing at the Terre Haute Action Track has replaced horse racing at the Four-Cornered Track and the Zorah Shrine Circus now performs at Hulman Center. The Banks of the Wabash Festival, first held in 1974 and now called the Wabash Valley Festival at Fairbanks Park, takes the place of street fairs of a century ago. Professional baseball is no longer played in the city, but more players, particularly boys and girls, are involved in baseball and softball than ever before. Now, many fans watch organized sports on television rather than attending in person. Some leisure activities have changed; others have not.

Street Fairs

November 2, 1897: *The merchants are determined to get into a field early for a street fair here next season . . . it is proposed to raise $6,000 and the intention is to give the greatest street fair ever seen in this country.*

October 13, 1898: *The great fair is on. The carnival of fun opened today at noon amid the toot of whistle, the ring of bells and the melody of numerous bands.*
— Terre Haute Gazette

Wabash Avenue was alive with people for this six-day event filled with parades, exhibits, daily balloon ascensions and free stage shows. Two large arches were constructed on the street in honor of Admiral George Dewey, leader of the attack which destroyed the Spanish fleet in Manila Bay earlier in the year. *The Gazette* (reported there was) *grand illumination by 3,500 electric lamps and powerful searchlights of the triumphal Manila and Santiago arches every night.*

October 10, 1899: *Street Fair is on . . the second annual celebration promised to eclipse the effort of last year. Bright and early Monday morning the ever faithful Ringgold Band paraded the streets and proclaimed to all that the reign of fun had begun.* — Terre Haute Express

Amusement Parks

Riverside Park

Innes' Orchestral Band
LAKE VIEW PARK, Terre Haute, Ind.
Sunday, June 3rd, 1906.

LAKE VIEW PARK---Beginning TUESDAY, JUNE 5th,
"LODGE WEEK"
DEVOTED TO UNIFORM RANK ORDERS.

Tuesday	Y. M. I. Night	Friday	Odd Fellows Night
Wednesday	K. of P. Night	Saturday	Company B., I. N. G. Night
Thursday	Woodmans' Night	FREE Exhibition Drills Each Night	

EXTRA ——— SPECIAL ENGAGEMENT ——— EXTRA
Anderson Boys Military Band
Afternoon and Evening Concerts.
Sensational Wall Scaling Exhibit
High-Class Vaudeville.
10 CENTS—GENERAL PARK ADMISSION—10 CENTS

Lake View Park

Harrison Park Casino, located just north of Collett Park, was a popular spot in the 1890s to enjoy vaudeville shows, stage plays and band concerts.

George C. Fischer, in his "Reminiscences of Old Terre Haute," described Lake View Park as *a big time amusement park located . . . about Twenty-ninth and Wabash Avenue . . . (with) a very high Rolley Coaster, Merry-Go-Rounds, a Dance Hall (and) an artificial lake.*

Riverside Park, also pictured here and in operation during the early 1900s, was *the headquarters for boatmen, pearl hunters, fishermen and pleasure seekers on the banks of the Wabash just over the Vigo County bridge.* Operated by Charles Denning and Frank Clark, the park offered gardens, amusement parlors, a zoo and a daily concert given by the largest phonograph made by the Columbia Phonograph Company. *both photos Terre Haute Parks and Recreation Department collection*

Terre Haute Sesquicentennial Celebration 1816-1966

Our Terre Haute Area Sesquicentennial Celebration is the result of the work of hundreds of persons working individually or as members of organizations in this tremendous, cooperative community-wide project . . . If the week serves to increase the community pride and the awareness of our heritage and the resulting responsibilities, and if the fun and fellowship bring us closer to our friends and others, the staff and committee will be highly pleased and well rewarded. Howard E. Potter, President, Terre Haute Heritage, Inc.

Meis Bros., Inc. president Salo J. Levite, Vice-president Lucien H. Meis, Jr., and employees observed the Sesquicentennial at their 624-634 Wabash Avenue store. The building was the site of the downtown Meis store until 1983.

The celebration included "special days" recognizing various groups in the city, a headquarters office at 666 Wabash Avenue, and a magnificent pageant at Memorial Stadium. Written by Joseph T. Newlin, the production included hundreds of local residents in the cast.

Dorothy J. Clark, then curator of the Historical Museum of the Wabash Valley, is shown here (upper right) in August, 1967, accepting the Sesquicentennial scrapbooks for a permanent record of the celebration.

Horses and Bicycles

A charter member of the Old Cycling Club of Terre Haute organized in 1884, J. Fred Probst, shown here two years later, described the bicycle as "a very effective formula for the cure of many human ills." These "unstable, uncomfortable and dangerous" high wheelers were soon replaced by the familiar "safety" models. Bicycling was one of the earliest recreational activities available to women; however by 1910, enthusiasts were beginning to switch to automobiles.

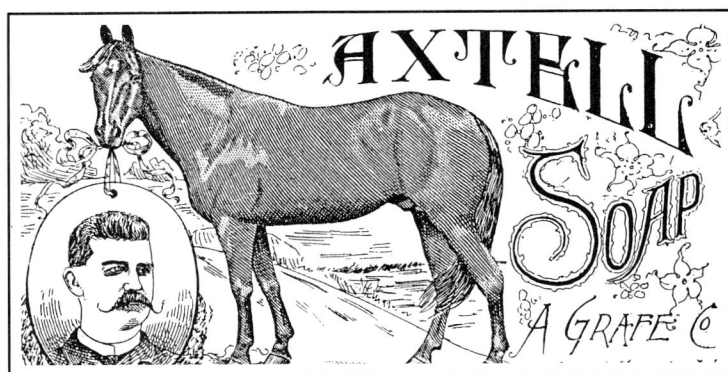

The A. Grafe Company, 34 North Sixth Street, manufactures the Axtell Soap, which appropriately to its name, is rapidly gaining ground among the users of laundry soap. Industrial America, 1892

Informal running and trotting tracks had been allotted in Terre Haute for many years before the first permanent trotting park was built on the Corbin Farm . . . in 1851.

W. R. McKeen . . . finally offered to the agricultural society 54 acres of land on which Terre Haute's famous "four cornered track" was to be laid in 1886 . . . the "square" which made the Terre Haute track world famous was the (one) on which Nancy Hanks, Axtell, Axworthy, General Watts and scores of other matchless animals were to make harness history. Axtell set a Terre Haute record for 3-year-olds, 2:12, in 1889. It is significant . . . that the Memorial Stadium . . . should stand on the spot where the city's first fame was won with the old race track. Neil Hines, Sports Editor, Terre Haute Star in The Wabash Valley Remembers, 1938

The Terre Haute Action Track at the Vigo County Fairgrounds south of the city opened in 1952 for sprint car (shown here) and stock car racing. The first Tony Hulman Classic was held in 1971 bringing 8,000 spectators, several celebrities and national television coverage to Terre Haute. In 1972 the Terre Haute Action Dragway opened adjacent to the dirt track. *Donald E. Smith collection*

Raymond Brown (1907-1982) rolled a 742 series in the American Bowling Congress tournament in Detroit in 1940 to become the national singles bowling champion. Brown first managed Jensen Bowling Alley starting in 1938, then Vigo Bowl, the oldest bowling alley in the city, until his retirement in 1969. A nephew of local baseball legend Mordecai Brown, he also played semi-professional baseball a number of years. *Sharon Milam collection*

The 1948 Soap Box Derby, an annual event during the late 1940s and early 1950s, took place on U.S. 40 east of the city. Co-sponsored by Downtown Chevrolet Sales, Inc. and the Tribune-Star Publishing Company, the event attracted 4,000 spectators to watch contestants in 24 races. George Compton, Garfield High School sophomore, won first place. *Lucille Miller collection*

Swimming, Golf and Tennis

Elvera Cullen Yontz collection

The slide at Fairbanks Park in the 1930s appears tame compared to the Deming Dipper now in use at Deming Park.

Recreational and competitive swimmers in Terre Haute use pools at the local high schools, the country clubs, the YMCA, YWCA and Voorhees, Deming and Sheridan parks.

Tribune-Star Publishing Company photo

Organized primarily for the playing of golf in 1898, the Country Club of Terre Haute was first located east of the city on property purchased from the Jenckes family. A nine-hole golf course and clubhouse, shown here in 1915, were constructed on the grounds. The club moved south to Allendale in 1918 and the Phoenix Club purchased the eastside facilities.

The Terre Haute Golf Association and Terre Haute Women's Golf Association sponsor adult tournaments annually at the public courses. Gene Verostko and Mary Alice Garmong hold records for most championships in the city tournaments.

Randy Ross taught tennis to youngsters in the early 1970s as part of the summer recreation program of the Terre Haute Parks and Recreation Department. The Rea Park Tennis Club (later the Terre Haute Tennis Club) was organized in 1951 to promote tennis as a lifelong sport and to sponsor tournaments for all ages. *Terre Haute Parks and Recreation Department collection*

Two Terre Haute Champions

Gregory C. Bell (1930-   ) won the gold medal in the long jump at the 1956 Olympic Games in Melbourne, Australia with a leap of 25 feet 8 and one-quarter inches and was No. 1 in world rankings 1956 through 1958. A graduate of Garfield High School and Indiana University School of Dentistry, Bell was named to the National Track and Field Hall of Fame in 1988.

Terre Haute's future track Olympians train with the Terre Haute Track Club organized by Pete Jones in 1965 as the Hyte Center Track Club. Several members have become Junior Olympic Champions and have earned athletic scholarships to colleges throughout the country. *Vigo County Public Library collection*

Terre Haute native Charles "Bud" Taylor (1903-1962) began his boxing career in 1920 at the Knights of Columbus Hall at Ninth and Ohio streets. He won the National Boxing Association bantamweight championship in 1927 though he often competed in other classes. He retired from competition in 1931 to become a boxing manager and promoter.

Boxing was popular in Terre Haute from the 1930s through the 1950s; large crowds attended the Golden Gloves tournaments for local amateur boxers sponsored by the Tribune-Star Publishing Company.

Two ISU Champions

Kurt Thomas (1956-   ), the first American gymnast in 46 years to win a gold medal at the World Championships in 1978, returned in 1979 to win two more gold and two silver medals. A victim of the United States' boycott of the 1980 Olympic Games in Moscow, the Indiana State University graduate is known for innovative and imaginative routines, particularly his "Thomas Flair" on the pommel horse. *1976 Sycamore yearbook photo*

In 1984, Bruce Baumgartner (1961-   ) became the first Indiana State University graduate to win a gold medal in the Olympic Games. The first United States wrestler to win three Olympic medals, Baumgartner won the silver in 1988 and again won the gold in 1992. *ISU Sports Information Office photo*

Football

Fans were treated to exciting and often unpredictable games at Memorial Stadium in the crosstown rivalry series between Wiley, Gerstmeyer, Garfield and later, Schulte. The annual Football Jamboree originated in 1953 and is still held at the Stadium; now the intense rivalries are between South, North and West Vigo with each school having its own football field.

The Vigo County Youth Football League was organized in 1969 to teach youngsters the basics of the sport. In 1992, 670 boys on 26 teams participated in the program.

Paul Moss (1909-), a graduate of Gerstmeyer High School, enjoyed an outstanding high school career in all sports, was All-American and All-Big Ten in football at Purdue, and played professional ball two years. Other Terre Haute men who have played or are playing in the National Football League include Paul Humphrey (Garfield), Jerry Sturm (Gerstmeyer), Craig Shaffer (Schulte), Anthony and Ernest Thompson (North Vigo) and Tony McGee and Mark Jackson (South Vigo).

Schulte defeated Gerstmeyer 26-7 in an exciting game at the Stadium in 1957. In 1960 Schulte became the first local school to have its own football field when Beech-Var Stadium opened on the school grounds. Named for Coach Pete Varda and Father Joseph Beechem, principal of the school, the field was made possible through the efforts of the Schulte Boosters Club.

Built in 1924 primarily for baseball, Memorial Stadium on East Wabash Avenue was also the site of home games for local high schools until 1971. Leased to Indiana State University in 1966, the football field became the first university operated outdoor facility in the world to be covered with AstroTurf in 1967. Total renovation was completed in 1970; of the original stadium, only the memorial Arch remains

The Indiana State Teachers College gymnasium at North Seventh and Eagle streets was packed the night Garfield High School defeated Bridgeport, Illinois in the final game of the 1945 Wabash Valley Tournament. The tournament was held annually from 1916 to 1972 and attracted teams from southwestern Indiana and southeastern Illinois. At one time, it was the largest non-state high school tournament in the country. Over the years, more than 120 different high schools participated in the final round of sixteen teams.

Basketball

Basketball first appeared in Indiana in 1892 and was played primarily at YMCAs and high schools. The establishment of a state tournament in 1911 which did not classify schools by size but provided competition between all entrants with one champion emerging has helped make basketball the most popular team sport in the state.

The 1953 Gerstmeyer Black Cats proudly display their state runner-up trophy at a parade in their honor. The team lost to South Bend Central in a game that has become a matter of "what if" speculation each year at tournament time. What if the official scorekeeper had not erroneously charged a fifth foul to Arley Andrews (the team's best shooter) instead of to his twin brother Harley? *both photos Vigo County Public Library collection*

Three Coaches

Duane Klueh (1926-), a graduate of State High School and Indiana State Teachers College, was Indiana State's first All-American, beginning his college career under Coach John Wooden during Wooden's two years at ISTC. The 1947-48 team was runner-up in the National Association of Intercollegiate Basketball tournament and Klueh was named most valuable player. He played professional ball two years and later returned to Indiana State to teach physical education, coach men's and women's tennis, and men's basketball. He was named Indiana Collegiate Conference Coach of the Year four times in basketball. Klueh retired in 1989 but continues to be active in tennis and has won several seniors tennis championships. In 1993 he was ranked among the top five tennis players over age 65 in the nation. *Indiana State University Archives collection*

Willard Kehrt (1912-), a graduate of Indiana University where he played basketball and baseball, came to Terre Haute in 1938 to coach and teach at Garfield High School. He took the 1947 and 1963 Garfield basketball teams to the state finals. The 1947 team was the first in state history to reach the final game undefeated; however, they lost to Shelbyville. While at Garfield, Kehrt coached Olympic gold medal winners Clyde Lovellette, Terry Dischinger and Greg Bell. He retired from coaching in 1964 to become assistant principal at Garfield and later South Vigo high schools. His career record is 450 wins-203 losses; Coach Kehrt was inducted into the Indiana Basketball Hall of Fame in 1973; he retired in 1979. *Willard Kehrt collection*

Howard Sharpe (1916-) holds the record for coaching victories in Indiana high school basketball; his 735th win in 1987 broke the long standing record of Marion Crawley. In Vigo County, he coached and taught at Honey Creek, Gerstmeyer and North Vigo high schools. Sharpe considers Gerstmeyer standout Bob Leonard to be the best player he ever coached. Leonard was a member of the 1953 NCAA championship team at Indiana University (along with Wiley's Dick White). Later, he was a player and coach in the Nationall Basketball Association, then coach and genreal manager of the Indinan Pacers. Coach Sharpe was inducted into the Indiana High School Basketball Hall of Fame in 1971 and named National High School Basketball Coach of the Year in 1975; he retired in 1987.

Three Olympians

Terre Haute's first Olympic gold medal winner, Clyde Lovellette (1929-   ) was the first basketball player to play on NCAA (1952), Olympic (1952) and National Basketball Association championship teams. A member of the 1947 Garfield High School State runner-up team, Lovellette was also a two-time All-American at the University of Kansas. During his 11-year professional career he played on three NBA championship teams (Minneapolis Lakers, 1954; Boston Celtics, 1963, 1964). Lovellette retired from the Celtics in 1965 and was elected to the Basketball Hall of Fame in 1988; he is director of the vocational educational program at White's Institute in Wabash, Indiana. *Willard Kehrt collection*

When Larry Bird (1956-   ) retired from professional basketball in 1992, *Tribune-Star* editor David Cox wrote: *No one individual has left such a prominent mark on this city as Larry Bird . . . he left an impression that will linger forever . . .* Three years with the ISU Sycamores, 13 seasons with the Boston Celtics, capped with a gold medal in the 1992 Olympic Games in Barcelona earned Bird award after award as he set numerous records. He also created excitement, pride and a loyal following among the people of Terre Haute as never before. His unselfish decision to stay at Indiana State to play his senior year, his student teaching at West Vigo and his support of the Terre Haute Boys Club are remembered along with his outstanding athletic achievements. *ISU Archives collection*

Terry Dischinger (1940-   ) was an Indiana High School All-Star, the first two-time winner of the McMillan Award for outstanding Vigo County athlete, high school letterman in four sports and a member of the 1955 Terre Haute Babe Ruth World Championship baseball team. He was also valedictorian of the Garfield High School class of 1958. He attended Purdue University on an academic scholarship. While at Purdue Dischinger was a member of the United States Olympic basketball team which won a gold medal in the 1960 Olympic Games in Rome. After a nine-year professional career in the NBA, he retired and became an orthodontist in Lake Oswego, Oregon. *Willard Kehrt collection*

IHSAA Honors

The Indiana High School Athletic Association was organized in 1903 to regulate competition and keep official records. In addition to team championships, a mental attitude award is given to senior participants in each sport at the finals tournaments and meets. Recipients must excel in attitude, scholarship, leadership and athletic ability. Several Vigo County athletes have received these awards.

Norman Cottom, Wiley High School All-American at Purdue, 1935

Mental Attitude Award Winners
1930-31-**Norman Cottom**-Wiley-boys basketball; 1946-47-**Ronald Bland**-Garfield-boys basketball; 1952-53-**Harley Andrews**-Gerstmeyer-boys basketball; 1962-63-**Gregory Samuels**-Garfield-boys basketball; 1972-73-**Stephen Cass**-South Vigo-golf; 1973-74-**Curtis Phillips**-North Vigo-boys baseball; 1974-75-**Mary Ann Shouse**-North Vigo-girls tennis; 1975-76-**Ben Schoffmann**-West Vigo-boys cross country; 1977-78-**Mara Hagen**-South Vigo-girls swimming; 1978-79-**Malcolm Cameron**-South Vigo-boys basketball; 1985-86-**Lisa Ridenour**-West Vigo-girls track

IHSAA Team State Champions
Only two teams from Vigo County have won state championships, both from North Vigo.
1972-73 - Boys Cross Country Team - North Vigo
1973-74 - Boys Baseball - North Vigo

Although a Terre Haute team has never won the state basketball championship, several have come close and local fans remember in detail when their favorite team "went to the Finals." (Prior to 1936, 16 teams went to the final round.)

1920 State High lost to eventual champion Franklin 30-8 in the first game.
1922 Garfield runner-up to Franklin 26-15.
1924 Wiley won two games, but was eliminated before the final game.
1931 Wiley again won two games, but was eliminated before the final game.
1947 Garfield runner-up to Shelbyville 68-58.
1953 Gerstmeyer runner-up to South Bend Central 42-41.
1954 Gerstmeyer lost to eventual champion Milan.
1956 Gerstmeyer defeated by Oscar Robertson and Crispus Attucks.
1957 Gerstmeyer again lost to Crispus Attucks.
1963 Garfield lost to South Bend Central 72-45
1977 South Vigo lost to East Chicago Washington.
1978 South Vigo runner-up to Muncie Central in overtime.
1979 South Vigo again lost to Muncie Central.
1991 South Vigo defeated by Indianapolis Brebeuf 52-39.

1953-54 Robert Holler-Garfield High School – boys golf-individual medalist
Willard Kehrt collection

Mara Hagen, Terre Haute South Vigo High School

Professional Baseball

Many major league baseball players have ties to Terre Haute. Terre Haute native Max Carey (1890-1976), inducted into the Baseball Hall of Fame in 1961, enjoyed a 20-year career as an outfielder for the Pittsburgh Pirates and Brooklyn Dodgers. He batted .458 in the 1925 World Series. Others include pitchers Cecil Ferguson, who played six years in the National League; Art Nehf, a Wiley and Rose Poly graduate who played from 1915-1929; Gerstmeyer's Bill Butland whose career was cut short by World War II; Vic Aldridge, elected state senator from Vigo County after leaving baseball; Harry Taylor, who still lives in Vigo County, played six years; and Dizzy Trout, who appeared in two World Series during his 15-year career. In 1993, North Vigo and Indiana State graduate Brian Dorsett was called up from the minor leagues to catch for the Cincinnati Reds (his fifth major league team since 1987).

A childhood injury to his right hand gave pitcher Mordecai "Three-Fingered" Brown (1876-1948) his nickname and a vicious curve ball. Brown's 14-year major league career (1903-1916) includes four World Series appearances for the Chicago Cubs; his career record is 239 wins, 131 losses. Born in Parke County, Brown began his career in 1901 with the Terre Haute Hottentots and returned to Terre Haute after leaving baseball to operate a service station at North Seventh and Cherry streets. He was inducted into the Baseball Hall of Fame in 1949.

Tommy John, Jr. (1943-   ) played Little League, Babe Ruth and American Legion baseball in Terre Haute and both baseball and basketball at Gerstmeyer High School. During John's remarkable 26-year (1963-1989) major league pitching career, he earned a lifetime won-loss record of 288-231. An injury threatened his career in 1974; however, reconstructive surgery on his left elbow enabled him to come back to win 20, 21, and 22 games in 1977, 1979 and 1980. *Thomas John, Sr. collection*

In 1901, 1902 and 1919 to 1956, except for a few years during the Great Depression and World War II, Terre Haute had a team in the Three-I (Indiana-Illinois-Iowa) League.

The 1950 Terre Haute Phillies pictured here won the league championship and post-season playoffs. *Terre Haute Parks and Recreation Department collection*

The traditional fire engine ride down Wabash Avenue was given to Terre Haute's World Champion Babe Ruth Team in August, 1955. Mayor Ralph Tucker and Coaches Glenn Staggs and Donas Dischinger are on the running board as team members wave to the cheering crowd gathered to welcome Terre Haute's first and, so far, only world champion baseball team. *Martin Photo*

Youth Baseball and Softball

The summer months in Terre Haute are filled with baseball and both fast and slow pitch softball games with players of all ages. Church, industrial, amateur, semi-professional and numerous youth leagues provide recreational opportunities for thousands of players ranging from T-ball for age six and under to the men's senior league for players over age 30.

Mayor Ralph Tucker gave the key to the city to Manager Wayne Myers and the Terre Haute American All-Stars in August, 1961, ten years after Little League was organized in Terre Haute. The first Little League team from Terre Haute to win a state championship, the Americans also participated in the Little League World Series, where they finished in fifth place. Just the week before, the Terre Haute Babe Ruth All-Stars had also won a state championship. *Wayne Myers Collection*

This young pitcher was participating in a Miss Softball America game in 1978. MSA was organized in Terre Haute in 1972; Jack Jones donated land for a playing field south of the city in 1978. In 1985, both the Senior and Major divisions won national championships at the tournament in Portage, Michigan. Ed Conley, enthusiastic local backer of the program, became the Indiana commissioner for Miss Softball America.

The Wabash Valley Girls Softball League was organized in 1989; their playing field at Eighteenth and Delaware streets was dedicated in 1993. Both leagues are members of the Amateur Softball Association. *The Spectator photo*

The future of the city is with its youth.

Treasure hunt at Charles T. Hyte Center, 1989. *Tribune-Star Publishing Co. photo*

Basketball in the snow, 1989. *Tribune-Star Publishing Company photo*

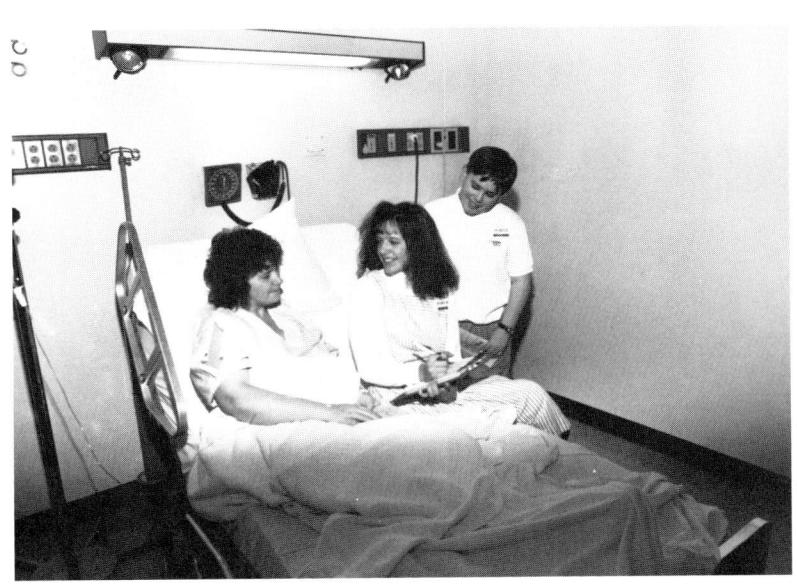

Volunteens at Union Hospital, 1993. *Union Hospital collection*

Cruisin' the 'Bash, 1989. *Tribune-Star Publishing Company photo*

Acknowledgements

The authors thank the Terre Haute First National Bank and the Vigo County Historical Society for their support of this pictorial history book and William Pickett, consulting historian, for his expertise and time given to this project.

The rich history of the Terre Haute area could easily fill the multiple volumes of an encyclopedia; but working within the limits of a 200-page pictorial book, we had to omit many individuals, groups and places. Rather we have attempted to capture some of the city's triumphs, tragedies and everyday living in the history of the city with the hope that a pictorial history of all Vigo County will follow at a later time.

The files of the Vigo County Historical Society were our major source of photographs; others came from the Vigo County Public Library Archives and the collections of individuals and organizations. These are identified as part of the accompanying captions. We are grateful to the many contributors for sharing their photographs and information for this sampling of Terre Haute history. We regret we could not use all photographs loaned for the project.

We also acknowledge the personal assistance of David Buchanan and Barbara Carney of the Vigo County Historical Society; Betty Martin, Clarence Brink, Susan Dehler, Nancy Sherrill, David Lewis and Mary-Margaret Iacoli of the Vigo County Public Library; Kenneth W. Martin, photographer; D. Omer Seamon, artist; Patti Krapesh of the Tribune-Star Publishing Company; B. Michael McCormick, our sports history consultant and Brad Baraks, the publisher.

And, finally, we thank our husbands, Bill Jerse and Pat Calvert, for their patience and sustained support.

Contributors

A P & S Clinic, Inc.; Mary Abrell; Sharon Akers; Dorisann Albright; Marilyn Allen; Frank Anshutz; James Boyer; Dorothy Braunschweiger Bilyeu; Norma and Marvin Bucy; Barbara Carney; Catholic Charities of Terre Haute; Centenary United Methodist Church; Tom Champion; Children's Theater of Terre Haute; Helen and Jim Clayton; Frank Day; Doris Dicus; R. Michael Dinkel; Ralph C. Dinkel; Michael Dowell; Logan Edwards; Peter and P. J. Ekstrom; Eugene V. Debs Foundation; William and Jean Farr; Robert Fiess; Glas-Col Apparatus, Inc.; Hamilton Center, Inc.; Andre Hammonds; Artie Harbaugh; Helen Harbaugh; Mary Harvey; J. K. Havener; Kenneth and Jane Hazledine; Shirley Hendricks; Historic Landmarks Foundation of Indiana-Western Regional Office; Clarence Hood; Indiana State University Archives; Indiana State University Sports Information Office; Indiana Vocational Technical College; Thomas John, Sr.; Robert E. Johnson, Sr.; Coyt Jones; Bruce Kasameyer; Willard Kehrt; Rochelle Kemp; Earl Kickler; Frank Kleptz; Jane King; Charles J. Kintz; Roxine Koenig; Thelma Lamb; Anne Temple Lambert; Larry Bird's Boston Connection; Sally Lowery; Wesley J. Lyda; C. Frank Martin; Kenneth W. Martin; Office of the Mayor; Glen and Hilde McHenry; Mental Health Association in Vigo County; Sharon Milam; Lucille Miller; Marilyn Miller; Max Miller; Helen E. Moore; Eugene V. Muench; Wayne Myers; Fred J. Nation; Leon Pitts; Helen Hanley Pollara; Reuben H. Donnelley; Rose Southside Child Care and Development Center; Rose-Hulman Institute of Technology; Rosetta Rardin; St. George Orthodox Church; Saint Mary-of-theWoods College; Jeffrey Schrink; Gladys Scruggs; John D. Sell; Sheldon Swope Art Museum; Donald Smith; Mary Frances Smith; Terre Haute Boys Club; Terre Haute Chamber of Commerce; Terre Haute Convention and Tourism Bureau; Terre Haute Day Nursery; Terre Haute Lions Club; Terre Haute Parks and Recreation Department; Terre Haute Police Department; Terre Haute Regional Hospital; Terre Haute YWCA; Terry Tevlin; Mildred Thurmond; Tribune-Star Publishing Company; Richard Unger; Union Hospital; United Child Care Center; United States Penitentiary—Terre Haute; United Way of the Wabash Valley; John Valle; Veterans Assistance Bureau; Vigo County Historical Society; Vigo County Park and Recreation Department; Vigo County Public Library; Vigo County School Corporation; WBOW Radio; Wabash Senior Citizens Center; Wabash Valley Broadcasting Company; Wabash Valley Goodwill Industries; Washington Avenue Presbyterian Church; Weston Paper & Manufacturing Company; Joe Wilkinson; Elvera Cullen Yontz; Karl and Allane Zucker

Bibliography

Allison, Harold. *The Tragic Saga of Indiana Indians.* Paducah, KY: Turner Pubg. Co., 1986.

"An Album of Early Terre Haute Street Cars." Central Electric Railfans Association, Bulletin 61, May, 1945.

Art Work of Terre Haute, Indiana. Chicago: Gravure Illustration Co., 1907.

Bailey, Gary L. *Losing Ground: Workers and Community in Terre Haute, Indiana, 1875-1935.* Ann Arbor, MI: UMI Dissertation Service, 1990.

Beckwith, H. W. *History of Vigo and Parke Counties.* Chicago: H.H. Hill and N. Iddings, 1880.

Biel, John G., Dorothy Clark, John K. Lamb. "Commemorative Book of Terre Haute, 1816-1966." Terre Haute: Moore-Langen Printing and Publishing Co., 1966.

Bradsby, H. C. *History of Vigo County, Indiana.* Chicago: S.B. Nelson, 1891.

Buntain, Rex. "Hometown Heroes." *Wabash Valley Magazine.* Feb/Mar, 1993, p. 13-46.

Burns, Lee. "The National Road in Indiana." reprinted from Vol. 7, No. 4, Indiana Historical Society. Public Library of Fort Wayne and Allen County, 1955.

Bush, Ned A. and John G. Biel. *Chronological History of Terre Haute and Vigo County, 1800-1974.* Terre Haute: Banks of the Wabash Festival Association, 1974.

Champion, Thomas E. *Terre Haute Fire Department, Terre Haute, Indiana, 1855-1975.* Shawnee Mission, KS: InterCollegiate Press, 1975.

Clark, Dorothy. "Revolutionary War Soldiers of Vigo County, Indiana." rev. ed., Terre Haute: 1981.

Clark, Dorothy J. *Historically Speaking.* Evansville, IN: Whippoorwill Pubns., 1981.

Clark, Dorothy J. *Terre Haute: Wabash River City.* Woodland Hills, CA: Windsor Pubns., 1983.

Combs, Charles N. *The History of Medicine in Vigo County, Indiana, 1818-1951.* Terre Haute: 1951.

Condit, Blackford. *The History of Early Terre Haute from 1816 to 1840.* NY: A.S. Barnes, 1900.

Cronin, William F., ed. *An Account of Vigo County from its Organization.* Vol. III in *History of Indiana* by Logan Esarey. Dayton, OH: Dayton Historical Pubg., 1922.

Eberson, John. "The Indiana Theatre, Our Achievement." opening night presentation folder, 1922.

Fatout, Paul. *The Canals of Indiana.* West Lafayette, IN: Purdue University Studies, 1972.

Fischer, George C. "Reminiscences of Old Terre Haute." Given before the Optimist Club of Terre Haute, Feb. 21, 1945.

Frye, O. B. "An Immigration Story—The Syrian Community in Terre Haute." unpublished manuscript, Special Collections, Cunningham Memorial Library, Indiana State University, 1991.

Furlong, Patrick J. *Indiana, An Illustrated History.* Northridge, CA: Windsor Pubns., 1985.

Gardon, F. J., compiler. *Twentieth Century Souvenir of Terre Haute Illustrated.* Terre Haute: Moore-Langen Prntg., 1903.

Harlow, Arvin C. *Old Towpaths.* Port Washington, NY: Kennikat Press, 1964.

Hassam, Loren. *A Historical Sketch of Terre Haute, Indiana, Its Advantages for Manufacture, and Attractions As a Home.* Terre Haute: L.M. Rose, 1873.

The Haute Magazine. Vol. 1, No. 1, Apr., 1904.

Hazledine, Jane Cunningham. *A History of the Community Theatre of Terre Haute, 1946-1991.* Terre Haute: 1991.

Historical Landmarks Foundation. *Vigo County Interim Report: Indiana Historic Sites & Structures Inventory.* Indianapolis: 1984

Historical Industrial Record of the Prairie City, 1823-1900. Terre Haute: Express Pubg. Co., 1900.

"Hoosiers Remember World War II: 50 Years Later." *Traces of Indiana and Midwestern History.* Fall, 1991.

Hoover, Dwight W. *A Pictorial History of Indiana.* Bloomington, IN: I.U. Press, 1980.

Hughes, Frances E. "History of the Terre Haute Day Nursery Association, 1888-1989." Terre Haute: Terre Haute Day Nursery Association, Inc., 1989.

Illustrated Industrial Souvenir of Greater Terre Haute. Louisville, KY: Natl. Pubg. Co., 1904.

Indiana High School Athletic Assn., Inc. *IHSAA 1991-92 Yearbook.* Indianapolis: IHSAA, 1992.

The Industrial Advantages of Terre Haute, Indiana. Terre Haute: Jas. P. McKinney, pubr., 1890.

Industrial America. Vol. I, No. 5. Chicago: Norton & Norton, 1892.

Jerse, Dorothy W.; Judith S. Calvert, Kenneth W. Martin, eds. *On the Banks of the Wabash: A Photograph Album of Greater Terre Haute, 1900-1950.* Bloomington, IN: I.U. Press, 1983.

Kent Avenue Women's Club. scrapbook, 1911-1961. Vigo County Historical Society archives.

Kubiak, William J. *Great Lakes Indians.* Grand Rapids, MI: Baker Book House, 1970.

Lingeman, Richard. *Theodore Dreiser at the Gates of the City.* NY: G.P. Putnam's, 1986.

Lyda, John W. *The Negro in the History of Indiana.* Terre Haute: 1953.

Lynch, William O. *A History of Indiana State Teachers College.* Indianapolis: Bookwalter, 1946.

Madison, James H. *Indiana Through Tradition and Change, 1920-1945.* Indianapolis: Indiana Historical Society, 1982.

Madison, James H. *The Indiana Way, A State History.* Indianapolis: Indiana Historical Society, 1986.

Markle, A. R. "Some Historic Schools Were Forerunners of Present System." *Terre Haute, Tribune,* May 2, 1948, p. 4.

Markle, A. R. "Early Buildings of Terre Haute." 4 Vols. unpublished, rev. by Dorothy Clark, 1965.

McCarty, C. Walter, ed.; A.C. Duddleston, assoc. ed. *Indiana Today.* n.p., Indiana Editors Assoc., 1942.

McCormick, Mike. "Glory Days." *Wabash Valley Magazine.* June/July, 1993, p. 30-38+.

McDonough, Irene Roberts. *History of the Public Library in Vigo County, 1816-1975.* Terre Haute: Vigo County Public Library, 1977.

Metheny, Nancy. "Terre Haute Indiana. The Faces. The Places." Terre Haute: Terre Haute Area Chamber of Commerce, 1986.

Oakey, C. C. *Greater Terre Haute and Vigo County.* 2 vols. Chicago: Lewis Pubg. Co., 1908.

Oakey, C. C. *Terre Haute Illustrated.* n.p.: H.R. Page, 1889.

Peddle, Juliet. "Types of Early Architecture Found in Terre Haute." *Terre Haute Tribune-Star,* Oct. 19, 1941, p. 16.

Phillips, Clifton J. *Indiana in Transition, 1880-1920.* Indianapolis: Indiana Historical Bureau, 1968.

Porter, David L., ed. *Biographical Dictionary of American Sports: Basketball and Other Indoor Sports.* NY: Greenwood Press, 1989.

Reichler, Joseph L., ed. *The Baseball Encyclopedia.* 6th ed. NY: MacMillan, 1985.

Rose Polytechnic Institute Memorial Volume. Cincinnati: Monfort & Co., 1909.

Roselli, Bruno. *Vigo: A Forgotten Builder of the American Republic.* Boston: Stratford Co., 1933.

Salvatore, Nick. *Eugene V. Debs: Citizen and Socialist.* Chicago: Univ. of Ill. Press, 1982.

Schlicher, John J. "Terre Haute in 1850." *Terre Haute Public Schools Bulletin No. 11,* 1917.

Taylor, Robert M., Jr. et al. *Indiana; a New Historical Guide.* Indianapolis: Indiana Historical Society, 1989.

Terre Haute Chamber of Commerce. "The Book of Terre Haute," Vol. 1, Nos. 2 (Sept., 1920); 5 (Dec., 1920); 7 (Feb., 1921); 8 (Mar., 1921).

Terre Haute Gazette. Art Souvenir of Terre Haute, Indiana, 1894. Terre Haute: Kelly Bros., 1894.

Terre Haute Northwest Territory Celebration Committee. *The Wabash Valley Remembers: 1787-1938.* Terre Haute: 1938.

Terre Haute Today. Terre Haute: J.A. Reid, Bookmaker, 1915.

Thomas, Bernice L. "Five and Dime Design." *Historic Preservation,* Jan/Feb., 1993, p. 62-70.

Thompson, Maurice. *Stories of Indiana.* NY: American Book Co., 1898.

Thornbrough, Gayle and Dorothy Riker, compilers. *Readings in Indiana History.* Indianapolis: Indiana Historical Bureau, 1956.

Vexler, Robert I. and William F. Swindler, eds. *Chronology and Documentary Handbook of the State of Indiana.* NY: Oceana Pubrs., 1978.

Wilkins, John E. "Recollections of an Old Terre Haute Fire Fighter." unpublished manuscript, Special Collections, Vigo County Public Library, 1910.

Wiley, William H. *Public School Education in Terre Haute, Indiana: One Hundred years of History.* Terre Haute: 1924.

Wood, Mary Elizabeth. *French Imprint on the Heart of America.* Evansville, IN: Unigraphics, 1976.

Writers' Program of the Works Progress Administration. *Indiana, A Guide to the Hoosier State.* NY: Oxford Univ. Press, 1941.

CITY DIRECTORIES: Directories for most years are bound and on microfilm at the Vigo County Public Library.

NEWSPAPERS: Terre Haute newspapers are on microfilm at the Vigo County Public Library.

Index

Abbott, Dr. Lyman 147
Abrell, Cpl. Charles Gene 61
Adams, Harry 83
Advocate 78
African-Americans 14, 112, 154
Afro-American Culture Center 28
agribusiness 77, 80-81
airplanes and airports 32, 33
Alden, Lyman P. 138
Alex TV & Appliance Sales & Service 124
Alexander, Dr. O. O. 131
Allen Chapel 45, 112
Allen Memorial Planetarium 161
Alliance for Growth and Progress 87
American Federation of Labor 64, 78
American Legion 58, 59, 62
American Revolution 8, 48
amusement parks 179
Anaconda Park 40
Anderson and Nichols law office 78
Andrews, Arley and Harley 187
Anshutz family 132
artists 167, 170
Asbury Chapel 146
Associated Physicians and Surgeons Clinic 131
authors 169
Axtell 182
Babe Ruth World Champions 188, 192-193
Baesler, Vera Diel 98
Baldwin, Harmon A. 149
Ball, Caroline Peddle 170
Ball, Spencer F. 43
Ball, Spencer F. 43
Ball, Susan 142
banking 94-95, 96
Banks, Mary Alice 143
Banks of the Wabash Association 46
Banks of the Wabash Chorus 123, 167
Banks of the Wabash Festival 177
Bannon, Dr. William G. 143
Barbazette and Sparks Cattle Feeders 80
barbers 98
Barhydt, Theodore 173, 175
Barnes, Dr. James 171
baseball 177, 191-194
BASF Corporation 75
basketball 177, 187-189, 190
Bauermeister, Charles W. Company 53
Baumgartner, Bruce 185
Baur, Mrs. Oscar 174
Baur, Sister Johanna M. 129
Baxter, Leo 176
Bayh family 76
Beach, Mary 142
Bear's Jack Frost 133
beauticians 98
Becker, Jacqueline 68
Becker's, David Peoples Pawn Shop 101
Beech-Var Stadium 186
Bell, Gregory C. 185, 188
Bement, Rea & Company 103, 152
Bemis Company 87
Benham, James R. 92
Best Theater 174
bicycling 182
Bidaman, Edwin 37, 63
Big Four Depot 28
Bird, Larry 126, 177, 189
Birney Safety Cars 29
Bledsoe, Walter A. 200
Blinn, John J. P. 48
Blumberg, Benjamin 54, 55, 132, 143, 169
Blumberg, Fannie Burgheim 169
BookNation 170
Borden's Pure Milk & Ice Cream Company 58
Bowers, Claude 169
Boy Scout Park 40
Boy Scouts 40, 58, 137, 142
Boyer, Earl, Jim, Jack 22
Boys Club 115, 137, 140
Boys' Vocational School 159
Braunschweiger, Martin 151
Brentlinger, Harry 13
Bricklayers Union Local #5, 78
bridges 19
Brighton, William 37, 69
Brittlebank Park 40
Bronson, David 133
Brown, Herman 32
Brown, Madame Edith 66
Brown, Mordecai 183, 191
Brown, Raymond 183
Brown's Business College 166
Bryant, Will H. 171

Bullitt, Cuthbert & Thomas 12
Bundles for Britain 58
Buntin's Hotel 20
Burnham, Daniel (architect) 30
buses 29, 31
business colleges 166
Calvary Cemetery 44
Camp Dick Thompson 49
Camp Krietenstein 142
Camp NaWaKwa 142
Camp Vigo 49
Camp Wildwood 142
Card, Joseph B. 85
Carey, Max 191
Carle, Elvira 68
Catholic Charities of Terre Haute 143
cemeteries 44
census, U.S. (figures) 14, 109, 110
Centenary Methodist Church 138
Centenary United Methodist Church 146
Central Catholic High School for Girls 157
Central Eastside Association 97
Central Labor Union 78
Central Presbyterian Church 146
Chadwick, Betty see Sullivan, Betty Chadwick
Chalos, P. Pete 35, 37, 93, 167
Chamber of Commerce 76
Champagne Velvet 53
Chappelle, Ralph 123
Charm Beauty Salon 98
Chauncey Rose Junior High School 159
Chauncey Rose School 134
Children's Learning Center 130
Children's Theater 174
Christian Science Church 147
Chunn, Major John T. 10
churches 110, 111, 112, 119, 122, 131, 145-148
Citizens for a Clean County 75
Citizens Trust Company 45, 96
city hall 36, 37, 47, 80
Civil War 48-49
Clabber Girl Baking Powder 88
Clark, Dorothy J. 168, 181
Clark, George Rogers 8, 13
Clark House 102
Clean-Your-Plate Campaign 58
Clear Creek Welcome Center 21
coal 7, 77, 79
Coates College 151
Coca-Cola bottle 86
Cochran, Landon 48
Cohen, M. D. & Son, Inc. 16
Collett, Josephus 40
Collett Park 40, 42, 45, 122, 123
Collett School 122
Colored Day Nursery 138
Columbia Records, Inc. 87
Columbian Enameling and Stamping Company 64
Combs, Dr. Charles N. 127, 131
Commercial Solvents Corporation 65, 126
Community Chest of Terre Haute 139
Community Theater 45, 167, 170, 174
Compton, George 183
Condit House 45
Condit, Rev. Blackford 9, 45
Confederate Soldiers Memorial 44
Conley, Ed 194
Constitutional amendments 47, 52-53
cooking schools 175
corruption 63, 66-67
Cottom, Norman 190
Coudert, Amalia Kussner 170
Country Club of Terre Haute 184
courthouse 13, 45
Cox, Claude 82
Cox, B. Guille, Jr. 200
Coy Park 41
Crawford, Dr. W. G. 131
Crawford, Mary Sinclair 151
Crawford School 151
Crittenton, Florence Home 135
Cromwell, Bud Orchestra 176
Cronin, William F. 92
Crossroads of America 15, 21
Crothers, Benjamin "Scatman" 167
Cruft, Charles 10, 48
Curtis Gilbert Park 41
dance bands 176
dance halls 176
dance schools 171
Danek, Dr. Victor 171
Davern, Lt. Joseph 39
Davis Gardens 81

day nurseries 138
Day, Vance 39
Debs, Eugene V. 7, 47, 51
Debs home 45, 51, 167
Decker, William J. and Reta 175
Dede Plaza 161
DeLane, John grocery 120-121
Deming Center 102
Deming, Demas 40, 94, 102, 165
Deming Hotel 102
Deming Land Company 41
Deming Park 40-41, 43, 140, 184
Dennis, J. W. Trucking Co. 46
dentistry 132
depots 28
depression, the - see Great Depression
DeVaney, Grace 160
Dewees-Preston-Smith house 14
Dickerson, Dr. George L. 23
Digital Audio Disc Corporation 87
dime stores 106
Dinkel, Captain Ralph 39
Dinkel, Thomas T. 200
Dischinger, Donas 192-193
Dischinger, Terry 188, 189
Dixie Bee Highway 21
Dobbs Memorial Park 41
Doxsee Food Corporation 81
Dreiser Square 126
Dreiser, Theodore 7, 19, 167, 168
Dresser Field 32
Dresser Park 42
Dresser, Paul 6, 42, 45, 19, 167, 168
Dressler, C. J. 28
Dubois, Tom 43
Duddleston, A. C. 34, 50
Dunbar, Arch 150
Dunbar School 154
Early, John D. 94
East Side Boosters Club 97
Eastern Motors Express, Inc. 83, 144
Eastside Businessman's Association 97
Eberson, John (architect) 175
Edgewood Grove 125
education 149-166
Edwards, William K. 36
Eglen Hovercraft 17
Ehrmann, Max 167, 169
Ehrmann Pork Packing Company 80
Elks Lodge No. 86, 10
Emeline Fairbanks Memorial Library 150
Ernestine Myers Dance School 171
Eugene V. Debs Foundation 51
Evans, Elmer 98
Evinger, Edward 78
Exchange Artesian Springs and Bath House 133
Fairbanks, Clara Home for Aged Women 135
Fairbanks, Crawford 42, 135, 150
Fairbanks, Henry 37, 42
Fairbanks Park 6, 17, 42, 43, 46, 60, 109, 141, 142, 168, 184
Farrington, James 94, 119
Farrington's Grove 45, 118-119
federal building 45, 46, 54
Ferguson, Marla J. 61
Fire Department 39, 58
fires 72-73, 74
First Baptist Church 127, 131
First Church of Christ, Scientist 147
First Congregational Church 45, 144, 147
First Financial Corporation 95, 200
First National Bank of Terre Haute 94
Fischer, Alfred L. 100
Fitch, Harry E. 32
Floating Palace 17
floods 70, 71
florists 81
Ford, Harvey W. 100
Fort Harrison 10, 11, 48, 145
Fort Harrison Country Club 10
Foulkes, John 99
Four-Cornered Track 177, 182
Fowler Park 11
Francis Vigo American-Italian Club 113
Frank Prox Company 79
Frank's Restaurant & Drive Inn 97
Franklin, Benjamin School 154
Frantz, Welby 83, 200
fraternal societies 114
Frey, Harry 93
Friend, Harold 47
Friendly Inn 130
Fuqua School 155

gambling raid 66
Garfield Gardens and Garfield Towers 123, 160
Garfield High School 123, 160, 161, 187, 189, 190
Garfield Theater 123
Garmong, Mary Alice 184
Garvin, Professor R. 166
gas companies 90
George, Mari Hulman 88, 89, 200
George, Tony 88, 200
Gerdink, Herbert R. 69
German immigrants 110
German Oberlandler Club 110
Gerstmeyer, Dr. Charles F. 159
Gerstmeyer High School 159, 161, 186, 187, 188, 190
Gibault School for Boys 137, 157
Gibson, Max 200
Gilbert, Curtis 11, 41, 94
Gillis Drug Store 103
Gillum, Dr. J. R. 131
Gilman, Ben Ives 80
Girl Scouts 56-57, 137, 142
Girls' Vocational School 159
Glas-Col Apparatus Company 85
golf 43, 177, 184, 190
Goodwill Industries 136-137
Gookins, James Farrington 167
Gookins, Judge Samuel Barnes 119
Gordon, Tyree 98
Gossom, James 37, 66
Grafe, A. Company 182
Graham Grain Company 81
Graham Park 42
Grand Opera House 173
Grand Theater 173
Grandview Cemetery 44
Gray, Richard 39
Gray, Samuel 125
Great Depression 47, 54
Great Northern Hotel 28
Grob, Rev. Theodore 137
grocery stores (neighborhood) 64, 124
Grover, Mary 44
Gulick, Flora 140
H.E.L.P. 68
Hagen, Mara 190
Hamilton Center 130
Hamilton, Katherine 127, 130
Hanley's, Charles Terre Haute Shoe Repair 101
Hanna, Kaleel 111
Hannaford, Samuel & Sons 13, 28
Harmony Hall 123
Harper, Ida Husted 52
Harrison Park 179
Harrison, William Henry 10, 48
Hart's Feed Store 80
Havens and Geddes 74
Hayworth, Reba and Ruth 50
Hazledine, Jane 68, 174
Hazledine, Ken 177
Hein, Edward Dairy 107
Hennecke, Keith A. 37
Herbert, Claude L. 74
Herz, Adolf 42, 76
Herz-Rose Park 42
Highland Lawn Cemetery 44, 45
Highway 40 - see U.S. Highway 40 & 41
Highway 41 - see U.S. Highway 40 & 41
Hippodrome Theater 45, 174, 175
Historical Museum of the Wabash Valley 6, 181
Holler, Robert 190
Home Packing and Ice Company 74, 80
Honey Creek Square (Mall) 7, 107, 166
Hoods Watch Shop 123
Hook Rehabilitation Center 129
Hook School 154, 158
Hotel Deming 102
hotels 102
House Trucking 83
Housewives Effort for Local Progress 68
hovercrafts 17
Howard, Edward N. 150
Hudson, Robert N. 119
Hulman & Company 88-89
Hulman & Cox 51
Hulman, Anton, Jr. 33, 42, 67, 88
Hulman, Anton, Sr. 88
Hulman, Antonia 128
Hulman Civic Center 167
Hulman, Francis 88
Hulman, Herman 76, 88, 165

Hulman, Herman, Sr. 44, 128, 154, 165
Hulman, Jacob 101
Hulman Links 42, 43
Hulman, Mary Fendrich 88, 128
Hulman Memorial Student Union 162
Hulman, Mrs. Anton, Sr. 33
Hulman Regional Airport 33, 61
Hulman School 154
Hungarian Hall 113
Hux Cancer Center 129
Hux Cardiovascular Center 129
Hyte, Charles T. Community Center 43, 112, 127, 195
IHSAA honors 190
Immanuel Lutheran Church 110, 147, 151
immigrants 109, 110, 111, 113
India Association 109
Indian Orchard cemetery 44
Indian Refining Company 121
Indiana Air National Guard 33
Indiana Bituminous Coal Operators' Association 79
Indiana Business College 166
Indiana Coal Trade Bureau 79
Indiana State College 45, 162, 163
Indiana State Normal School 7, 43, 158, 162, 167
Indiana State Teachers College 47, 162, 163, 187, 188
Indiana State University 5, 7, 126, 127, 162-163, 167, 170, 186
Indiana State University School of Nursing Clinical Education 129
Indiana Theater 175
Indiana Vocational Technical College 164
Indiana Wood Preserving Company 85
Interstate 70, 7, 21
interurbans 29, 30
Irish immigrants 18, 110
Irwin, Dr. Glenn 132
Jenckes, Ray and Grace 44
Jenckes, Virginia 47, 52
Jerry's Bakery 99
Jett, Dr. F. H. 131
Jewish people 111
Jobe, Thelma B. Stress Center 128
John, Tommy 177, 191
Johnson brothers 32
Johnston, Judge Harold R. 69
Jones, Harvey E. 38
Jones, Jack 194
Jones, Max E. 140
Jones, Pete 185
Julia Lambert WAVE platoon 55
Kadel, Robert 33
Kasameyer Glass, Inc. 23
Kehrt, Willard 188
Kennedy, John 39
Kent Avenue Women's Club 117
Kerman Grotto 114
Kesler & Kesler 4, 49,94
Kidder, Willard 77
King Classical School 151
King, J. D. drugstore 97
King, Lawrence 42
Kintz, Raymond Lumber Co. 46
Kivits Brothers 100
Klueh, Duane 188
Kolsem, Charles 55
Korean War 61
Kresge, S. S. Company 104, 106
Krietenstein, George 142
Ku Klux Klan 109
Kussner, Amalia see Coudert, Amalia Kussner
Labor Temple Association 78
Laboratory School 47, 163, 170
Ladies Aid Society 62, 127, 134
Lake View Park 179
Lamb, John K. Center 128
Lang, Hermann 98
Larrison, Leland 37, 66
Larry Bird's Boston Connection 126
Laska, John Joseph 167
Lasselle, Hyacinth 12
Lederer, Julius Liquor Store 53
Leonard, Bob 188
Levin Brothers 96
Levin, Sidney 143
Light House Mission 144
Lincoln School 112, 154
Lindley, Jonathan 12
Linton, David 14
Little League 194
Lockwood, Lewis 133
Lone Tree cemetery 44

Loudermilk, Gerald 75
Lovelace Truck Service 83
Lovellette, Clyde 188, 189
Lowery, Norman L. 200
Ludowici & Hulman 88
Magnetic Mineral Springs 133
Mahaney, Patsy Candy Shop 50
Malooley, Joe 40
manufacturing 7, 77, 84-89
Maple Avenue United Methodist Church 122
Markle, Abraham 12
Mars, William 36, 38
Martin, Ken 92
Martin, Steve 69
Marx, Joan 68
Masonic Temple 114
mayors 36-37
McDonagh, J. P. 78
McIntyre, Terry 91
McKeen, Riley 131
McKeen, S. C. 125
McKeen, W. R. 125, 182
McLaughlin, Ross 39
McLean Junior High School 155
McLean, William E. 48, 155
McMillan, Vernon R. 37, 65
Meadows Center 107
Meadows School 155
Medal of Honor 48, 61
media 92-93
Meis Bros., Inc 180-181
Memorial Hall 4, 45, 49, 94, 170
Memorial Park 42
Memorial Stadium 63, 79, 181, 182, 186
Merchants Distilling Corporation 86
Merchants National Bank 122
Methodist Temple 150
Mexican War 48
Meyer, Dr. Ramon 171
Miller and Yeager (architects) 37, 46
Miller-Parrott Baking Company 99, 144
Miner's Picnic 79
Minshall, Deloss W., Charles, Helen 130, 138
Miss Softball America 194
Mitchell, Dr. Albert M. 32
Model Milk & Ice Cream Company 22, 23
Monninger, A. R. 28
Moore, Ted 140
Morey, Glen H. and Ruth K. 85
Morgan, Major Willoughby 10
Morrissey, Ernestine Myers 171
Moss, Paul 186
Motor Freight Corporation 83
Motor Springs Service Company 100
mound builders 8
mussels 16
Myers, Major George 62
Myers, Wayne 194
N A A C P 112
National Council of Jewish Women 111
National Register of Historic Places 44, 45
National Road 15, 20, 21, 102
National Youth Administration 58
Native Americans 8, 9, 16
Naylor's Opera House 172
Neoteric-USA-Inc. 199
New York Central railroad 27, 28
Newcomers Club of Terre Haute 116
Newlin, Charles 96
Newport, Richard D. 139
newspapers 11, 92
Niemeyer, Maynard F. 83
Niemeyer, William 83, 200
Nitsche, R. F. 55
North Baltimore Glass Company 86
North, Glenn W. Construction Co. 46
North Vigo see Terre Haute North Vigo
Northwest Territory 8, 13, 149
Oakley Economy Stores 124
Oakley, H. N. 54, 124, 142
Oakley, Hollie and Anna Foundation 42
Oakley Park 42
Oakley Plaza 127
oil 79
O'Leary, Patrick 200
Olympic champions 185, 189
"On the Banks of the Wabash" 168
opera house 167, 172
Optimist Club 115
organized labor 78
Osborn, Grover C. 139
Osborn, J. W. 11, 14
Ouabache School 122

Overland Motor Car 82
overpasses 27
Owen, Judge DeWitt H. 113
Owen, O. Keith, Sr. 81
Owens-Illinois Glass Company 86
P S I Energy 91
P W A 135
Packard automobile 23
parks 40-43
parochial schools 157
Patterson, Herb 144
Paul Cox Field 32, 161
Payne, Robert L. 37
Peddle, Juliet A. 121
Pennsylvania Railroad shops 24-25, 27, 77
Persian Gulf War 61
Pfeifer, Paul E., Inc. 53
Pfister, Mrs. J. P. 60
Phillips, Walter 123
Phoenix Club 78, 111, 184
Phoenix oil well 79
Pierce Branch Nursery 138
Pierce, Dr. H. J. 131
pioneers 9, 11
Police Department 38, 58
pork packing 80
post office 11, 45, 46
"Prairie City" 34
Prairie House 102
Preston House 14
prison - see U.S. Penitentiary
private schools 151
Probst, J. Fred 182
Prohibition 7, 47, 77, 53
prostitution 66
Public Works Administration see P W A
Pugh, C. G. Bicycles 2
Quaker Maid Company 83, 84
radio 93
Ragle, John W. 200
railroads 7, 15, 24-28, 77
Ramsey, S. V. Veterinary Hospital 22
Rankin, Alan C. 66
Rea Park Golf Course 43
Rea Park Tennis Club 184
Rea School 122, 152-153
Rea, William S. 43, 152
Recipe Foods, Incorporated 81
Reely, Cleon R. 38
Reiman, Stella 118
Reinking, Edith 131
Religion in American Life award 69
Reuben H. Donnelley 126
Rhyan & Goodman funeral directors 97
Ridge, Jack 91
Riggs, E. A. "Gus" 32
Riley, James Whitcomb School 154
Ringgold Band 167, 178
Riverside Park 179
Roberts, Donn 37, 63
Romeo 16
Root, Chapman II 200
Root Glass Company 86
Root, William R. 32
Rose, Chauncey 7, 27, 42, 47, 94, 102, 127, 134, 165
Rose, Chauncey Memorial 46, 54
Rose Dispensary 127, 134
Rose Orphans Home 134, 138
Rose Polytechnic Institute 7, 41, 93, 134, 159, 165, 170
Rose Southside Day Care and Development Center 138
Rose-Hulman Institute of Technology 7, 165-166
Roselawn Memorial Park 44
Ross, Randy 184
rotogravure 92
Ryan, Peter J. 48
S.S. Terre Haute Victory 60
Sacopulos Johnson Carter and Sacopulos 170
Sacred Heart Catholic Church 113
Sacred Heart School 157
St. Agnes Academy 128
St. Andrew Roumanian Orthodox Church 113
St. Ann Catholic Church 113
St. Ann's School 157
St. Anthony Hospital 128
St. Benedict Catholic Church 110, 148
St. Benedict's School 157
St. George Orthodox Church 111
St. Joseph Academy 157
St. Joseph Catholic Church 110, 148
St. Joseph Cemetery 44

St. Joseph School 157
St. Margaret Mary's School 157
Saint Mary-of-the-Woods College 7, 156
St. Patrick Catholic Church 110
St. Patrick's School 157
St. Stephen's Episcopal Church 146
Salvation Army 54, 144
Sam's Popcorn Stand 123
Sarah Scott Junior High School 56-57
Saratoga Restaurant 94
Saturday Evening Post article (1944) 65 (1961) 63, 67, 69
Schaal, George 125
School Reorganization Act 149
schools 149-166
Schulte High School 157, 186
Schultz, Abraham 101
Scott, Malcolm 159
Scottish Rite 45
Scudder, Janet 170
Seamon, D. Omer 4
Seeburger, Edward 39
service clubs 115
Sesquicentennial Celebration 180-181
Shackelford, Jane Dabney 169
Sharpe, Howard 188
Sheldon Swope Art Museum 170
Sheridan Park 43
Shewmaker, Uriah 16
shopping centers 107
Simeon House I and II 143
Simms, J. T. 125
Simplicity Pattern Company 84
"Sin City" 47, 68, 69
Sisters of Providence 156
Sky King Airport 32
Smith, Donald E. 95, 200
Smith Hardware 101
Smith, J. J. 109
Smith, Ralph E. 137
Smith, Virginia L. 200
Smock, John B. 38
Soap Box Derby 183
soccer 177
Society for Organizing Charity 127, 130, 139
softball 194
Soldiers and Sailors Monument 49
Sony, U.S.A. 87
South Vigo see Terre Haute South Vigo
Southside Day Nursery 138
Spalding & Rodgers Circus Co. 17
Spanish-American War 49
Spectrum Industries 130
Spencer F. Ball Park 43
sports 182-194
Staggs, Glenn 192-193
Stahl-Urban Company 84
Standard Machine Company 82
Standard Malleable Castings Company 82
Standard Wheel Company 82
State Bank of Indiana 94
State High School 163, 190
steamboats 17
Steeg, Henry 37, 41
Stevenson, Thomas 39
Strawberry Hill 48, 119, 151
street cars 29
street fairs 178
Sullivan, Betty Chadwick 93
Swafford, Dr. Benjamin 129
Swan Theater 123
swimming 184
Swope Art Museum 167, 170
Swope, Sheldon 65, 170
Syrian immigrants 111
T H R O W, Inc. 142
Tajimi, Japan 109
Talley, Cora 116
Taxay, Rabbi 54
Taylor, Charles "Bud" 185
Taylor, Zachary 10, 48
technical schools 164
telephone companies 91
television 93
Temple B'Nai Abraham 111, 143
Temple Israel 111
Temple Laundry 100
Templeton Coal Company 85
tennis 177, 184
Terminal Arcade 30, 31, 45
Terre Haute Action Dragway 183
Terre Haute Action Track 177, 183
Terre Haute and Richmond railroad 7, 15, 27

Terre Haute Board of Aviation Commissioners 32
Terre Haute Brewing Company 53
Terre Haute Center for Medical Education 127
Terre Haute City Lines 29, 31
Terre Haute Commercial College and Telegraphic Institute 166
Terre Haute Convention & Visitors Bureau 21
Terre Haute Day Nursery 138
Terre Haute Decorating Company 99
Terre Haute Drawbridge Company 19
Terre Haute Electric Traction Company 29
Terre Haute First National Bank 1, 94-95, 200
Terre Haute High School 158, 170
Terre Haute House 21, 59, 102
Terre Haute Housing Authority 126
Terre Haute Land Company 7
Terre Haute Lions Club 115, 140
Terre Haute Malleable Manufacturing Company 85
Terre Haute North Vigo High School 159, 161, 177, 188, 190
Terre Haute Oratorio Society 167
Terre Haute Ordnance Depot 59
Terre Haute Parks and Recreation Department 184
Terre Haute Phillies 191
Terre Haute Regional Hospital 128
Terre Haute Rotary Club 137
Terre Haute Sanitarium 129
Terre Haute Savings Bank 14, 78, 96
Terre Haute School of Watchmaking 164
Terre Haute Society for Organizing Charity 139
Terre Haute South Vigo High School 32, 158, 161, 177, 190
Terre Haute Street Railway 29
Terre Haute Symphony Orchestra 167, 171
Terre Haute Tennis Club 184
Terre Haute Tornado 60
Terre Haute Track Club 185
Terre Haute Traction & Light Company 29, 30, 90
Terre Haute Vitrified Brick 46
Terre Town School 155
theaters 175
Thomas, Kurt 177, 185
Thomas, Raymond F. 32
Thompson, Col. Richard W. 43, 108
Thompson Park 43
Thornhill, Claude 176
Thornton, Jack, Jr. 177
Tillotson, Elijah 36
Tirey, Ralph N. 162
Tokyo Ballroom 176
Tony Hulman Classic 183
tornadoes 70, 71
Torner House 127
Torner, Rebecca 140
Townsley, Madge Polk 174
transportation 15-35
Tri-Industries, Inc. 126
Trianon Ballroom 84, 176
Trout, Charles M. 96
trucking 83
Tucker, Ralph 17, 37, 40, 67, 69, 93, 192-193, 194
Tuesday Literary Club 116
Turman, Hazel Dodge 33
Turman, William T. 167
Turner Brothers Glass Company 86
Twelve Points 122-123
Twelve Points Park 43
Twelve Points State Bank 122
U S O 55
U.S. Highway 40 and 41 - 7, 20, 21,
U.S. Penitentiary 46
Union Depot 28
Union Hospital 129, 195
United Child Care Center and Pre-School 138
United Hebrew Congregation 111
United Mine Workers District No. 11 79
United Way of the Wabash Valley 127, 139
University School 163
urban renewal 126
utilities 90-91
Van Gilder, Jake 98
Vandalia Railroad 7, 26, 27, 28, 133
Vendel, John C. 124

Verostko, Gene 184
veterans housing 60
veterans organizations 62
Viet Nam War 61
Vietnamese Resettlement Project 109
Vigo American Clay 46
Vigo County 13
Vigo County Association for Mental Health 130
Vigo County Central Labor Union 78
Vigo County Council on the Aging and Aged 143
Vigo County Historical Society 6, 168
Vigo County Home 135
Vigo County Medical Society 127
Vigo County Public Library 150, 158
Vigo County School Corporation 149, 155, 161
Vigo County United War Veterans Council 62
Vigo County Youth Football League 186
Vigo County Youth Soccer Association 177
Vigo, Francis 13
Vigo Ordnance Plant 59
Visiting Nurse Association 132
Volunteers of America 52, 127
Voorhees Park 43
Voorhees, Senator Daniel W. 7, 43, 44
Vrydagh, Jesse A. 44, 172
W P A projects 42, 46, 47, 54, 160, 163
W T H I Radio-TV 84, 93
Wabash & Erie Canal 18, 110
Wabash Avenue 2, 29, 101, 103, 104-105, 106
Wabash Commercial College
Wabash Fibre Box Company 87
Wabash Mills 77
Wabash Movie House 45
Wabash River 9, 15, 16, 19, 145
Wabash River Ordnance Works 59
Wabash Senior Citizens Center 111, 143
Wabash Valley 8
Wabash Valley Basketball Tournament 187
Wabash Valley Central Labor Council 78
Wabash Valley Festival 177
Wabash Valley Girls Softball League 194
Wabash-Brown College of Commerce 166
War of 1812 48
Warren, Chauncey 94
Warren Park Farm 107
Washington Alternative High School 161
Washington Avenue Presbyterian Church 119
Washington, Booker T. School 161
Washington Park 43
Weinstein, Dr. J. H. 131
Weinstein, Dr. Leo 129
Weldin Talley Memorial Playhouse 174
Welfare League 127, 139
Western Register & Terre Haute Advertiser 11, 14, 17
Western Tar Products 85
Weston Paper and Manufacturing Company 87
Whalen, Edward 33
White, Dick 188
Wildy & Poths 82
Wiley High School 150, 158, 160, 190
Wiley, William H. 154, 155, 158
Williams-Warren Zimmerman House 45
Williamson, Lisa 35
Wilson, Captain R. E. 60
Wilson, Gilbert Brown 170
Woman's Department Club 116, 119
woman's suffrage 52
Women Ordnance Workers 59
women's clubs 116-117
Woodlawn Cemetery 44
Woodrow Wilson Junior High School 149, 170
Woolworth, F. W. 106
Works Progress Administration see W P A
World War I 50
World War II 55-60, 77
Y M C A 141
YWCA 141
Yeakle, Edwin 39
Young Men's Civic Club 112
Zimmerman, George S. 45
Zorah Shrine Circus 177
Zorah Shrine Temple 114, 164

Directors

First Financial Corporation and Terre Haute First National Bank
Front row left to right: Walter A. Bledsoe, Welby M. Frantz, Mari H. George, Donald E. Smith and Virginia L. Smith. Back row left to right: Chapman J. Root II, Thomas T. Dinkel, Norman L. Lowery, Tony George, William A. Niemeyer, John W. Ragle, Patrick O'Leary, Max Gibson and B. Guille Cox, Jr.

Evolution of the First Shield

The shield that serves as the symbol for First Financial Corporation's family of banks is one of the oldest and most widely recognized trademarks in the Wabash Valley. It originated with the Terre Haute National Bank, which was organized in 1905.

In 1932, following several mergers, Terre Haute First National Bank was born. Around that time, the National Charter number that was issued to the bank's predecessors by the federal government in 1863 was added to the shield.

Terre Haute artist Phil "Pinky" Powell designed the First shield as it appears now. He replaced the bank's name with the word "First," rendered in the distinctive script that has become as familiar as the shield itself.

Today all the affiliate banks of First Financial Corporation use the First shield as their emblem. This tangible link with the past remains a proud symbol of First's ongoing commitment to serving the people of the Wabash Valley.

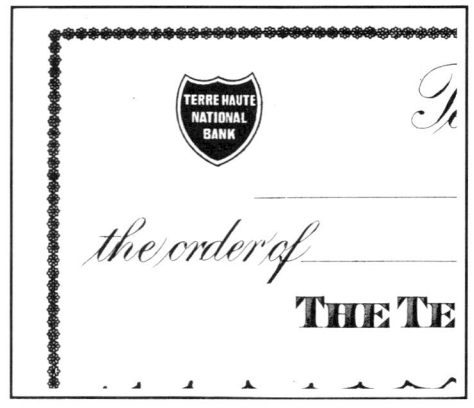
Promissory note dated 1915

Savings envelope from the 1950s

The First shield today

NO BREAD CAN BE BETTER THAN
H-O-L-S-U-M
Improves the Health and Reduces Expense. TRY IT!
IDEAL BAKING COMPANY

DOWNTOWN CHEVROLET SALES INC.
AUTHORIZED **CHEVROLET** YOUR CHEVROLET DEALER
SALES — C-1341 — 24 Hour Service at 120 N. 8th St.
SERVICE — C-5019 — 323 OHIO ST.

For Your Favorite Drink...
in a Friendly Atmosphere...
RACE TRACK TAP
30 So. 7th St.
"A WINNER EVERY TIME"
CHOICE DRINKS -:- GOOD FOOD

TAXICABS
Phone WABASH **4905**
BOWER'S TAXI SERVICE
O. J. SEXTON, Prop.
FIVE AND SEVEN PASSENGER CARS
PROMPT SERVICE DAY OR NIGHT
Phone WABASH **4905**

WILLIS & WILLIS
Chiropractors — Palmer School Graduates
OFFICE 1267½ LAFAYETTE AVE.
HOURS: 9 to 12 A. M. / 2 to 5 P. M. / 7 to 8 P. M.
Sundays by Appointment
Residence 1312 Second Ave. Telephone Wabash 3030
Telephone WABASH **1563**
"KEEP SMILING"

Our Fiftieth Year 1893–1943
Rx *Dickerson Shoes*
BEDFORD
"WALK IN COMFORT"
HORNUNG'S
X-Ray Fitting.   28 So. 7th St.

E. H. Bindley & Co.
WHOLESALE DRUGGISTS AND JOBBERS OF DRUGGISTS SUNDRIES

WASSELL INN
2808 WABASH AVE.   PHONE C-8824
Complete Your Nights Entertainment at WASSELL'S

Smith-Alsop Paint and Varnish Company
PAINT MAKERS
Factory, 104-110 Wabash Avenue
Salesroom, 11 South Seventh Street
Phone Wabash **6018**

TICK--TOCK TUCKER
814 Wabash Ave.
AT THE SIGN OF THE CLOCK
IN THE MIDDLE OF THE BLOCK
Diamonds, Watches, Silverware, Cut Glass and Jewelry

A TIP-TOP TOP
That will give you long and satisfactory service will be one made to your order by
F. B. THOMAS
That is the only kind we build—the different, distinctive, better.
904-906 POPLAR STREET   PHONE, WABASH 995

C. R. SAPPINGTON TRANSFER & MOVING
(The "Preacher"—the Original Sappington Movers—14 years)
PERMITS Ind.—442 Mo.—5368 I. C. C.
STORAGE — CRATING — PACKING
We Specialize in Long Distance Moving
Personal Attention on all Work
ALL LOADS INSURED
1637 S. 3rd C-8246
STORE—26 S. 3rd C-8205
RES.—1412 S. 3rd . Harrison 3254
LARGE ENCLOSED WATERPROOF and DUSTPROOF VANS

FURS-- Fur Service Steiger's
Phone **C-3221**
Cold storage vault and complete fur factory on the premises. Certified Furriers.
CLEANING
STORAGE
RELINING
REPAIRING
RESTYLING
STEIGER'S FUR SHOP
22 N. 6th St.   C-3221
"Terre Haute's OLD Reliable Furrier"

ARTISTS AND ENGRAVERS
TERRE HAUTE ENGRAVING CO.
7TH AND OHIO
TERRE HAUTE, IND.

PHONES WABASH **6500**
ERMISCH—MY—CLEANER
THE OLDEST FIRM OF ITS KIND IN TERRE HAUTE
DRY CLEANING AND DYEING
RELIABLE AND PROMPT SERVICE
106 NORTH SEVENTH STREET

FOX & PFISTER
687 OHIO STREET.   PHONE WABASH 195

A. ROWE SONS CO.
Wholesale Meats
First and Linden Sts.   Crawford-2306

TAKE HOME A BOX OF
McWhinney's **GENEROUS CHOCOLATES**

DE SOTO AND **PLYMOUTH**
SALES
SERVICE & PARTS
COLE AUTO CO.
133 S. 6th St.   C-5685

THE APPLE CLUB
Mrs. Marie Gregory
Specializing in CHICKEN-STEAK & ITALIAN DINNERS
Phone for Reservations
1st & Davis, West of Airport   C-2047

"**Dagwood**" Sandwiches and **Mint Coca-Colas**
NEW TASTE THRILLS
at the **PARKMORE**
37th and Wabash.
The Parkmore Entertained 1,500 Guests Last Sunday.

BUSINESS FURNITURE
The town's largest and best stock of Office Furniture is here
Desks
Filing Cabinets
Chairs
Tables
Costumers
You will find these in oak and mahogany in all the standard sizes and styles.
THE VIQUESNEY CO.
Printers and Office Outfitters
614-616 OHIO ST.   Phone 3303   TERRE HAUTE, IND.

CALLAHAN'S..
24 HOUR AMBULANCE SERVICE
● LARGEST AND MOST MODERN FUNERAL HOME IN THE MIDDLE WEST....
Air Conditioned

Crawford **4351**

Simplex Shoe Repair Shop
Quality Up and Price Down

Ed Nash
CIGARIST

Men - Ladies - Children
Terre Haute's Finest Selection of Beautiful Footwear
BEN BECKER
525 Wabash Ave.

Carney Tire Co.
KELLY SPRINGFIELD TIRES
ROAD SERVICE
Battery Recharging
Tire Repairing
1600 Wabash Ave.   C-8300

1920 - 1949

Baggage
BLACK & WHITE CAB CO.
C-3064
25¢ CABS 25¢

Freitag-Weinhardt, Inc.
36 Years' Experience
Plumbing, Hot Water, Steam and Vapor Heating — General Repairing
30 North 6th St.   Crawford 2394

WALKER ELECTRIC SUPPLY CO.
Motor Repairs and Machine Work
656 Walnut   C-6835
Night Phone H-3756

Always Open
MACE
6½ & Ohio
Free Parking With Purchase
AUTO-B-MY SERVICE
C-1367